The COMEDY Bible

From Stand-up to Sitcom—

the Comedy Writer's Ultimate

How-to Guide

Judy Carter

A Fireside Book

Published by Simon & Schuster

New York   London   Toronto   Sydney

FIRESIDE
Rockefeller Center
1230 Avenue of the Americas
New York, NY 10020

Designed by Ruth Lee

Manufactured in the United States of America

30 29 28 27 26 25 24

Library of Congress Cataloging-in-Publication Data

Carter, Judy.
    The comedy bible : from stand-up to sitcom : the comedy writer's ultimate
how-to-guide / Judy Carter.
        p.   cm.
    1. Wit and humor—Authorship. 2. Comedy—Authorship. 3. Stand-up
comedy. I. Title.

PN6149.A88 C37 2001
808.7—dc21   2001032047

ISBN 0-7432-0125-6

PHOTO CREDITS
Aaron Rapoport/HBO (top), Leslie Slavin (bottom): p. 34
Karin Martinez: p. 39
Susan Maljan: p. 54
David Steinberg: p. 72
Courtesy of *The Drew Carey Show* and Warner Bros.: p. 95
Richard Baker: p. 101
J. P. Williams (top), Pam Springstein (bottom): p. 107
Randy Holmes/FOX (bottom): p. 108
Joan Marcus: p. 216

Acknowledgments

It takes a lot of people to make a book like this happen, especially if the writer is someone who got a D in high school English.

Special thanks to:

Chuck Adams, my editor and friend, who by this time could headline at any comedy club. Jandy Nelson, my agent at Manus & Associates Literary Agency, who showed me that lunch with an agent could be a lot of fun, especially if you don't remember where you've parked your car.

Margot Black, for assisting in arranging interviews. Kathy Fielding, for transcribing everything, and Julie Gardner, for all her assistance in running comedy workshops and putting up with me when I'm not so funny.

Ben Richardson, for your talent, jokes, commas, and breaking me out of a record-breaking writer's block.

Gina Rubinstein, who next time will be more careful before saying, "Sure, I'll give it a read."

All of my students, who taught me much more than I taught them.

The comedy professionals who contributed time and material to this book—Bernie Brillstein, Bruce Hills, Bruce Smith, Carol Leifer, Cathy Ladman, Chris Adams, Chris Mazzilli, Christopher Titus, Cindy Chupack, Dean Lewis, Debbie Kasper, Delilah Romos, Diane Nichols, Ed Yeager, Ellen Sandler, Emily Levine, Gabe Adelson, George Wallace, Greg Proops, Irene Penn, Judi Brown, Kathy Griffen, Kathy Anderson, Leigh

Fortier, Lilly Walters, Mark Travis, Michael Hanel, Michelle Marx, Phyllis Diller, Richard Jeni, Richard Lewis, Rob Lotterstein, Robin Roberts, Robin Schiff, Rocky LaPorte, Steve Marmel, Sue Kolinsky, Susan Leslie, Sybil Adelman Sage, T. J. Markwalter, Tim Bagley, Tom Dreeson, Tom Shadyac, Wendy Kamenoff.

In memory of

who made us all laugh and showed me
what was truly important

Contents

About This Book

In the beginning, God created heaven and earth.

Great opening line—but unfortunately, already been used. And thou shalt not steal material, especially from God. But then, that's an entirely different kind of "bible," at least in most respects. What *that* Bible and this bible have in common is wisdom. Wanna learn how to love thy neighbor? Read that one. Wanna learn how to make thy neighbor laugh? Read this one. This version of the bible will show you how to discover your originality, craft it, and turn your sense of humor into a moneymaking comedy career—no joke! *The Comedy Bible*—don't be funny without it.

If you're serious about comedy, then here's why you need this book:

- Because you hear others say, "Hey, you're funny, you should be a comedian."
- Because you want to quit your day job and make money being funny.
- Because you would like to turn those ideas jotted down on scraps of paper into sitcom scripts.
- Because you think that you're as funny as the schmucks you see on TV.
- Because sometimes when you see a new sitcom or hear a comic tell a joke you say, "I thought of that!"
- Because you think people are stealing your comedy ideas, and you'd do something about it but you can't get off the couch.

Some of the funniest people I know are waiting tables, cleaning houses, temping in offices, and whining about their lack of success while less gifted comics and writers are making millions. Why not you? No matter what your day job is now, you could make a living doing comedy, although very seldom does real success come over night.

Even the best comics started out doing something else. Jay Leno started out as an auto mechanic. The late, brilliant Sam Kenison was a Catholic priest before he started doing stand-up. Writer/producer Barry Kemp, Emmy-nominated writer of *Taxi* and producer/creator of *Newhart* and *Coach,* started as an insurance salesman in Phoenix. Rodney Danger-field was selling house paint before he became famous—which might be why he didn't "get no respect."

If you have a talent for making people laugh, there are a lot of opportunities for fun and profit just waiting for you. And a person can make it in the funny business without ever getting onstage. Comics express themselves in many different ways. Many, of course, do get onstage, acting and doing stand-up, but others write sitcoms, screenplays, and songs, while others express themselves through cartoons, advertising, and more. People who know the craft of comedy writing are pursued and paid well for their talent. From politicians to manufacturers, everyone has got something to sell, and comedy sells it best. It's no wonder, then, that many politicians have a staff of comedy writers working for them so that they don't become big jokes themselves. They know also that ideas presented with humor become the sound bites that make the six o'clock news. And of course, advertisers know that commercials that make a jaded TV audience laugh will move merchandise more effectively than any other method. Even Hallmark employs comedy writers to write their humorous cards.

Humor can even get you dates. Just look at the personal ads—"sense of humor" is the number one requirement of many people seeking a mate. But the big question is, how do you go from being one of the guys who gets drunk at parties and lights his farts to being a Jim Carrey, who gets paid over $50 million a year to light *his* farts?

After ten years of running comedy workshops, coaching over five thousand comics, and doing stand-up at thousands of events myself, I have developed an understanding of what it takes to be successful in comedy—and it isn't luck, relatives in the business, or a boob job. Those things may get you in the door, but they aren't going to make people laugh—unless, of course, it was a really bad boob job. What it takes to make it as a comic or as a comedy writer is a combination of talent and craft. If you have a gift for comedy, then I can show you how to shape your gift into the sort of "funny" that will get you noticed and paid. The proof? After taking my eight-week course, many beginning stand-up comics have been signed, often after their first performance, by some of the biggest and most powerful agents, managers, and studios. And some stand-up students who have gone on to become successful writers found that their scripts read more humorously and sold more easily because they could pitch funny.

Of course, just as there are specific things you can do to make your career happen, there also are things that will kill and sabotage your success. This book will tell you which is which. Believe me, I know, because I've done it all—the good, the bad, and the unfunny.

About Me

I have been very fortunate to make a living doing what I love most—comedy. I've worked at only one nine-to-five job in my life—teaching theater for two years at a private boys' school in Los Angeles. Other than that, for twenty-five years I've made a living performing, writing, and teaching comedy (all of which is not bad for a twenty-nine-year-old). For the first ten years of my career I did clubs and television shows. At the height of my performing career I was on the tube every week and on the road forty weeks a year as a headliner in comedy clubs and concert venues. I was nominated for Atlantic City's Entertainer of the Year award for my performances at Caesars Palace. I have produced and written television shows. I've written books that have won awards (OK, *one* book that won *one* award), seen my film scripts optioned and my plays produced.

Sometimes I look at the things I own and marvel: "This outfit cost me three jokes." "This home cost me one script—but ten drafts!" After all these years, I still am amazed at being able to make a living off my sense of humor.

But this book is based only partially on my successes. In fact, it's based mostly on my mistakes and failures. Like when I had too much time in the greenroom before going on national TV and decided at the last minute to throw all my material out the window and do something new—and unfunny. Like the time I spent doing material that I didn't believe in because I wanted to be what I thought was commercial. The time I didn't sign with a major manager because I was scared of success. The time I finally had an audition with a top television producer and let my fear crush my craft. The time I inappropriately used profanity in my act during the taping of a network television show and really f**ked up. The time I slept with a bartender who looked exactly like a producer at NBC—but wasn't. And like all the times I brutally judged myself, squashing my creative process. I have learned a great deal from my mistakes and so can you.

If you have a modest amount of ambition and talent, you can create the opportunity to show your funny stuff to someone who can change your life. But to make it work to your advantage, you will need to be very well prepared. It used to be that an agent or manager would spot raw talent, work with that person to become his or her best, and then present their find to the industry once that person's talent and persona had matured. But today's fast pace and the overwhelming neurosis of show business seldom allow that to happen anymore. Few agents, managers, or producers really know if they themselves are going to have a job next year—or even next week—and in this state of paranoia and insecurity there's little room for long-term bets on talent. These talent finders want someone prepackaged, predefined, and predisposed to deliver the goods on a moment's notice. Given this environment, comedy performers and writers can no longer afford the fantasy of waiting to be discovered. Instead they need to discover themselves and become masters of their craft, so that when opportunity knocks they are ready and able to deliver the goods.

Talented funny people need guidance if they are to demystify the creative process, get out of the way of their own success, and make a living. *The Comedy Bible* is an instructional guide, aimed not only at showing you how to express your humor but also at guiding you to pay attention to your ideas so that others will too. If you're going to succeed you have to learn how to discover your talent (and how to exploit it) rather than wait to be discovered. In *The Comedy Bible* you'll learn how to hone your persona; how to master your craft and be able to meet the demands of success; how to stop waiting for that agent to come into your life and, instead, to make it happen yourself; how to market yourself; how to take your talent and career into your own hands and put your comedy vision out there in a powerful way. This is the kind of book I wish I had had when I started out, because the pathway to success doesn't have to be a secret.

Part One: Warm-up—Is There Any Hope for You?

A comedy career is not for everyone. It's one thing to be the funny dentist, able to get your patients through their most excruciating moments, and quite another to have a career in comedy. Let's face it, it's harder when the audience *isn't* on laughing gas. In this part you will take tests to find out what fields of comedy best suit you, learn how to collect and organize your ideas to get started, and discover how to get beyond fear that can stop you in your tracks.

Part Two: Comedy Workshop

Great works of art don't come from divine inspiration but from ordinary, day-to-day activities and observations. Your life is a joke—and that's the good news. Wake up and smell the comedy around you—in your relationships, your breakups, and your dilemmas. You might find your entire act, screenplay, or sitcom tonight at the dining room table. I will show you how to transform the raw material of your life into commercially viable comedy projects—whether a stand-up act, a one-person show, a situation comedy, or a magazine piece.

Part Three: Funny Money

By the time you read this part, you will have an act or a script or some piece of comedy material in development. Now it's time to get out of the house and present yourself and your material to others who are in a position to appreciate your work. Showbiz *is* business, so here you will find tips from the stars on how they carved out successful careers in comedy. It's nice that your drinking buddies think you're funny, but wouldn't it be funnier—and lots more lucrative—if the entire state of New York thought so as well? It's time that you were not the world's best kept secret.

Let's begin . . .

PART ONE

Warm-up—

Is There Any Hope for You?

What Do You Want to Be When You Grow Up?

"When adults ask kids, 'What do you want to be when you grow up?' they're just looking for clues themselves."

—PAULA POUNDSTONE

There are a lot of ways to make a living from comedy. You can perform it, write it, draw it, or manage it. From the list below, check which ones you're interested in or think you know you're good at.

Performing Comedy

❑ **Stand-up comic**
   Depending on the quality of your act, you can work at comedy clubs, hotels, concert venues, colleges, or corporate meetings, on cruise ships, at open mikes, or at your aunt Thelma's eightieth birthday party.

❑ **Improviser**
   Sketch TV shows such as *Saturday Night Live* and *Mad TV* scout improvisers from improv troupes such as Second City (in Chicago and Toronto) and the Groundlings (in Los Angeles), as well as improv festivals (Austin, Texas, Montreal, Canada). Improvisers are in demand for acting and TV commercials as well as for voice-over work, feature animation, and game shows.

❑ **Commercial actor**

Funny people who can add sizzle to ad copy are cast in high-paying TV commercials.

❑ **Voice-over performer**

Comedy timing and technique are required in this field, which needs comics to add funny character voices to cartoons, TV commercials, and feature animation.

❑ **Warm-up for TV shows**

Most TV shows hire a comic to warm up the live studio audience before and during the taping of TV shows and infomercials.

❑ **Radio comedy**

Funny song parodies turned unknown "Weird Al" Yankovic into a famous and rich man. Radio stations buy prerecorded song parodies, impersonations, and other comedy bits produced by small production houses that specialize in creating this type of material.

❑ **Radio talk show host**

As more talk shows fill the AM and FM airwaves, radio producers are turning to comics to keep their listeners laughing and listening.

❑ **Cruise ship entertainer**

Imagine doing your act for your grandmother—that's the kind of act you need to work cruise ships. If you've got four different twenty-minute *clean* sets and don't mind living with your audience for a few weeks, then this could be for you.

❑ **Corporate humorist**

If you can make people laugh with clean material, then entertaining at corporate events might be just your thing.

Writing Comedy

❑ **Customized stand-up material**

Some stand-up comics who perform supplement their income by writing for other comics. And then there are those funny people who have never done stand-up themselves but who write it for others, such as funnyman Bruce Vilanch, who writes for Bette Midler and the *Academy Awards show.*

❑ **TV sitcoms**

Comics are hired to staff sitcoms or develop sitcoms for stand-up comics who have development deals. Many of the most successful sitcoms are based on stand-up comedy acts. Stand-up comics Larry David and Jerry

Seinfeld became billionaires when they turned their stand-up acts into one of the most successful sitcoms ever—*Seinfeld.*

❏ **Punch-up**

TV and film producers hire comics for the important job of punching up, or adding laughs to, a script.

❏ **Screenwriting and directing**

Comedy directors often start their careers with live performances. Betty Thomas started in an improv troupe and went on to direct features such as *The Brady Bunch Movie.* Tom Shadyac, director of *Patch Adams, Liar, Liar,* and *The Nutty Professor,* actually started out in my stand-up workshop. Two years later, he directed his first feature, *Ace Ventura.*

❏ **Literary writing**

"Funny" can also translate into books, magazine articles, and newspaper columns. George Carlin turned his unused stand-up material into the book *Brain Droppings.* Comedy director/screenwriter Nora Ephron *(You've Got Mail, Sleepless in Seattle)* wrote short funny magazine pieces that later became a popular book, *Mixed Nuts.* Dave Barry expresses his "funny" in a nationally syndicated column and in books.

❏ **Development and producing**

Funny ideas often translate into projects for commercial TV and film. Paul Reubens's character Pee-wee Herman started out as a character in an improv show at the Groundlings. It turned into an HBO special, two feature films, and an award-winning children's TV series.

❏ **Animation writing**

All major studios actively look for funny people to write and punch up their TV and feature animation projects. Irene Mecchi began as a comedy writer, writing comedy material for Lily Tomlin. Now she works for Disney animation and was the screenwriter of *The Lion King.*

❏ **Internet work**

Because a good laugh can stop an Internet surfer at a Web site, companies such as Excite, Yahoo!, and AOL hire comics to write catchy copy.

❏ **Speechwriting**

Many CEOs and politicians turn to comedy writers to provide sound bites so that they get noticed, win over their audiences, and don't get stuck with their foot in their mouth.

"I know what they say about me—that I'm so stiff that racks buy their suits off me."

—AL GORE, 1998, WRITTEN BY MARK KATZ

Marketing Comedy

❏ **Merchandising**
Funny ideas can turn into funny products, such as Pet Rocks, screen
savers, or greeting cards. Skyler Thomas, who started writing jokes in my
class, put his jokes on T-shirts. They became major sellers and he now
runs a multimillion-dollar T-shirt business called Don't Panic, with stores
nationwide.

❏ **Ad copy**
Who do you think writes those funny bits in ads that get your attention?
Comedy writers.

"Most relationships don't last as long as the L.A. Marathon."
                                          —L.A. BILLBOARD

❏ **Managing and booking**
Many agents and managers started by putting shows together for themselves and ended up booking others.

Right now, of course, you don't need to make a commitment to any
specific comedy field. Actually, no matter which field of comedy you are
interested in at the start of this book, be open to the possibility of shift-
ing winds. You might be totally committed to performing stand-up until
someone offers you a $50,000-a-year job writing funny ads for toilet
cleaners. It could happen.

You might start off thinking you want to be a stand-up comic and end
up discovering that you have a lot of ideas that can work as sitcoms. Billy
Riback started out doing *stand-up* at the Improv at $25 a night, and now he
produces comedy TV shows making millions. Conan O'Brien and Garry
Shandling were both sitcom writers before they became comedy stars. In
1978 David Letterman was a joke writer for Jimmie "Dy-No-Mite" Walker.
The Zucker brothers and Jim Abrahams, who created and directed the
movies *Airplane!, Naked Gun,* and *Ghost,* began their careers in a comedy
improv troupe in Madison, Wisconsin, called Kentucky Fried Theater.
And then there's Gary Coleman, who started off as a comedy actor starring in his own sitcom and ended up as a security guard. Go figure!

The various fields of comedy can morph into one another. Sometimes
a comic's act becomes the basis for a sitcom *(Roseanne),* or a screenplay

becomes a sitcom (*M*A*S*H, Suddenly Susan*). Even jokes have become merchandise: Rosie O'Donnell's slingshot toy has sold over 2 million units.

I became a stand-up comic thanks to United Airlines. I started off as a funny magician working at the Magic Castle in Hollywood—I levitated celery, sawed a man in half, and performed a death-defying escape from my grandmother's girdle. United Airlines changed the course of my career when I arrived in Cincinnati and my act arrived in Newark. That night I walked onstage without my tricks, without an act. I was so scared that I just started babbling about what happened, and to my surprise, I got laughs. I then ranted about all the humiliations of my life and the laughs got bigger, and before I knew it, my twenty-minute set ended. It was then that I learned the biggest lesson about comedy: truth is funny and shows up even when your luggage doesn't. I became a stand-up comic, because why schlepp around a bunch of props when people will pay you just for your ideas? Recently I've added to my work schedule by doing funny motivational speaking at Fortune 500 companies. Who knew?

The bottom line is, funny people are not limited to one field of comedy, and many of them overlap. For right now, you don't need to know what you want to be when you grow up—all you need is your sense of humor. But first, let's make sure you have one.

The Right Stuff— Do You Have What It Takes?

Some people, no matter how hard they try, just aren't funny. It takes a certain disposition to do comedy. So, how do you know if you have the right stuff?

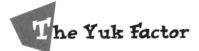

The Yuk Factor

Circle the answers that describe you best.

yes no Do you think that you're funnier than most of the schmucks you see on TV?

yes no Every time you open your mouth, does an inner voice say, "You should be writing this down"—even during sex?

yes no Are you jealous of everyone who makes a living from comedy?

yes no Could you think of funny jokes even at a funeral?

yes no Do you ever think that you are the only sane one in your crazy family?

yes no When you get angry, do you get funny?

yes no Would you tell people your most embarrassing moments and inadequacies if you could get a laugh?

yes no Do you notice the quirks of life that other people miss?

yes no Do you study the minute details of life, such as lint?

yes   no   Do you sometimes imagine a future full of the improbable? Such as, *"What if* men got pregnant?" *"What if* you were born old and grew young?"

yes   no   Do you think you look funny when you're naked?

yes   no   Do you talk back to your television?

yes   no   Did you grow up in a family where few things were really discussed and communication was at a minimum?

yes   no   Do you imitate your family behind their back?

yes   no   Do you have opinions about everything?

yes   no   Do you get accused of exaggerating?

You Are As Funny As You Think

Garry Shandling, famous comic, would answer all twenty questions "Yes." Teri Aranguen, my accountant, answered only four "Yes." If you answered more like Garry and less like Teri, then give up the spreadsheet—you have a comic's disposition. You might be working as an accountant but you are thinking like a comic. It's not how you currently make your living that makes you a comic but how you think—how you see the world, your attitude about the absurdity surrounding you, and of course, how you can make people laugh. If you imitate your family members behind their backs, you're not being rude; you're doing what we call *act-outs.* If you are funny when you get angry, you already know how to deliver with *attitude.* If you have opinions about the service in a restaurant, the new TV season, interest rates, don't think of yourself as a know-it-all; you have a *hit on a topic.* And if you are insanely jealous of other comics' success, it just might be a healthy expression of your own desires for success. But if you want to watch other comics in clubs, follow them home, and watch them through binoculars, you're not an observational comic—you're a stalker. Get help.

We funny people are not normal. In my workshops, the normal ones are not the funny ones. We think differently. For instance, having a hard time at work? Normal people think, "What a bad day." Comics think, "A bad day . . . *and* material!"

> "I used to work in an office. They're always so mean to the new girl in the office. 'Oh, Caroline, you're new? You have lunch at nine-thirty.' I worked as a receptionist, but I couldn't get the hang of it. I kept answering the phone by saying, 'Hello, can you help me?' It's so humiliating to go on job interviews,

especially when they ask, 'What was the reason you left your last job?' 'Well, I found that after I was hired, there was a lot of tension in the office. You know, I found it difficult sitting on the new girl's lap.' "

—CAROLINE RHEA

Jerry Seinfeld

Normal people express their sense of humor by memorizing jokes; comics transform their life experiences into punch lines and write their *own* jokes.

We funny people are a strange sort. We like laughs, even at our own expense. We funny people were the cave people who probably slipped on the banana peel just because we were certain that it would get a laugh. We think a lot about little things, such as lint or hotel soap.

"I like tiny hotel soap. I pretend that it's normal soap and my muscles are huge."

—JERRY SEINFELD

We think slanted—out of the box.

"A lot of people are afraid of heights. Not me—I'm afraid of widths."

—STEVEN WRIGHT

Most people hide their defects; we comics show them to the world. Matter of fact, the more people who know about how fat we are, how bald, how insecure, the better we feel—as long as we get a laugh.

"I have low self-esteem. When we were in bed together, I would fantasize that *I* was someone else."

—RICHARD LEWIS

We love to expose stupidity.

"Please, if you ever see me getting beaten up by the police, please put your video camera down and help me."

—BOBCAT GOLDTHWAIT

Bobcat Goldthwait

We generally grew up in a family where few things were really discussed and communication was at a minimum, but we remember every humiliating thing that happened.

> "I don't feel good about myself. I recently broke up with this woman. Why? I felt she wasn't into me. I said, 'I love you. I adore you. I worship you.' And she said, 'Ain't that a kick in the head.'"
>
> —RICHARD LEWIS

We've kept a mental record of our family's weirdness because we knew even at an early age that they were a source of material.

> "Both my parents got high my entire life. We used to go on family trips together without even leaving home. I don't have childhood memories. I have flashbacks. I think that's why I hate to travel, because we never went anywhere. Oh wait, we did . . . rehab. That was fun."
>
> —VANESSA HOLLINGSHEAD

We usually think that we are the only sane ones in our families, but usually we are sorely mistaken. We are not normal. We are comics.

Most people have misconceptions about what comics are like. Comics are not necessarily funny, happy, outgoing, laugh-getting clowns. I have a friend who had the misplaced idea that she would have a really fun dinner party by inviting a bunch of comics. She anticipated a laugh-a-minute kind of night. Wrong! It was a Nietzsche sort of night: her cooking was analyzed, two people felt too depressed to talk, and three others felt too fat to eat. At one point, when the conversation turned to creative ways to commit suicide, the hostess decided that this would be a good time to go to a movie and asked that we lock up when we left.

> "If I ever commit suicide I'm going to fling myself off the top of a skyscraper, but before I do I'm going to fill my pockets with candy and gum. That way when the onlookers walk up they can go, 'Oh, Snickers, hey!'"
>
> —PATTON OSWALT

Being a comic or a comedy writer is not for normal people. It's a way of looking not only at your life but at your dreams. If you are a comic, you probably even dream funny. It's a discipline to pay attention to ideas that come at all times, even during sex. "Hold it right there, honey, I've got to write this idea down." It's about living in the funny zone twenty-four hours every day—watching life, having opinions, recording them, and fleshing them out to a finished piece. That's the discipline.

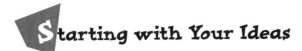tarting with Your Ideas

We all have funny ideas. We wake up with them; we get them in our sleep, or while drinking coffee or driving our car, and even in times of grief.

Ellen DeGeneres is an example of someone who managed to turn tragedy into comedy. A close friend of hers had died, and while alone and grieving in her fleabag apartment, she was inspired to write a routine that would one day make her a star—"A Phone Call to God."

> "I don't understand why we have fleas here because fleas do nothing at all beneficial. But I thought at times like this when we can't figure it out for ourselves . . . wouldn't it be great if we could pick up the phone and call up God and ask him these things. Just pick up the phone and call up God—'Yeah, hi God, it's Ellen . . . Listen, God, there's certain things on this earth. I just don't understand why they're here. No, not Fabio. No. But there are certain things, I mean, Jesus Christ. No, I didn't mean that. That was great. We're still talking about that. No, I was thinking more about insects. No, bees are great. The honey. That was clever. You're welcome. I was thinking more about fleas . . . they seem to have no beneficial . . . [*waiting*] No, I didn't realize how many people were employed by the flea collar industry . . . not to mention sprays. Well, I guess you're right. Of course you are . . .'" [*edited*]

Whenever I tell someone that I'm a comic, they bend my ear about *their* idea for a sitcom, a screenplay, or a joke. "You know, a lot of people tell me that I'm funny!" the person will say.

"OK, and please install my cable, Mr. Funnyman."

So, what is the difference between someone making a living from their ideas and someone who sees their ideas on TV and says, "Hey, I thought of that?"

It starts with paying attention and writing your ideas down. Many funny people aren't even aware that the ideas flying through their minds have the potential to become successful creative ventures. Some people are so overwhelmed with the day-to-day struggles of life that they don't even pay any attention to that quiet insightful voice, the one that says,

"This is really funny, I should write it down," and the voice that says, "This would be a great television episode." You might say to yourself that these ideas are nothing. But look what Jerry Seinfeld did with "nothing." There are a thousand little observations about the details of life that fly past us every day. Don't let them go to waste.

PRO TALK *with Carol Leifer, stand-up and writer/producer on* Seinfeld

"I get my ideas from life. I was out at dinner and ordered a bottle of wine and the waiter gave me the cork to smell, and I felt stupid sitting there sniffing it. 'Yeah, that's a cork.' And then the waiter laughed, so I wrote it down and put it in my act—'You feel like such an idiot, the guy hands you the cork and it's like, "I don't know what I'm supposed to do . . ." Like, "uh, yeah, yep, that's cork." ' "

Buy Comedy Supplies

- ❑ pen
- ❑ small notebook (one that fits in a pocket)
- ❑ large binder
- ❑ 100 index cards
- ❑ small tape recorder (digital is the best to save your ideas as individual sound bites)

Exercise: Keeping an Idea Book

You've probably been thinking up ideas for many, many years. Well, now it's time to write them down. Get yourself a notebook that you keep by your bed and another, smaller one that can fit in your pocket. Carry this, a working pen, and a small tape recorder with you all day. You don't want to lose the next major sitcom hit that will boost the profits of NBC because that day you didn't have a pen that worked. Write down all ideas within a few minutes of thinking about them.

Divide the big book into sections—for example, jokes, sitcom, film, and career ideas. Each morning before you get out of bed, before you pee, spend just ten minutes writing down fresh ideas. If you don't have any, then just keeping writing about anything—your dreams, your revenge fantasies, anything. They don't have to be funny. Just the act of writing down these ideas will keep the mental pipeline open.

The morning is the best time to write. Keep the paper and a pen by your bed so that when you wake up, all you need to do is reach over and start writing. If you need coffee badly, then prepare it the night before and put it in a thermos by your bed. Any activity that you put between you and writing will give you an excuse not to do it at all. If you have to go to work early, set your alarm ten minutes earlier. It's a start.

Do not get out of bed before concluding this brief writing period. And do not give in to any self-negotiations, like "I'll skip today because tomorrow I'll have the whole day to write." This line of thinking is a formula for sabotage. Very few writers write the whole day. It's unrealistic. Can you write for ten minutes? It might not seem like much, but if you fill three pages a day, in a week you'll end up with twenty-one pages. At the end of a year, that's a book, a screenplay, an act.

These morning writings are not supposed to be masterpieces. Occasionally you'll produce an incredible idea, wonderful dialogue, hysterical jokes, but for the most part it will be drivel, and that's OK. Get the juices going, the records in place, and the discipline in gear. The more pages you have, the more likely you are to hit on some truly inventive stuff. As anyone in sales knows, it's a numbers game. The more darts you throw, the more likely you are to hit something. The more people you date . . . You get the idea. It's like Amway.

PRO TALK *with comic George Wallace*

"I write my joke from seeing stupid things. Stupid signs. 'Quiet Hospital Zone.' And there's nothing making noise but the ambulance—a big siren going 'Woooo.'"

If something does strike you as a workable idea, put it on an index card. These index cards will come in handy when outlining a sitcom or putting together your stand-up act.

Richard Lewis

PRO TALK *with comic Richard Lewis*

"I carry a pad of paper everywhere and if something strikes me funny I write the premise down. Over the course of a few months I will have thousands of these premises and I circle those that really make me laugh, and think about how I can actually say it onstage. Over the course of a tour, premises develop and grow into routines and oftentimes strong one-liners. I tape every show and if I ad-lib, I add that to the show."

Some suggestions about this free-form writing:

- Do not judge it.
- Be messy.
- Do not *try* to be funny.
- Don't go back and reread your stuff for at least a month. That way you'll be able to reread it with fresh eyes.

Habits: Honoring Your Ideas

Ideas are starting points and are neither good nor bad. There are half-baked ideas, crazy, wild, tiny, and big ideas, but none of them should be judged before you take each for a run. One of the mistakes neophyte comics make is that they are too quick to label an idea bad, wrong, or stupid before they investigate it.

For instance, which of these ideas is "bad"?

- Idea for a sitcom—"How about a sitcom where a nun has a big hat that makes her fly?"
- Idea for a film—"It's the middle of the Korean War. Everyone is getting blown to bits. But the doctors are really funny."
- Idea for a joke—"I'm so depressed I want to kill myself. I wonder if there is a punch line here?"

All of those ideas led to comedy that made money:

- *The Flying Nun* was a popular TV series starring a very young Sally Field.
- *M*A*S*H* was a wildly popular film directed by Robert Altman and served as the basis for a long-running and very successful sitcom.
- One of comic Paula Poundstone's signature pieces was about suicide.

> "I tried using carbon monoxide, but my building has a big underground parking garage so it was taking a really long time. I had to bring along a stack of books and some snacks. People would go by and tap at the window and say, 'How's that suicide coming?' and I'd say, 'Pretty good, thank you, I felt drowsy earlier today.' "
>
> —PAULA POUNDSTONE

Exercise: Writing Your Ideas

What are the ideas that you've been carrying with you?

Remember, ideas are starting points. If you are like most creative people, you probably have been carrying around a lot of ideas. Whether you are interested in stand-up or scripts or something for the printed page, it's good to explore different forums. Write at least one idea in your notebook

- for a joke
- for a sitcom
- for a magazine article
- for a film

Studying what makes you and others laugh is a great starting point for understanding comedy. Sometimes it's someone's attitude, the way they say something, the combination of different points of view, an argument, or simple stupidity. Carry around your idea book with you for the next forty-eight hours and write down exactly what you saw, heard, or said that got a laugh or a smile. Telling a joke does not count, unless it was a joke that you wrote. Rather, your laugh-getting comment could be an off-the-cuff remark you made while at your therapist's office, at a party, at the office, or at the dinner table. Get off the couch, out of the house, and pay attention!

Make a list of what got laughs.

_____

_____

_____

_____

_____

_____

Describe what it felt like to get laughs. Be descriptive rather than just say-ing, "It felt good."

Look over the lists you just made. You might have noticed that when you are getting laughs, there is something that you are doing differently that is making you funny. It's important to know what that something is. For example, if you got a laugh while telling a friend a painful story about something that happened to you, did you exaggerate the humiliation? Did you make up things that didn't really happen? Did you make your-self more of a victim?

Find five things you or someone else did that heightened the "funny," and write them here.

 he Funny Zone

"People ask me, 'Steve, how do you get so funny?' I say to them, 'Before I go onstage I put a fish in each shoe. That way I feel funny.' "

—STEVE MARTIN

Look over your list about the feelings you get from making other people laugh. Are the following some of these words on your list—*alive, present, playful, angry, imaginative, energized*? If so, then you know what it's like to be in the funny zone.

Steve Martin

All of us funny people have been there. You're at a party and the subject of bad dates comes up. You join in with stories about your own dating hell, but you're in the funny zone and you're getting laughs. Matter of fact, the more horrible the story is, the more everyone laughs. You ride it, and you get a feel for controlling the laughs, exaggerating just the right amount, acting out your date, adding the perfect amount of sarcasm—you are in the zone. And that is how you create comedy material. It was spontaneous and it worked. The trick is to write it down as soon as you can, before you forget what you said. Keep track because life is full of comedy material.

> "I hate singles' bars. Guys come up to me and say, 'Hey, cupcake, can I buy you a drink?' I say, 'No, but I'll take the three bucks.' "
>
> —MARGARET SMITH

Have you ever had a fight with someone that turned funny? There you are, both yelling at each other when suddenly you take a turn into the funny zone—still angry, but funny. You might be still fighting, but you are also creating great comedy dialogue. Write it down. And you'll probably win the fight, too. We are more likely to win fights with a punch line than a punch-out.

Margaret Smith

> "Does it hurt your back to kiss your own ass like that?"
>
> —FROM NBC'S *WILL AND GRACE,* WILL'S RETORT TO A FRIEND WHO IS BRAGGING ABOUT WHAT A LADIES' MAN HE IS

Looking in the mirror you notice that you've gained weight, but instead of calling yourself a worthless tub of lard you start playing with your bulging midriff and start seeing some advantages to being fat. You have leaped into the zone. And you write it down.

> "I used to think it was weird that dogs had nipples on their stomach . . . then I looked at myself naked."
>
> —JUDY CARTER

 etting into the Zone

My experience as a comedy coach has been that when students bring in material that they carefully plotted out on their computers, it can be clever and smart but sound too literary and contrived to get laughs. The best way to write killer material, the kind that will rock a room and threaten to create hernias from laughing too hard, is to capture and expand upon spontaneous moments. That means that you want to create material when you are in the funny zone.

As children we play and joke and aren't worried about what others think. Put a comic and a kid onstage and the audience invariably will watch the child, because children are always in the zone. You can write comedy while sitting alone at a computer, but it might end up sounding forced and devoid of energy. This doesn't mean you necessarily need to be standing, talking, writing, and improvising all at the same time when you create comedy material. It's different for everyone. You need to find for yourself what it takes to put you in the zone.

For me, it's working in front of another comic—someone who doesn't judge me and understands that 80 percent of my attempts at comedy material are going to fail. Someone who keeps the energy going. I almost never create material alone or sitting down. I need to be standing up. I am not funny in a chair. I also never fully write my material down. Instead, I jot notes on the back of unopened junk mail envelopes. That is what works for me. What works for you may be very different.

Exercise: Finding Your F-Zone

Look back at the exercise "Writing Your Ideas" on page 40, where you listed what you were saying when you made others laugh. Describe the circumstances. Were you standing? Was there music on? What else? Recreating these circumstances will help to put you in the f-zone no matter what kind of mood you are in.

_____

_____

_____

_____

_____

But getting into the zone is just a start. Whether it's a joke, a script, or a greeting card, comedy takes work. I've seen a lot of very funny, talented people quit when the going got tough. Comedy can get scary.

Comedy . . .
Be Afraid,
Be Very Afraid

Does the thought of standing alone onstage trying to make a sea of strangers laugh scare you? Do you get a knot in your stomach at the words "Well, I read your script and I have some comments"? Does sitting in front of a computer with no ideas whatsoever fill you with thoughts of "Well, maybe working at Staples wasn't that bad!"

If comedy scares you, then congratulations—you get it. Comedy *is* scary. A survey taken by *USA Today* noted that the number one fear people share is not the fear of dying but the fear of standing in front of people—and dying, so to speak. Just look at the words comics use: "I died." "I killed them." "I slayed them." Comedy can be violent. Or at least it can feel that way. So, if you aren't frightened of doing comedy or writing comedy, take your pulse—you might be dead.

You also might have some "neggie" voices turning up the volume when you try to do something creative. Do any of the following criticisms have a familiar ring to them?

> "You're no good."
> "You're stupid."
> "You're doing it wrong."

Some of us have had our creativity so beaten down by others—most likely parents—that we annihilate our own ideas before they can take form. Let's say that when you were a child you built the most wondrous sand castle. You were absolutely committed to translating the vision in your head into reality. Then let's say your dad comes along and tells you that you are doing it wrong. "Castles don't look like that," he says. "Do it this way." How do you think you are going to feel the next time you are in the sand? You don't want to do it wrong, so you just don't do it. How many times did something like that happen to you? Take those experiences and multiply them times a million and you might understand what's blocking your creative free expression of your ideas. It becomes safer not doing, not trying, not taking the risk of being wrong. You become another person, sitting on a couch drinking beer and criticizing others, saying things like, "This guy sucks. I could do it better than him."

But you don't do it at all.

Fear—It's a Good Thing

It's worth spending some time on the topic of fear. I see so many very talented comedy neophytes quit because they let fear get the best of them. One student in my class was so terrified of going onstage that he made his beeper go off as if he were being paged. Each time, he said, "My wife is having a baby." By the third class, we knew something was up, or that his wife was having triplets and it was a very long labor. Many students won't admit that they are frightened. They just stop showing up.

Fear is not the problem. The problem lies in the way we deal with it—or rather don't deal with it. A lot of times we don't realize when we are frightened, even though our actions and decisions are based solely on fear. For instance, we might not go to a party because we are frightened to go alone, but what we tell ourselves is, "I'm too tired, I have a big day tomorrow."

Your unexpressed fears could be holding your creative process hostage. You might stop reading this book because you feel uncomfortable about failing, but what you say to yourself is, "It isn't practical for me to do comedy," or, "I'm wasting my time," or, "I'm the leader of the free world; I should be focusing on Iraq." And slowly but surely the "practicality" that cloaks our fears pounds our dreams into dust.

Brave people are *not* unafraid. What distinguishes them is that they act *despite* the fear. And funny people don't necessarily find it easy to pop off before an audience of two thousand. Actually, people who are self-confident and even saintly aren't the funniest people in the world. You might notice that there are not many spiritual gurus who have achieved cosmic consciousness hanging around open-mike nights at comedy clubs. Also, insecurity is funny. Woody Allen is at his funniest when he's most neurotic.

> **"I don't mind death—I just don't want to be there when it happens."**
> **—Woody Allen**

So if you're waiting to get more confidence before you perform—forget it. Do the following instead.

Exercise: Judy's 5-Step Fear Management Program

Step 1. Admit Your Fears to Yourself

Stand-up Comedy Fears

Imagine yourself doing stand-up. Write all thoughts of fear, impending doom, anxiety, apprehension, dread, foreboding, or panic in the right column. And be honest, not funny.

Judy's Fear List	Your Fear List
Bombing	
Having hack material	
Looking fat	
Incontinence	
Running out of material	
The audience doesn't get me.	
I make a fool of myself.	
I have to follow someone who really kills.	
They'll hate me.	

Scriptwriting Fears. Imagine you're writing a script. What are your fears?

Judy's Fear List	Your Fear List
I won't have ideas.	
I'm wasting time.	
I'll be bored.	
It's lonely.	
I'll discover that I have no talent.	
Someone will steal my idea.	
I won't be able to sell it.	
My script sucks.	
My characters suck.	

Step 2. Evaluate Your Fears

Now go back over these lists and cross off all unrealistic fears. For instance, if one of your fears is dying onstage, you can X that out. More people have died from clogged pores than from doing stand-up. Although performing might make you sweat and grunt, dying is not an option even when you wish it would be.

Step 3. Confide in a Friend

Then call a friend and tell him or her your *realistic* fears. Fear loses a lot of its power when it's out in the open. Plus you might also get a few laughs. Some of the best material comes from outbursts of honesty. With the right twist, those neggie thoughts of yours can turn into comedy gold.

> **"This guy told me he thought I was attractive. When I get a nice compliment I like to take it in, swish it around in my brain . . . until it becomes an insult."**
> **—SHEILA WENZ**

Step 4. Golden Opps

In this exercise we are going to play out our realistic fears and, step by step, give them a positive spin. For instance, one of my fears is, "Nobody will understand me." Write one of your fears here: *Your* fear is

_____

_____

On the left column I play out each step of *what will happen* with my fear, playing it out until it turns positive. You fill in the right column. Write as many or as few as you can think of.

Judy's List	Your List
If nobody understands me . . .	If . . .
then I'll feel misunderstood	then . . .
then I'll feel bad	then . . .
then it will get back to my agent	then . . .
then I will lose my agent	then . . .
then I'll get a better agent	then . . .
then I'll have better gigs	then . . .
then I'll have a better career	then . . .
then I'll be performing at places where everyone understands me	then . . .
	then . . .

Step 5. Take Action

Fear is like the school bully who's made you his target. You can try to avoid him by walking home a different way, but he will always find you. Are you going to let the fear of losing your lunch money dictate where and how you live? Or will you do the scary thing and deal directly with the bad guy? Successful people are not necessarily less frightened than you—they just do things in spite of being frightened.

Phyllis Diller

Pro Talk *with Phyllis Diller*

"For fifteen years I was terror-stricken. Try flop sweat that ended up in your shoes! I never had to soak my feet, they got soaked every night. In fact, I am still wearing the same very expensive Herbert Levine boots and the inside leather lining has been eaten by the acid of my flop sweat. Just because you are frightened doesn't mean that you are never going to make it. In my case, I had to do it—I had five hungry children. Poverty and motherhood together are the greatest motivation in this world."

Most human beings are afraid to look stupid, and when doing comedy, we take that risk in a big way. There is only one way to deal with this fear—do something stupid.

Pick something that you are scared of doing and go do it—something legal, of course. It won't help to say something like, "Oh, Officer, I robbed the bank because I'm working on my comedy career."

Pick something to do that is out of your comfort zone. It doesn't even have to be about comedy. It can be:

- "I'm going to call and ask someone out."
- "I'm going to ask for a raise."
- "I'm going to eat lunch with a stranger."
- "I'm going to tell my parents I'm gay." (Even if you're not.)

Or it can be something to further your comedy career:

- "I'm going to perform at an open mike."
- "I'm going to call an agent."
- "I'm going to write new material."

Exercise: Taking Action

Write down five actions that you would like to do today were you not blocked by fear.

_____

_____

_____

_____

_____

Now pick one and do it!

After you take action on one of your fears, write how it felt. Was it as scary as you thought? Can you do something tomorrow that is even scarier?

_____

_____

_____

_____

_____

Comedy Buddies: Finding Your Fun Mate

I strongly recommend working through this book with a comedy buddy. Jay Leno, Dennis Miller, and Rosie O'Donnell don't develop material alone and neither should you. Most often sitcom writers are hired in teams. It's important to have someone to bounce your ideas off. I can always identify the students in my workshops who work alone; after they deliver their jokes, the class stares blankly at them, going, "Huh?" Running material by a comedy buddy before going public assists comics in eliminating all the this-is-relatable-only-to-myself-and-my-cat jokes. So, until you have your own staff, find at least one buddy you feel comfortable with, someone you can get stupid with and can bomb in front of—because sometimes comedy is not pretty.

You have to be careful about who you choose. Some people make you feel funnier just by being around them. Others make you wonder if you've ever been funny in your life. Your grandmother might make you nice cookies but she may not get your sense of humor.

A good comedy session is like a hot game of tennis. You want to play with someone who is going to return your ideas and maybe even put a new spin on them. If you keep serving and your comedy buddy never returns the ball, think about working with someone else.

PRO TALK *with comic George Wallace*

"I started stand-up in New York with Seinfeld and we always bounced material off each other. When we had a bit that wasn't working, other New York comics would say, 'Try this and try that.' In New York, comics tend to hang out together and network and get other jobs, where in L.A., they have cars and they've got to get back to their respective counties."

Exercise: Finding the Right Comedy Buddy

Make a list of five friends who you would feel comfortable working with.

1. _____

2. _____

3. _____

4. _____

5. _____

Can't think of anyone? Then go hang out at a comedy club and talk to people. We can also help you on-line. To find a comedy buddy in your neck of the woods, post a notice on our Web site at *www.comedyworkshopS.com.*

Quit While You're Ahead

Stand-up students are always asking me, "Do you think I have what it takes to do stand-up, or should I quit?" I never can answer this question. I am often shocked at who does and doesn't make it. After ten years of teaching, I've learned that it's not always the person with the most talent who succeeds—it's the one with the most endurance.

"Hey, Judy, I haven't even begun. Why bring up quitting now?"

Planning when you quit is better than quitting in reaction to a bad audience, a writer's block, or a lack of progress. How many projects have you started and never finished? Probably quite a few. Sometimes we quit because we get bored, or because we don't have time, or the going gets rough, or we start having a hot affair and are doing our best just to get out of bed. Most likely you won't make a conscious decision when to quit working on comedy; rather, your enthusiasm will just fade away.

Quitting is not necessarily a bad thing, if *you* control it. Jerry Seinfeld quit after nine years of a highly successful TV series, *Seinfeld,* even though NBC offered him $5 million an episode. Seinfeld listened to his inner comic. "I felt the moment," he said about his decision to retire the show in 1998. "I knew from being onstage for years and years and years, there's one moment where you have to feel the audience is still having a great time, and if you get off right there, they walk out of the theater excited. And yet, if you wait a little bit longer and try to give them more for their money, they walk out feeling not as good. If I get off now, I have a chance at a standing ovation."

Actually there is another reason Seinfeld stopped short of a tenth season: nine is his lucky number. "He's very superstitious," his mother, Betty, told magazine writer Debra L. Wallace. "Everything has to be divisible by nine."

PRO TALK *with comic Richard Lewis*

"I didn't make money at doing stand-up for a long time, but I never thought about quitting. I did it purely for the passion of it all."

Being successful in comedy means making a commitment to your creative process. That means deciding at the starting gate where your finish line is and committing to run the entire race.

PRO TALK *with Jim Carrey*

"Before *Ace* [*Ventura, Pet Detective*] came out, I spent fifteen years on the comedy club circuit. I once had a repertoire of a hundred and fifty impressions, and promises of fame and promises of glory that faded away. Too often I'd heard studio executives saying, 'You've had your chance,' and wham!—I was out of the light into the dark again."

Exercise—Examining Your Commitment

Answer these questions in your notebook. As of right now . . .

- Why do I want to do comedy?
- Am I better off quitting?
- What are the consequences of quitting?
- What are the consequences of *not* quitting?

PRO TALK *with comic George Wallace*

"There was one time I thought about quitting—all I ever wanted to do when I started was to work a showroom in Vegas. And I was lucky—one and a half years after I started, Diana Ross had me open for her at Caesars Palace. I walked out one night, got a standing ovation in front of Diana Ross, and I thought, 'I could go back to advertising sales because I've reached my goal.' Then I thought, 'Hell no!' "

Exercise: When Will You Quit?

(* Denotes all the things that have happened to the author.)

❏ When you can't think of an answer to exercises in this book?

❏ When your life gets too "busy" to finish this book?

❏ When your comedy buddy turns out to be a flake and doesn't get together with you?*

❏ After you bomb at your first open mike?*

❏ After you kill at your first open mike?

❏ At the first signs of writer's block?*

❏ When you get your first paying gig and the check bounces?*

❏ When you showcase for a famous agent who says, "Keep your day job"?*

❏ When you see other comics stealing your material?*

❏ When you've been doing comedy for three years and still don't have enough money to cover your rent?

❏ When you're making a great living headlining in comedy clubs?*

❏ When your parents threaten to disinherit you for choosing comedy as a career?

❏ When you get your first television job and then get cut out of the show at the last minute?*

❏ When a club owner develops a grudge against you and faxes everyone in the business to tell them not to hire you?*

❏ When you get a development deal and nothing happens?*

❏ When the agent who was excited about signing you stops returning your calls?*

❏ When your agent dumps you and you can't find another agent?*

❏ When a producer turns your act into a sitcom—and then wants someone *else* to play *you!*

❏ When you sell your screenplay but the producers hire another writer for a rewrite?*

❏ When you get your own sitcom and you're the lowest-paid person on it?*

❏ When you get picked to act in a TV pilot—your big break—and it doesn't get picked up?

❏ When your sitcom makes it onto the air—with low ratings?

❏ When you're fired from the show that *you* created?

❏ When they offer you $5 million an episode to keep your sitcom on the air, but you're already a millionaire and you want more time off?

❏ After reading this list?

So, when are you going to quit? I thought at first that I would quit when the phone stopped ringing. But when the phone stopped ringing, I hired a publicist and made it start ringing again. Every seeming roadblock has a detour that will eventually get you back on course.

I'm quitting comedy after my first stroke. Then again, since I'm a gadget head, I could still write funny stories with my specially equipped eyeball-controlled computer. So I'll quit when I'm dead. Unless I'm a funny spirit and can channel jokes to some up-and-coming comic.

When you are going to quit? Make a conscious commitment here and now—in *ink!* Aim high. For example, "I'm going to keep doing comedy until my tenth million is safely in the bank." Or, "After my third Academy Award." Or, "When my dad actually laughs at one of my jokes."

I'm going to keep doing comedy until

_____

_____

_____

_____

_____

PRO TALK *with comic Richard Jeni*

"At the beginning you're always kind of quitting. If you're starting out and it's horrible and everyone hates you and nobody wants to talk to you and you feel like a total worthless piece of crap every minute, then you're on schedule. At the beginning, you know the audience doesn't like you, and the club owners don't like you because the audience doesn't like you, and you don't like you because the club owners and the audience don't like you. It's a very rocky hard time. There's no getting around that boot camp period."

Richard Jeni

ommitment Contract

Now that you know when you are going to quit, that means you have made a commitment. If you're like me, you find it harder to break a commitment if someone else knows about it. Have you ever avoided telling a friend about a project because they might hold you to it? Telling someone else that you are going to do stand-up or write a sitcom can strengthen your own commitment. We at Comedy Workshops are committed to your comedy process and we would like you to make a commitment with us.

We will track your progress and give you assistance along the way with encouragement, practical tips, and new exercises.

Fill in (in ink).

I commit to doing comedy until _____
_____ .

Signed _____ Date: _____

E-mail: _____

Address: _____

Now copy this page and fax or e-mail it to *(fax)* 310-398-8046 or *(e-mail)* info@comedyworkshopS.com.

The Comedy Bible's
Ten
Commandments

Follow these ten commandments and you just might get to comedy heaven. Forsake them and you could spend your entire career in open-mike purgatory or spec script hell.

1. Thou shalt not covet thy neighbor's jokes, premises, or bits.

Throughout this book there are examples of jokes from my students and the pros. This material is for educational purposes only. It is copyrighted material and should not be reproduced or stolen. When you rip off somebody else's material, you are not only robbing them; you're also stealing from yourself because you're not pursuing your own creative process. You might think of another comic's material while reading this book, but don't delude yourself by pretending that you thought of it. You'll cheat yourself from developing your own unique perspective. Don't swim in those waters.

Someone else's material might help to get your foot in the door, but you'll soon find some comic's foot in your butt. Word will get around fast that you steal material, and since a lot of comics book clubs, you will get blacklisted and never again work. Your own material—don't do comedy without it.

2. Honor thy mother and father, but don't hesitate to put them in your act or scripts.

Some beginning comics think it's disrespectful to poke fun at their parents. They're right. But being a comic is not about being nice and polite—it's about being funny. Those little irritating habits of your parents can be comedy gold. Actually, students are surprised to find that their parents are flattered to be included in their act. But no guarantees here about staying in the will.

3. Thou shalt not bear false witness.

Be authentic with your point of view and explore topics that you really care about. The old days of doing disingenuous jokes for the sake of being funny will sound hack. Humiliating your wife or husband for the sake of a laugh won't make you famous and might make you single. Can you say "divorce"?

4. Thou shalt notice how stupid God made the world.

Funny is all around you. Keep your eyes open. Write down all the weirdness, stupidity, and oddness you see.

5. Thou shalt get a comedy buddy.

Material that you write by yourself is guaranteed to make *you* laugh—and usually, that's about it. If you want to make sure it will make someone *else* laugh, why not have someone with you while you write it? Working with someone can help you find new slants on the old stuff and keep cranking it out when you want to nap.

6. Thou shalt choose a comedy writing day and keep it holy.

Make the time to get together with your comedy buddy as important as your appointment with your therapist, lover, or plastic surgeon. Don't break your dates with your comedy buddy.

7. Thou shalt carry around a pad and a pen at all times.

Because you never know when "funny" will happen, carry a small notebook in your pocket, bag, or backpack. When weirdness happens, write it down. You may think that you will remember it, but chances are you won't.

8. Thou shalt not skip any of the exercises in Part One.

They may seem silly or pointless, but those exercises will help you form a stockpile of raw material that you will later turn into killer stuff. Don't waste time getting critical of your ideas. Even the flimsiest of ideas can lead to something extraordinary.

9. Create a stand-up act even if you just want to write sitcoms.

In the kernel of a joke lives the underlying structure of all comedy forms. If you know how to write a joke, you will be able to translate that skill into writing scripts, articles, and other comedy forms.

If you're wondering where the tenth commandment is, then congratulations. You're already starting to notice the weird, the stupid, and the odd.

Exercise: Your Creative Process

Where are you the most creative? In the living room, bed, or maybe on the toilet? To get the creative juices flowing, do you need quiet, your stereo blasting, or just more fiber in your diet?

What is the best environment for your creative process? (A lot of this book was written on a laptop in the lobbies of cheap hotels.)

_____

_____

_____

What is the best time of day for you to work? (I do it in the morning or I don't do it at all.)

_____

_____

_____

Who is your best choice for a comedy buddy? (Relatives are generally not a good choice.)

_____

Action Checklist

So far I've

❑ passed the funny test

❑ got my comedy supplies—pen, small notebook, large binder, index cards

❑ written down ideas for a joke, a sitcom, a magazine article, and a film

❑ examined what makes me laugh and what puts me in the funny zone

❑ completed Judy's 5-Step Fear Management Program

❑ signed and mailed in the commitment contract

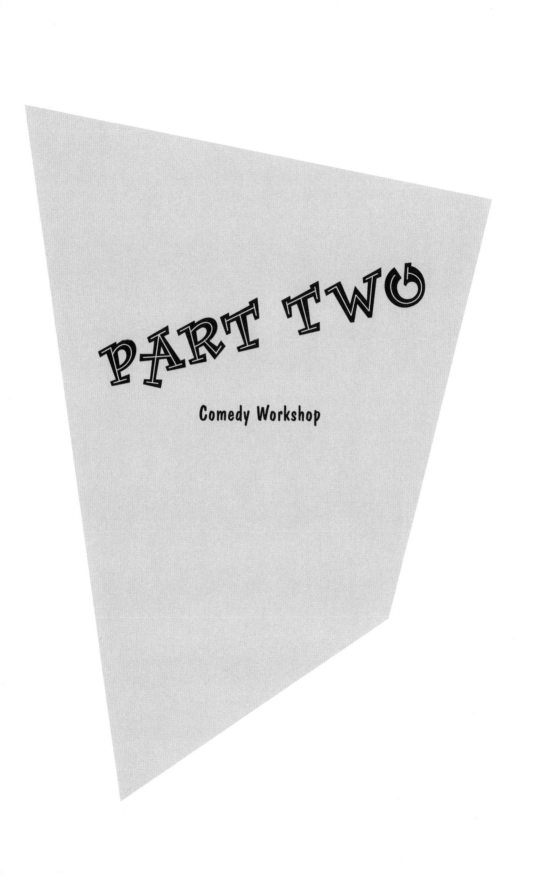

PART TWO

Comedy Workshop

26 Days to Killer Comedy Material

That's right, twenty-six days from now you are going to know how to write jokes based on your life experiences and perform them. Many of my students who have followed these techniques have ended up as working stand-up comics and comedy writers. Why not you?

Note. The instructions in this book are suggestions only. Joke writing is a very elusive art form and there are many different ways of approaching it. There might be some exercises that will do nothing for you and some comedy theories that you will find stupid and of no help. That's good. You're funny—you're supposed to find things stupid. I always say, use what works for you and leave the rest. And if nothing works for you, well, sorry, no refund.

"But Judy, I'm really a writer. I have no intention of performing. The idea of getting up onstage makes me want to projectile-vomit."

> **PRO TALK** *with Rob Lotterstein, sitcom writer, TV producer, former stand-up student*
>
> "My goal wasn't to be a stand-up comic, as anyone who saw me perform could tell you. But doing stand-up taught me how to pitch jokes and story ideas which get me work. And from working in front of an audience I got a real feel of what makes people laugh."

Even if it's scary and you have no intention of being a stand-up comic, you'll get a lot out of giving performing a try. Stand-up comics are very often hired to write sitcoms, political sound bites, books, and screenplays, as well as to direct and write movies. Why? Because *stand-up is the most condensed form of comedy,* and if you understand the basic principles of the simplest of jokes, you will be able to translate that skill to many different domains, whether writing, performing, or marketing. Because it's all about making an audience laugh. And whether that audience is sitting at a nightclub, watching your sitcom on TV, or reading your script, you have to make them laugh.

All comedy forms have basically the same structure. A joke is just the sparest version of that form. As elegant as a haiku, a joke has a setup, a turn, and a tag. A sitcom has act one, a turn, and a resolve. A screenplay has the same elements—it's just a longer form. And look at a greeting card: the front cover is the setup; open it and there's the punch. Many comedy professionals started out by doing stand-up. Thus it's not too surprising that major motion picture comedy director Tom Shadyac (who directed *Liar Liar, Ace Ventura, The Nutty Professor,* and *Patch Adams*) started in stand-up—in my class! TV comedy writers Rob Lotterstein *(Dream On, Caroline in the City)* and Davey DiGeorgio *(Late Show with David Letterman)* jump-started their careers by doing stand-up in my workshop. Comedy actors Paul Reiser, Roseanne Barr, and Michael Keaton all started by performing stand-up—but not in my class.

PRO TALK *with Tom Shadyac, feature director*

"Having started as a stand-up comic, I can truly understand the concerns of the actors I work with, such as Jim Carrey, Robin Williams, and Eddie Murphy. It really helps."

Sometimes a joke becomes the premise for a sitcom. It then gets made into a movie, becomes a cartoon strip, and before you can zip open the lock top, becomes licensed merchandise.

Seth MacFarlane, creator and executive producer of the animated show *Family Guy,* did stand-up when he was in college. When one of my students, Davey DiGeorgio, was interviewed for a staff writing position on the *Late Show with David Letterman,* his written material was not enough; they wanted to see the video of his stand-up showcase. And if you look at the staff of the top TV sitcoms, most of the writers and producers started by doing stand-up.

PRO TALK *with Seth MacFarlane, creator and executive producer of* Family Guy

"I developed many of the voices for the characters in *Family Guy* in my stand-up act."

But it's not just important to know how to *write* jokes; it's vital to get up and *perform* jokes. Since most jokes end up being spoken rather than read, it is necessary for comedy writers to get the direct experience of performing their material. Performing stand-up in front of an audience will give you a direct, immediate feel of what is funny that you can't get from sitting in front of your computer. And although the joke examples in this section are mostly from stand-up comics, later you will learn how these joke writing principles apply to *all* forms of comedy—sitcoms, articles, essays, and so on.

"There are a lot of ways to make people laugh. Why is it so important to start as a joke writer?"

Here's one important reason: an invention that has changed the human mind forever—the remote control. When you have that little baby in your hand, you are God, controller of what you see and hear. And how long does it take before you get bored and change the channel? Two seconds, if you're patient. That means your material has to dazzle an audience in a very short period of time. And in the comedy business, an audience can be anyone—a drunk watching your act, a producer reading your script, a studio executive listening to a story pitch. Once you know the construction of a joke you will know the principles of grabbing and holding the attention of *any* audience you may have to face.

"But I don't have time to work on this every day. Should I wait until I have more time?"

Students who wait until they have enough time usually wait themselves out of doing it altogether. Note that *these twenty-six days do not need to be consecutive days*. The creative process doesn't necessarily happen on a rigid time schedule. When I skip a few days of writing—OK, a week—it might appear as if I am a slacker, especially when I'm on my snowboard. But I find that I need that time to process ideas in my subconscious mind. I need to dream my ideas, and then, when I get back to the actual writing, it flows. Thinking about writing *is* working. However, if you are taking more than four days off, you are a slacker and need to do something to get yourself back on course. If you find yourself really stuck, go back and redo Judy's 5-Step Fear Management Program (page 46) to rejuvenate your creative process.

Let's begin . . .

Day 1: Get a Gig

Time allotment: one hour to one month, depending on how much you procrastinate. Book yourself doing three minutes at two different open mikes.

"Oh no! I don't even have an act yet! I'm going to skip this one."

Comedy is not for wimps. To paraphrase the old saying, "To procrastinate is human, to perform is nuts." Or something like that. If you are like most human beings, you are one big procrastinator. That is why all our comedy workshops, even the ones for novices, end with a showcase. Knowing that they will have to perform in public makes the students really do the work—now. And committing to *two* open mikes is important, because writing comedy is about reworking material.

Yes, it's scary, but booking yourself *before* you have an act is a great way to make sure you develop an act—in this case your fear works *for* you. Face it, no matter what you do, you are going to die anyway, so you might as well take a leap of faith and get yourself some gigs.

"What is an open mike?"

An open mike is a place where amateurs are permitted to perform—typically for free. Comedy clubs will often set aside one night for amateurs, and many bookstores, bars, and colleges have open mikes where people can sign up and perform without having to audition. Sometimes in L.A. and New York you will find pros working out the kinks in their new material, but mostly it's for people who are just beginning their comedy careers.

"How do I find a place to perform?"

- Call your local comedy club and find out when they have an amateur night.
- Check your local paper for open mikes in coffeehouses, bookstores, bars, organizations, and so on. If you live in Los Angeles, San Francisco, or New York it's best to stay clear of the major comedy clubs for the first year and do open mikes in low-profile places.
- See if there is an open mike at your college.
- Go to our Web site *(www.comedyworkshopS.com)* to find out if there are any open mikes in your area, and post a query in our comedy forum.
- Hang out at a comedy club and ask other comics to suggest places where you can perform.
- If all else fails, start your own open mike. When I was a kid magician, I produced a show in my backyard for charity. I printed up tickets, went door to door inviting people to my show. I actually got it featured in the *L.A. Times.* Not bad PR for a ten-year-old.

"Are some open mikes better than others? What should I watch out for?"

All open mikes aren't created equal. Some are not set up for comedy, so no matter how funny you are, you won't get laughs. Here's what to look for when choosing a venue in which to perform.

- Can the audience see the stage? A lot of open mikes are not really set up well for comedy and have all sorts of obstacles blocking the audience's view. When I was starting out, I performed in a revolving bar at a Holiday Inn. By the time I got to the punch, I had a different audience. Not a good room.
- Is it a rowdy room? Sometimes you discover too late that a place is too rough—like when you're already in the ER having bullet fragments removed from your kidneys. So here are a few tips: A sports bar during the World Series makes a lousy open mike. And if you see a sign that says, "All the beer you can drink and comedy too!" don't expect the crowd to laugh at Nietzsche jokes.
- Is your act right for the room? It might be hard to get a Harlem audience at a Def Jam comedy night to empathize with how hard it was for you to pay off your student loans for Harvard, just as your routine about how hard it is to get laid might not get laughs at an open-mike night at the Saint Maria Goretti Catholic Church.
- Is there a sound system setup? This is very important—especially if there are hecklers. At least with a mike you will be louder than them. Informal

open mikes at coffeehouses or bookstores rarely have mikes, but that's OK because they rarely have alcohol. And sober people tend not to toss out such witty retorts as "You suck!"

So, save money on therapy and check out a venue *before* you commit to performing there.

PRO TALK *with comic Diane Nichols*

"I was performing at the student union at UCLA and next door was a bowling alley. Every time I got to a punch line somebody would bowl a strike!"

Exercise: Committing to Performing

To successfully do the stand-up course, you will need to book one open mike twenty-one days from today and a second one two weeks later.

Because you are working alone, it might be hard to take this course seriously. In our workshops, when students don't show up, we page them. To get a bit more real, make a commitment and sign your pledge below—in *ink.*

First gig

I commit to perform at _____ (name of place)

on _____ (date)

Second gig: (14 days from above date)

I commit to perform at _____ (name of place)

on _____ (date)

Booking Comedy Buddy Sessions

In this twenty-six-day program to get your act together, you will need to commit to ten meetings with your comedy buddy at certain points in the process. Take out your Palm Pilots and commit to a schedule.

Day 3 (time and date) _____ place _____
Day 5 (time and date) _____ place _____

Day 7 (time and date) _____ place _____

Day 9 (time and date) _____ place _____

Day 10 (time and date) _____ place _____

Day 11 (time and date) _____ place _____

Day 13 (time and date) _____ place _____

Day 14 (time and date) _____ place _____

Day 15 (time and date) _____ place _____

Day 19 (time and date) _____ place _____

Day 1 Action Checklist

❑ I booked two open mikes.

❑ I arranged comedy buddy meetings.

DO NOT GO ON TO DAY 2 UNTIL THE ABOVE IS COMPLETED, EVEN IF IT TAKES YOU TWO MONTHS.

Day 2: Learn Joke Structure—the Setup

Note. Read all joke examples out loud so you know what they *sound* like, rather than what they *read* like.

Today you are going to

1. learn comedy structure
2. write setups
3. get serious about comedy

The structure of stand-up is very simple. Jokes are broken down into five parts.

ATTITUDE + TOPIC + PREMISE + ACT-OUT + MIX + ACT-OUT

Attitude
Topic   **THE SETUP (SERIOUS)**
Premise

Act-out
Mix   **THE FUNNY (FUNNY)**

The setup is not the funny part of a joke, but it is the most important part. If you can't get the audience interested at the beginning of a joke, they are not going to be there at the end of the joke. Audiences make up their minds very quickly, so on every joke it's important to *first* capture their attention, *then* make them laugh.

Setups are usually very serious and authentic—meaning that they have a ring of truth and honesty. Look at these serious setups from some very funny people.

> [*Setup*] "I hope you're in love and I hope you feel good about yourself, because I am not in love and I don't feel good about myself. I recently broke up with this woman."
>
> —RICHARD LEWIS

> [*Setup*] "My doctor told me that I had cancer and I was going to have a hysterectomy."
>
> —JULIA SWEENEY

When you seem sincere and personally revealing in your setup, it gets the audience to relate to what you're talking about. Then, when you jump to the funny part, it creates a surprise that makes people laugh. If you *start* funny, there is no way to *build* to the laugh.

> [*Setup*] "My doctor told me that I had cancer and I was going to have a hysterectomy. [*funny part*] Why do they always have to remove a part of your body you need? Why can't people get cancer of fat? 'Julia, you've got cancer of your fat and we are going to have to take it all out.' "
>
> —JULIA SWEENEY

I challenge you to be as serious and unfunny as possible when doing today's setup exercises.

"I don't want to be bogged down with structure. I just want to get up there and be funny."

PRO TALK *with His Holiness the Dalai Lama, Tibetan Buddhist spiritual leader and Nobel Peace Prize recipient*

"Learn the rules so you know how to break them properly."

Before you break the rules, you need to know what they are. Trying to be funny without first knowing the structure will be a hit-and-miss experience. Stand-up is a highly structured craft. When done well, it looks like the comic is just improvising off the top of her head. But really, all professional comics have a thorough understanding of what makes material work or not work. Don't kid yourself. Funny stuff takes work. If it was as easy as the pros make it look, many more people would be quitting their day jobs.

> <u>**Pro Talk**</u> *with comic Greg Proops*
>
> "No one is a natural—you have to work at being a natural."

Comedy Structure: The Topic

Attitude + TOPIC + Premise + Act-out + Mix + Act-out

Each joke is always about something, and that something I call a topic. Unless the audience is clear about *what* you are joking about, they're not going to laugh. Later we will go into great detail about how to pick your topics, but for the sake of this exercise, I'm going to assign you a topic and we will work on the process of developing a joke together. My topic is "body piercing." Your topic is "drugs."

"But I don't want to joke about drugs."

Shut up.

Comedy Structure: The Attitude

ATTITUDE + Topic + Premise + Act-out + Mix + Act-out

Our next step is to add attitude to the topic. Attitude gives a joke energy and direction. Just as actors never say their lines without emotion and intent, neither does a stand-up comic say a joke without attitude. Even when *writing* comedy, each joke needs to be connected to an attitude or an emotion. That's why comedy writers often work with a partner or a tape recorder, reciting jokes out loud with attitude, and *then* write them down. Jokes without attitude can end up sounding too literary, perhaps humorous but not funny enough to get the big laughs.

Here are the four basic attitudes that are useful for working with this book—and writing jokes for, say, the rest of your career:

1. "weird"
2. "scary"
3. "hard"
4. "stupid"

Memorize these words. Say them out loud right now. Elongate them as you say them. *"Harrrrrrrrd!"* These words are a comic's tool to get the really big laughs. You might have a funny idea for a joke, a great topic, a funny character, but without attitude it will remain just that—a funny idea. You gotta season your raw material by marinating it in attitude. Adding attitude to a joke is like putting gas in your car—now it can go someplace. Attitude provides the energy that moves a topic from idea to joke. I cannot emphasize this enough.

Robin Williams

"Piercing is weird. I come from San Francisco, where there are a lot of people into body piercing. They get to where they look like they've been mugged by a staple gun. Fifteen earrings here, a little towel rack there."

—ROBIN WILLIAMS

The attitude "weird" drives Williams's joke and in the end he tells us just how weird piercing is.

Sometimes the attitude is said in the form of a question.

"Isn't dating hard? I asked this one girl out and she said, 'You got a friend?' I said yes and she said, 'Then go out with him.' "

—DOM IRRERA

The hardest part of performing is engaging the audience. Posing the attitude+topic as a question is one powerful way to get the attention of an audience.

It is also important to hold the attitude or the emotion throughout the entire joke.

*"Why use such **negative words?** What about **love?"***

Nobody in their right mind will pay cover and inflated drink prices to hear what comics or writers *love*. Look at Howard Stern's high rating and you can see that people tune in to hear someone say all the stuff that most people are too polite (or scared) to talk about—the things that scare them, that are stupid, and so on. And depending on your topic, the end result can be positive: "Racism is stupid." Get it?

"Not all comics say these attitude words before or in each joke. Hey, Judy . . . what's up with that?"

Professional comics always use attitude, even if they don't actually *say* the attitude word itself. Usually the attitude is implied. When Jay Leno says, "What is going on with the president?" the attitude implied is that what is going on with the president is something "stupid." He doesn't need to say, "Do you know what's stupid?" Attitude can be conveyed in the comic's puzzled expression or in his tone of voice. When creating material it is imperative that comics starting out (like *you*) actually *say* the attitude words when creating material. In my workshops, I found that if I let students slide and not say the attitude words, the attitude almost always vanishes from their act, along with the laughs. When you've done enough comedy that having attitude in your material becomes second nature, then you can stop worrying about having the attitude words. Seinfeld and Leno are at that point, but chances are that you aren't. So, at least for now, trust me.

"What about other attitude words, like hate, suck? *I don't want to sound like everyone else."*

There is only one reason I use these words when coaching—they work. In the process of doing countless workshops, I've discovered two things: these attitude words bring about the best results, and even when everyone starts with similar attitudes and the same topics, they all create totally different jokes. Even Beethoven started out playing scales on the piano. This is the beginning of the creating process. Later there will come a time when we take these attitude words out, but for now, stick with the program.

Exercise: Getting Attitude

Add each of the four attitude words to your topic, "drugs," posing it as a question. For instance, if your topic were "body piercing" your list would look like this:

1. You know what's *weird* about *body piercing?*
2. You know what's *scary* about *body piercing?*
3. You know what's *hard* about *body piercing?*
4. You know what's *stupid* about *body piercing?*

Now write your four questions here, using "drugs" instead of "body piercing."

_____

_____

_____

_____

Practice saying the above list, emphasizing the attitude. Do not be funny here. Keep it simple.

Comedy Structure: The Premise

Attitude + Topic + PREMISE + Act-out + Mix + Act-out

Now you are going to add a premise to your attitude+topic combo, to create what is called the setup.

SETUP = **Attitude + Topic + Premise**

A premise is also called an opinion, a hit, a slant, a spin, a point of view. The premise must clearly and precisely answer the question of the *attitude+topic.* It's usually more insightful than funny.

Here is the setup to a Robin Williams joke; the topic is "having kids" and the attitude is "hard."

[*You know what's hard about having kids?*] "When you have a baby, you have to clean up your act."

Williams's premise—"When you have a baby, you have to clean up your act"—clearly and specifically answers the question "What is *hard* about having kids?" It's not funny, but it is true and insightful. A comic wants the audience to relate to his premise, to feel, "Oh, yeah! I know what you are talking about!"

It's only *after* Williams states his premise that he reveals the funny part of the joke:

> "You can't come in drunk and go, 'Hey, here's a little switch. Daddy's going to throw up on you.' "

What makes a good premise?

- A good premise is *insightful*.

> [*What's stupid about freebasing?*] "Freebasing, it's not free. It'll cost you your house—it should be called homebasing."
>
> —Robin Williams

- A good premise is an *original* observation.

> [*It's weird that*] "We've gotten to the point that over-the-counter drugs are actually stronger than anything you can buy on the streets."

Denis Leary

That's Denis Leary's original hit on the topic of "drugs." It's a simple, logical answer to "What's weird about drugs?" It's also not funny. Only after stating the premise does Leary go to the funny by getting specific:

> "It says on the back of the NyQuil box, 'May cause drowsiness.' It should say, 'Don't make any plans.' "

- A good premise is very specific about what *exactly* is hard, weird, stupid, or scary about the topic.

> [*What's weird about health food stores?*] "It's weird how everyone in health food stores looks sick."
>
> —Debbie Kasper

Premise Pop Quiz

Practice by coming up with premises about *"relationships"*: *Do you know what's weird (hard, stupid, scary) about relationships?*

Premise examples:

- *"The first person who says, 'I love you,' loses power."*
- *"When you break up, everyone always blames the other person."*
- *"Romance goes out the window after the first year."*
- *"Once you have sex, they don't treat you as nice."*
- *"You get better gifts before you sleep with someone."*

Now try coming up with five premises about *"relationships"* on your own.

_____

_____

_____

_____

_____

A premise provides the foundation for smart material, not just for stand-up but for sitcoms, humor essays, and commentary. Later, in the chapter on writing sitcoms, you will find that each sitcom can be reduced to a single-line premise. That's why it is extremely valuable for writers who aren't necessarily going to be doing stand-up as a career to learn how to write original premises now.

Hack Attack: Common Premise Mistakes

- **A hack premise is general rather than specific.**
  "What's *hard* about relationships is men are weird." This premise—"men are weird"—is too *general.* Rather, set up exactly how "men are weird." Get specific because the funny is in the details. A more detailed setup would be, "What's hard about relationships is that men are always comparing their girlfriends to their mothers." Building on that setup, student Sharon King went on to create this joke: [*acting out boyfriend*] "You don't do nothing. My mother had two jobs and raised five kids." [*Sharon*] "Why can't I meet a man who's mother just sat on her ass all day?" *First* she wrote a serious premise and *later* she found the funny part.
- **A hack premise doesn't *answer the attitude+topic question.***
  "Do you know what's *hard* about relationships? I was on-line and after five minutes in a chat room, this woman thought we were married!" Look at the logic of this—or lack thereof. "I was on-line" doesn't answer "What

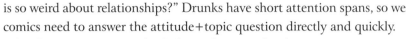
is so weird about relationships?" Drunks have short attention spans, so we comics need to answer the attitude+topic question directly and quickly.

■ **A hack premise is one that's been done to death.**
"What's weird about men is that they leave the toilet seat up." "Isn't it weird how dogs and cats are really different?" "It's weird how people pick their noses in their cars." Hack! "Isn't it weird how comedy writers use tired old lines and expect to have a career?"

■ **A hack premise is one that is untrue.**

Wrong way:

"The weird thing about being from Canada is that people stereotype you. Everyone thinks that everyone from there is funny. Mike Myers, John Candy, Michael J. Fox are all funny. That's a lot of pressure."

This is a hack premise because most people don't "think that everyone from there is funny." The truth is that most Americans don't think anything about Canada. Try a more truthful premise about Canada.

Right way:

"What's weird about Canada is that Canada has no personality. It's like America Lite."

All setups need to sound authentic and plausible. As comic Tom Dreeson, a comic veteran of fifty-nine *Tonight Show*s, once said, "Your setup needs to lead the audience down the path of *truth* and *then* surprise them."

"*[True part]* I grew up very poor with eight brothers and sisters. My mother used to buy us discount clothing. You know what I'm talking about? Rejects. *[made-up part]* She'd buy me these reject pants with the zipper on the side and the pocket in the front. One day I got arrested looking for change."

—TOM DREESON

Tom Dreesen

■ **A hack premise is one that tries to be funny rather than genuine.**
"What's weird about drugs is that they make you fart!" Stupid and hack. Usually my students' minds go blank in trying to *think* funny. Or in *trying* to be funny, they come up with stupid shock humor, the kind that was funny in third grade. Since the setup is the part of the joke that *sets up* the funny part, it's usually serious and unfunny—but

genuine. Many comics agree that the setup is more important than the funny part because this is where the audience decides if they like you or not. Even when writing sitcoms, many funny scripts are rejected because they sound jokey and aren't authentic to the characters. Whether writing or performing, if your setup seems jokey it can turn the audience off.

Here is another example of a hack premise from Tom Dreeson.

Wrong way:

"I was standing in my backyard and these aliens landed and probed me."

Hack! This premise tries to be funny and winds up sounding stupid and jokey. There's also no attitude, and this is less like a premise than like a story because it uses past-tense verbs—"I *was standing.*" The audience is thinking, "Oh, how am I going to bear five minutes of this idiot?"

There's a way to set up this premise so that it works.

Right way:

"My uncle is so *weird* he thinks aliens landed in his backyard and probed him."

This way the setup is credible and your uncle is the weird one—not you. Or you could do it this way:

"Did you read that *stupid* article in the *National Enquirer* where this guy thought aliens landed in his backyard and probed him?"

Thinking in terms of what is weird, stupid, scary, or hard, rather than thinking about what is funny, will free your creative process.

■ **A hack premise is about *you* rather than an insight about *others.*** "Isn't it weird how my girlfriend doesn't want to have sex?" What do I care? I don't even know your girlfriend.

Chances are if you are using the words *I, me,* or *my* in the premise, it's too self-absorbed and won't interest the audience. Start general and then get to something specific about yourself.

"[*General*] These days you have to be married or have a steady girlfriend because you can no longer have casual sex. [*specific*] Of course, I have never believed in casual sex anyway. I have always tried as hard as I could. No woman has ever said to me, 'Hey, you're taking this casually.' That's because I usually wear sweatpants. I have black cork I put under my eyes."

—GARRY SHANDLING

Once the audience is interested, you can bring in specific personal elements. But don't make it into a story about "you." Comedy writing is an intense investigation into what it means to be a *human being*—not what it means to be *you.*

"[*General premise*] You can't spank your kids anymore because they've got the 1-800-CHILD-ABUSIN' line. [*personal*] My parents were so strict, my mother would say, 'Go ahead and dial that number if you want to. Go ahead, the phone is right over there. 'Cause I'll be out of jail long before you are out of the hospital.' "
—GEORGE WALLACE

■ A hack premise is one that *describes* something that happened (story) rather than *gives an insight* about what happened.

The most common mistake that beginning comics make is confusing a *story* with a *premise.* Stories don't work in stand-up because they take too long to tell.

Wrong way:

"Do you know what's weird about relationships? I was dating this girl and she dumped me. I've been really lonely. I don't know how to cook or do the bills and I'm really desperate. I want to find someone new and I've been going out every night trying to find someone and nothing is happening. Girls don't like me."

"Oh waiter . . . check please." Stories are too long and boring. When the setup poses a question—"Do you know what's weird about relationships?"—the next sentence *must* answer it. "I was dating this girl and she dumped me" does not tell the audience what is *weird* about body piercing.

Right way:

"Do you know what's weird about relationships? You never meet someone when you really want to."

See how the above cuts to the chase with the insight and avoids the tediousness of having to hear "what really happened"?

Got it yet? A premise is not a description of what happened. It's a cut-to-the-chase, get-to-the-point, original observation. For instance, what premise could you gather from this faulty setup?

"The Internet is just too slow. You can't download anything without taking a long time."

This is just a statement of *what happened,* with *no* attitude and *no* premise. The first step is to give the topic—"the Internet"—an attitude: "weird."

Then drop the story and replace it with a premise, an original observation about something specific, such as:

"You know what's weird about the Internet? It's changed what women want in a guy—women now rate men by who's got the fastest Internet connection."

For right now, you don't need to know how you are going to make a premise funny. Fresh observations are easy to make funny.

"Women used to want a guy with a slow hand, now they want a man with a fast hard drive. 'Ohhh, you've got a T3 connection? I like a man with a lot of RAM and who knows how to use it.' "

Understanding the difference between a story about "what happened" and a premise is the key to successful comedy writing. It's also what makes it hard. Anyone can recite something that happened, but it takes imagination and insight to come up with a good premise.

"But Judy, a lot of my stories are really funny. I had a crowd in stitches at a party."

This is one of the hardest facts of comedy writing for my students and other beginning comics to get: something that works at a party, a dinner table, or a bar doesn't always work on a stage. Many think that it's important to tell audiences about something that "really happened." Wrong. Stand-up comedy is *premise-based,* not story-based. Students who are obsessed with having to tell their stories usually get no response and end up with "Well, I guess you had to be there" as their punch line. Not funny.

Even when writing scripts or essays, the same rule applies. A written piece might be based on something that actually happened, but professional writers rarely limit their writings to the simplistic retelling of a story. Structure, imagination, and artistry need to be applied to transform any story into a piece that works.

"But my *stories are* really *funny."*

OK, be stubborn. Tell your *really* funny stories. Then, after you bomb on your first open mike, come back to this lesson and learn how to write premises so you end up getting laughs.

Exercise: Writing Premises

Remember how I gave you the topic of "drugs" earlier? Write down all premises below. A few tips:

- Directly answer the attitude+topic question ("Do you know what's weird about drugs?").
- Keep it in present tense. (Don't use the verbs *were, was,* and so on.)
- Don't *try* to be funny.
- Avoid using the words, *I, me,* or *my* in the premise.
- Come up with a strong opinion, an insight, an original observation.

Judy's Premises on "Body Piercing"	Your Premises on "Drugs"
Piercing is stupid. It's painful enough just to be in a relationship. There is no need to add to it.	
It's hard to have everything pierced because when you are getting dressed in the morning, you have to decide not only what earrings to wear but which rings to put in your nose, your belly button, and even down there.	
It's hard being pierced when you go through metal detectors at the airport.	
It's hard to understand what people are saying when they've got hardware in their mouth.	
It's weird to see older people with nose rings.	
It's scary for parents to see their ten-year-olds get their bodies pierced.	
It's scary that nose rings are now an acceptable business accessory, like cuff links or a tie clip.	
It's scary that kids hurt their bodies as a way to rebel against their parents.	
It's stupid because it looks so unattractive.	
It's hard because if you have everything pierced, you have to buy more jewelry.	

Day 2 Pop Quiz

1. What are the four attitude words? _____
2. Every joke is about a _____
3. A premise is _____

Day 2 Exercise: Making a Date with Your Comedy Buddy

Make a date to get together with your comedy buddy and do what all pros do—have a comedy jam session to work on the funny part of the joke.

"I'm just going to do it myself because I don't know anyone who wants to learn joke writing."

Even if you are a hermit writing comedy alone in the Ozarks, you still need to jam your material with someone. You are creating material *for* people, and it needs to be written *with* people. If there's no one nearby, you can jam material by phone, but don't do it by e-mail. When jokes are first written instead of spoken, they usually end up sounding literary (and unfunny) when performed. If you need to find a comedy buddy and have access to the Web, go to *www.comedyworkshopS.com* and post a notice in our "Looking for Comedy Buddy" section. And if you truly don't know anyone, get a therapist. At least you'll have someone to talk to for an hour.

Day 2 Action Checklist

- ❑ Went over the four attitude words.
- ❑ Wrote ten premises with the topic "drugs."
- ❑ Made a date to get together with my comedy buddy.

Day 3: Learn Joke Structure—
the Funny Part (Comedy Buddy Day)

Today you and your comedy buddy will have a comedy jam session and

- read through the lesson
- hone your premises
- add act-outs

- add mixes
- fill out index cards

Exercise: Premise Check and Reworking Your Premise

Chances are that many of your ten premises on drugs are unclear, muddled, and incomprehensible. Sometimes things that make sense to *us* don't make sense to anyone else. It's hard to find the funny part of a joke if your premise doesn't work. That's why it's important to do a buddy check with each other's premises *before* creating the funny part of the joke. But it's not enough for your premise to be clear just to you and your buddy. Drunken strangers have to be able to get it too. Arriving at a clear premise usually takes a bit of work. Good, authentic premises generally require a lot of ranting and raving and plenty of assistance from your comedy buddy. Think of your original ten premises as a starting point.

Rewrite your original ten premises on "drugs" by having another jam session with your comedy buddy. Turn your tape recorder on and try standing up in front of your comedy buddy and pacing, or walking, while you talk. Movement helps get the energy going. When it comes to getting into your funny zone, use anything that works except heavy drugs. They don't really work anyway, except maybe with other people who are on them, and it could get very expensive making sure that your whole audience is always wasted. You and your buddy can take turns being the comic and the coach.

What does a comedy coach do?

- Helps his buddy get unstuck by repeatedly asking, "What's *weird, stupid, hard,* or *scary* about that?"
- Keeps asking, "What do you mean?" until the premise is *specific* and *clear.*
- Helps his buddy find an original, specific truth or insight about his topic.
- Keeps his buddy's energy up.
- Eliminates these words from his buddy's premises: *me, I, my.*
- Is generous with his time and energy. (I found that the more I assisted others, the more I learned about writing jokes for myself.)

A coaching session on premises should play out something like this:

COMIC: Do you know what's *weird* about piercing? It hurts.
COMEDY BUDDY: Well, it's true that it hurts, but that doesn't answer the question "What's weird?" Tell me something that's specifically *weird* about it.
COMIC: It's *weird* because . . . well, maybe it's not *weird* but it's *stupid.*

COMEDY BUDDY: OK. Why is it *stupid?*

COMIC: It's *stupid* because why would someone choose to do something to themselves that hurts?

COMEDY BUDDY: You're answering a question with a question. *Why* is it *stupid?*

COMIC: It's *stupid* because between being in a relationship, working for a stupid boss, and paying taxes, there's already so much pain in your life, there is no need to add to it.

COMEDY BUDDY: OK, that makes sense. Good. That's clear, write that down. Let's work on another one.

COMIC: Piercing is weird because I know this weird guy at my school and he got his private parts pierced and—

COMEDY BUDDY: Stop. That's a story. Cut out the *I* and don't tell me what happened. Just say what's weird or stupid about it.

COMIC: Another reason it's *stupid* is that I can understand piercing ears, but not other body parts.

COMEDY BUDDY: OK, but cut out *I* and tell me *specifically* why it's *stupid.*

COMIC: It's *stupid* because . . . Well, maybe it's not *stupid,* but it's *hard* to have everything pierced because when you're getting dressed in the morning, you have to decide not only what earrings to wear, but what rings to put in your nose, belly button, and even down there.

COMEDY BUDDY: Great. That will lead to something. How about *hard?* What's *hard* about being pierced?

COMIC: It's *hard* to go through metal detectors at the airport when you're pierced.

COMEDY BUDDY: Good, that makes sense. I'll write that down.

Write your reworked premises on "drugs" below. Make sure you *include* an attitude word in each premise and *exclude* the words *I* and *my.*

_____

_____

_____

_____

_____

_____

_____

_____

_____

_____

Comedy Structure: The Act-out

Setup (unfunny) ➜ Act-out (funny part)

So far you and your comedy buddy have developed some premises about "drugs." But they shouldn't be funny . . . yet. Now it's time to add what I call an *act-out* to each premise. In an act-out, the comic acts out the situation of the joke and scores the big laughs. Instead of *talking about* someone or something, you *perform* it. You turn into the people or things you mentioned in the setup—actually act them out. And finally, you get to be funny.

In the vaudeville days of stand-up, jokes were strictly setup punch lines.

"Take my wife . . . please!"

—HENNY YOUNGMAN

But now, with the popularity of improvisation and the intimacy of TV, the punch line has gone the way of eight-track tapes and has been replaced with an act-out. Act-outs give comics the chance to show off their ability to do voices and characters.

[Crack is stupid.] "I would never do crack. Would never do a drug named after a part of my own ass. Someone says, *[act-out]* 'Do you want some crack?' I say, 'I was born with one, pal, I really don't need another one. Thank you very much. If I want the second crack I'll give you a call. For right now, I'm sticking to the solo crack-ola.' "

—DENIS LEARY

Act-outs can be short.

[It's weird that everyone is on a drug.] "My drug of choice is the antidepressant Zoloft. I think of it as an air bag for my mind. As soon as things start getting too rowdy . . . *[act-out]* 'Poof! . . . Aaahh . . . ' "

—DANA GOULD

Act-outs can be long, such as in Ellen DeGeneres's "Phone Call to God" (abbreviated version on page 36), where Ellen acts out a six-minute phone call to God asking why He made fleas. Robin Williams does a long act-out of a baseball player pleading his case to the grand jury:

"Everybody's doing cocaine now. Baseball players having to go in front of grand juries. *[act-out]* 'Yeah, I did cocaine. Can you blame me, though? It's a slow goddam game. Come on, Jack, I'm standin' out in left field for seven innings and there's a long white line going all the way to home plate. I see the guy puttin' it out goin', "Ha ha ha." And that damn music. "Dit dit di dit. Dit dit di dit." I don't know whether to slide or do a line, you know what I'm sayin'? People are slidin' into home headfirst. Yeah! "You're out!"—"Doesn't matter, baby, I'm up now." ' "

—ROBIN WILLIAMS

Act-outs are where you can work in your celebrity impressions without being a hack.

[*When people take drugs.*] "They try and drive. They've got this idea that [act-out] "Yeah, I can drive. I've got it together, dude. I'm OK. If I can just find my feet I can drive.' Then they get out, they're in the car . . . haulin' down the freeway, they're movin' fast. They think they're goin' at light speed. They think Scotty's sittin' next to them goin', [act-out] 'Jim, you can't push it any faster. It's a Chevrolet, Jim, you can't drive it any faster than that.' "

—ROBIN WILLIAMS

"But Judy, I'm not very good with doing voices or characters."

That's OK, neither am I. Act-outs don't have to be wild, they can be just as effective and funny if they're low-key.

"Babies don't need a vacation. But I still see them at the beach. It pisses me off. When no one's looking, I'll go over to a baby and ask, [*act-out*] 'What are you doing here? You haven't worked a day in your life.' "

—STEVEN WRIGHT

Don't worry about accuracy if you are acting out your mother or father. The comedy patrol isn't going to yank you offstage and say, "His mother sounds nothing like that."

Acting out means that you *perform* what you are talking about instead of just talking about it. For instance, see what telling a joke without an act-out would sound like.

Wrong way:

"It was hard having a dad as a lawyer. I had to motion for a puppy."

Although this is a funny idea, it didn't get a laugh. I suggested acting out the scene of asking for the puppy.

Right way:

"It was hard having a dad as a lawyer. When I wanted a puppy I had to go, [*act-out*] 'Dad, motion for puppy!' [*act-out in father's voice*] 'Motion for puppy denied.' 'Sidebar, Dad.' "

—BARRY PRESTON

In most jokes there are two characters that can be acted out. In the setup, the comic talks to the audience. In act-out, he's talking to an imaginary character in a scene. For example, in the premise "It's *hard* being pierced, going through metal detectors at the airport," the two characters are the *pierced person* going through the metal detector and the *security guard*. The act-out would then be:

" 'Buzzzzzz!' [*security guard*] 'Please remove all of your jewelry, miss.' [*pierced person*] 'Oh, OK! [*Then act out, removing a lot of rings in weird places.*] Can you help me with this one?' " [*You'll have to use your imagination for where I'm pointing.*]

Act-outs are not meant to be written out on paper; they're funny in the way that they're *performed*.

"People would think before they kill someone if a bullet cost five thousand dollars. [*act-out*] 'Man, I would blow your f**king head off if I could afford it. I'm going to get me another job, I'm going to start saving some money, and you're a dead man. You better hope I can't get no bullets on layaway.' [*second premise*] Even if you get shot by a stray bullet, you don't have to go to no doctor to get it taken out. Whoever shot you'll take that bullet back. [*act-out*] 'I believe you got my property.' "
—CHRIS ROCK

The characters in act-outs don't have to be people. They can be animals, vegetables, minerals, or even God.

Richard Pryor

"What is hard about dating is when you like someone, sometimes they don't like you back. God is messing with you. 'Please, God, can I have him?' [*in deep voice*] 'No. I'm going to keep you liking him and he will never like you back.' "
—FALEENA HOPKINS

Robin Williams gives voice to a chair.

"I wonder if chairs go, 'Oh no! Here comes another asshole!' "

Richard Pryor's heart talks to him in this joke:

[*Heart attacks are weird.*] "Your heart gets mad. 'Thinking about dying now, ain't you? You didn't think about it when you was eating that pork.' "

"I noticed that a lot of comics say, 'I.' I thought that you said not to use the words I, me, *or* my *in the premise."*

Yes, that is true for the premise, but not for the act-out. A joke starts out general so everyone can relate, and after the premise is the time to bring in the *specifics* about you. The lead-in to the act-out is where you get very, very specific. If the premise has the word *people* in it, the act-out has to have exactly *which* people because you can't act out people in general.

For example, student Maz Jobrani starts out general.

"It was hard growing up Iranian American . . ."

He then brings in exactly what was *hard* for *him* and then acts out his mother.

"I could never get anyone to spend the night at our house because everyone was afraid we were going to take their kid hostage. My mom would get on the phone with my friend's dad. 'Hello, Mr. Johnson? Hi, this is Maz's mother. I am just calling to let you know that your son Kenny is going to spend the night at our house. You know, he is such a handsome boy. He has a million-dollar smile. Hello? Hello?' "

If you are a writer who has no intention of becoming a stand-up comic, it is still extremely necessary for you to be able to create and perform act-outs. Especially for script writers, acting out different characters is a skill that is necessary when writing dialogue, pitching story ideas, and creating characters.

Act-out Common Mistakes

Mistake #1: Mentioning Someone in the Setup and *Not* Acting Them Out.

You have to be consistent. If someone appears in the setup, they have to be shown in the act-out. Anybody mentioned in the set-up needs to be acted out.

Wrong way:

"[*Setup*] It's weird when you break up with someone and your friends are more upset about it than you are. [*act-out*] I broke up with my boyfriend and my mother was screaming at me, 'I liked him. It's you I can't stand.' "

This is a poorly constructed joke because the comic set up her *friends* but acted out her *mother*. Here's a better act-out for the same setup.

Right way:

" 'Oh no! That's terrible that you guys broke up. [*beat*] Do you have his phone number?' "

Or:

" 'Oh no, you can't break up with him! He's the one with the Laker tickets!' "

Paul Clay sets up a joke that takes place at a Bruce Springsteen concert. So in this joke he acts out *Springsteen* and *the audience.*

"[*What's weird is*] Bruce Springsteen has kids and now he doesn't give any more of those four-hour concerts. After an hour and a half, he says, [*act-out*] 'Are you ready to rock and roll?' And the audience answers, 'No, Bruce, we've got sitters.' And he says, 'Oh, shit, me too. Good night.' "

Mistake #2: Setting Up One Thing and Then Acting Out Another

The act-out must naturally emerge from the premise. You cannot switch attitudes or topics midstream.

Wrong way:

"I think tobacco and alcohol warnings are too general. They should be more to the point. My father said, 'Drinking will ruin your health.' I thought drinking would just make me become the asshole my father was."

This joke is flawed because the setup is about *tobacco* and *alcohol* warnings, but the act-out then is a warning from a *father.*

Right way:
[*Warnings are stupid.*] "I think tobacco and alcohol warnings are too general. They should be more to the point: 'People who smoke will eventually cough up brown pieces of lung.' And, 'Warning! Alcohol will turn you into the same asshole your father was.' "

—GEORGE CARLIN

George Carlin

Not having the same characters in your act-out is like watching an improv scene where the audience says, "Do a scene with a *doctor* and the queen of England on the *moon*," and the troupe performs a scene with a *lawyer* and the queen of England in *New Jersey*. Just as, in a restaurant, you expect to eat what you ordered, the audience expects you to deliver exactly what you set up. So if your attitude in the setup was "weird," your act-out needs to express exactly how weird it is. And that weirdness needs to be exaggerated.

> "It's *weird* when men change a baby's diapers. 'Cause when a woman changes them, you might hear: [*act-out of woman cooing sweet baby talk*] 'Oh my little baby, coo-coo baby.' But when a man changes it, you always hear: [*act-out of a man getting really* weird] 'OH MY GOD! Sit still! Don't move . . . AAAHHHHHH!' "
>
> —Jules Roenitz

Mistake #3: Going into a Story

A lot of my workshop students really want to put a "this really happened" story into their act. They make up a premise to give them an excuse to tell the story.

> "You know what's weird about drugs is that they make people stupid. I was at this party the other night and this guy comes over and he tells me that I'm really ugly. And I was so insulted, so then I . . ."

What they do is bomb, because poorly crafted stories can suck the energy out of a room.

"How do I know if I'm telling a story?"

- If you are not at an act-out within three lines—you're telling a story.
- If you are using the phrase "so then I"—you're telling a story.

But there is a way to structure story into stand-up. Add act-outs and a retort.

> "You know, what's weird about drugs is that they make people stupid. I was at this party the other night and this guy comes over and goes, [*acting out a stoned guy*] 'Man, you are some ugly woman.' Can you believe that? So I said, [*acting out yourself stoned*] 'Here's my phone number.' Yeah, drugs do make you stupid."

When adding an act-out to a joke, the rule of thumb is that first someone says something and *then* the other person (usually you) answers with a snappy, unexpected retort. It's best to work with your comedy buddy in coming up with these funny retorts.

Mistake #4: Go Back and Forth with Dialogue Without a Laugh

Some beginning comics mistake a joke for a play and run on and on.

Wrong way:

"My mom hates my hair, and the first thing she always says to me when she sees me is, 'Oh my God! Look at your hair. It looks like a rat's nest.' [*comic*] 'Mom, just stop it. You don't look so good yourself.' [*mom*] 'Last time I was here I thought that you were going to cut it.' [*comic*] 'The only thing I want to cut is you.' [*mom*] 'I am going home if you keep talking like that. All I asked you to do was to cut your hair.' [*comic*] 'Not until you shave that beard!' "

By the time you finish, nobody is going to remember what the setup was. If you act out someone saying something stupid, *you* have to have the final say. In most cases your snappy retort ends the joke. In order to find the best retort you should try different lines because the initial one might not be the best one. After you have explored a lot of different lines, narrow it down to the funniest one and get to it.

Right way:

"My mom hates my hair, and the first thing she always says to me when she sees me is, 'Oh my God! You still haven't cut that hair!' And I go, 'Sweet Jesus! You still haven't shaved that beard!' "

—NANCY MAGNELLI

Notice in this Robin Williams joke that every retort is a laugh.

"They handed me my son. They held him up and I went, 'My God, he is hung like a bear.' [*retort*] 'That's the umbilical cord, Mr. Williams.' [*retort*] 'Don't cut that, let him dream for a while.' "

Mistake #5: *Describing* the Act-out Rather Than *Doing* It

Beginning comics are often reluctant to play a character, and so instead of acting out the dialogue, they describe the situation.

Say out loud the following two jokes. Notice the different way it *feels* when you do *act-outs*.

[*Without act-outs*] "It's hard being a single dad because you get the neediness and the pouting and the whining and the crying. Then there's my son and *his* needs."

[*Same joke with act-outs*] "It's hard being a single dad because you get the neediness and the whining— [*whining*] 'I'm hungry. This food sucks. [*crying*] You don't pay me enough attention.' And then there's my son and *his* needs."

—BRUCE BLACK

In the first example the comic *describes* what happens, and in the reworked example he *acts out* what happens as it is happening now.

Exercise: Adding Act-outs

The way to create good act-outs is to get yourself into the comedy zone, cut loose, and perform the situation verbally and physically. It's best not to write out your act-outs—they tend to end up sounding too literary and rigid and, worst of all, not funny. The best act-outs come from mindless ranting—where you pace and talk nonstop (with attitude) about your topic into a tape recorder. Don't *think* funny, but rather *be* funny. After creating my act-outs this way, I'll jot down a short phrase to remind me of the act-out, for example, "going through airport." Or I say it over and over again until I get it just right, and then I write it down. But I never *create* my act-outs on paper.

Give this a go using your ten premises on "drugs" as a starting point. Get up in front of your comedy buddy and be playful and loose. Say one of your premises out loud, emphasizing the attitude, then jump into an act-out—and I mean that literally. Actually jump. Physical movement will help you to get over self-consciousness. If your act-out includes your grandmother, physically become her, open your mouth, and see what comes out of it.

"My grandma could never go to a sperm bank. [*with heavy Jewish accent*) 'What's the matter here? Everything's frozen? Nothing fresh? Oy!' "

Explore a lot of opinions for your act-out and then narrow it down to the best one. Keep it short—have someone say something, and then you respond. Don't go on too long. Get in the act-out, get out of it, and nobody gets hurt.

Judy's Premises on "Body Piercing"	Judy's Act-outs
It's stupid because just being in a relationship hurts so much, working for a stupid boss hurts, paying taxes hurts. There is no need to add to it.	"Oh gee, I'm just not feeling enough pain in my life. I think I need to pierce my tongue."
It's hard to have everything pierced because when getting dressed in the morning, you have to decide not only what earrings to wear but what rings to put in your nose, belly button, and even down there.	"Let's see, I got my nipple ring, my nose ring, my eyebrow ring." "Please, I can't even decide what to wear in the morning, much less accessorize my nostril!"
It's hard to understand what people are saying when they've got hardware in their mouth.	"Arrrg, ooh, gump, hummp." "Excuse me, but could you take that bolt out of your tongue and tell me the specials again?"
What's weird is that in some cities like San Francisco it's a popular fashion.	"I'm going to an elegant ball. Do you think this dog collar matches my nipple studs?"
What's scary is when your kids come home with their body pierced.	"Jimmie, that Batman pin is for your jacket, get it out of your eye!"
It's scary when people in professional jobs show up with nose rings.	"We'll take your appendix out in a moment, Mr. Johnson; I just got to get the fishhook out of my ear first. I wouldn't want to catch your spleen on it."
It's scary that kids hurt their bodies as a way to rebel against their parents.	"I'll show Mom and Dad. I'll stick sharp objects in my nose, my tongue, my belly button, my nipples . . ." Yeah, that will show them. Show them that they're right—you are a complete idiot.
It bugs me because it looks so unattractive.	"Judy, how do I look?" "Like a porcupine."
It's hard because if you have everything pierced, you have to buy more jewelry.	"Do you take this woman to be your wife?" "I do." "Now please put the ring on her nose . . ."

You might not be able to come up with act-outs for each joke, and they all won't be winners. But the more you have, the more likely you are to come up with at least a few finished jokes.

Now you try it.

Your Premises on "Drugs"	Your Act-outs on "Drugs"

Comedy Structure: The Mix

**Attitude + Topic + Premise (unfunny) ➜
Act-out + MIX + Act-out (funny)**

Not all jokes have mixes, but it's a great way to sponge a couple more laughs out of your setup. A good mix is where a comic connects two elements that people don't associate with each other. The laugh comes from the way the comic connects them.

"Auto mechanics always have attitude and they make us feel guilty. [*act-out of auto mechanic*] 'Look at this. This is a mess. I mean, you got your oil mixed in with your water. How'd you let it get to this point? This is pathetic. I can fix this for you for, like, two grand.' [*mix*] Can you imagine this guy as a preschool teacher going up to some poor helpless four-year-old? [*act-out of child*] 'Teacher, I finished my finger painting. Do you like it?' [*auto mechanic voice*] 'Look at this. You got your oranges mixed in with your greens. You're coloring outside the lines. This is a mess. How'd you let it get to this point? It's pathetic. I could fix this for you for, like, two grand.' "

Mixes generally start with "Can you imagine if" or "What if," and are almost always followed by another act-out. In the previous joke, Dave DeVos talks about how *hard* (attitude) it is to deal with an *auto mechanic* (topic) because they always *exaggerate everything* (premise), and he acts that out. Then he mixes in "Can you imagine this guy as a preschool teacher?" and does a second act-out.

Drew Carey

"Dolphin-safe tuna. That's great if you're a dolphin. *What if* you're a tuna? Somewhere there's a tuna flopping around a ship going, 'What about me? I'm not cute enough for you?' "

—DREW CAREY

Laughter is a natural response to the surprise of the mix. The following mixes are too ordinary to make people laugh.

Wrong way:

- a 911 operator—who is concerned
- an impersonator—who does an impression of Elvis
- a pothead—who is a biker

Right way:

These mixes are surprises.

- a 911 operator—who is self-obsessed: "So you're being held at gunpoint, and you think *you've* got problems? You, you, you. It's always about you!"
- an Elvis impersonator—who stutters: "Get off of my blue suede sh, sh, sh, sh . . ."
- a pothead—who is your grandmother: "Grandma is crocheting a lovely cover for her bong."

Here student Missy Pyle starts off talking about what is "hard" about being an "unemployed actress" and she mixes in another topic—"plumbers."

> "It's hard being an unemployed actress. When I'm at a party and people find out that I'm an actress they always ask, 'Oh, is there something I would have seen you in?' Do people ask plumbers that? 'Oh, you're a plumber, is there a drain that you've unclogged that I could have seen?'"

Most amateur comics think that the way to be *different,* unique, and creative is to pick a weird or shocking topic, but a true talent can take an ordinary topic and create brilliant mixes.

Cathy Ladman

> "*Marriage* is very difficult. Marriage is like a five-thousand-piece *jigsaw puzzle.* All sky."
> —CATHY LADMAN

Later in this book you will understand that mixes are a necessary ingredient for all forms of comedy—scripts, speeches, essays, articles, and more. Writers use mixes as a way to stir in imagination, surprise an audience or a reader, create interesting characters, and push an idea to its extreme.

Exercise: Practice Mix

This exercise is not for your act, but a practice to get this notion of mixing together two different things. *Finish this sentence: "Sex is just like a pen because . . ."*

Examine the following jokes and write down what the mixes are.

"Frankenstein was a weird monster. As a kid, I never understood him. He never caught any black people. No Mexicans, either. He only went after very scared white people. Frankenstein was obviously suffering from hemorrhoids. You can tell from the way he walked. 'Oh shit, let me catch somebody slow.' He never went into the ghetto. A black guy with Nikes would have run circles around his ass. 'Yeah, come on, Frankie, bring your green ass over here.' If Frankenstein went into the barrio, the Mexicans would've taken those bolts right out of his head. 'Well, thanks, man, we need that shit for our tires. I'm glad you showed up, man. My wheel was loose.' "

—PAUL RODRIGUEZ

The mix is _____ and _____.

"Where I sit it appears that life can be absolutely f**king brutal. I view life like a big desperate bear loose in a campground. I try to avert its gaze because if you lock eyes with it, it thinks you want to play; it doesn't know its own strength and it just starts beating the living shit out of you. All in the name of good, clean Kodak fun."

—DENNIS MILLER

The mix is _____ and _____.

"I view a visit to the therapist in much the same way I view a visit to the hairdresser . . . When I leave the office my head looks great; around an hour later, it's all fucked up and I can't get it to look that way on my own. 'Excuse me, doc, can I get a little mousse for my id?' "

—DENNIS MILLER

The mix is _____ and _____.

"Dinner with my parents is a nightmare. The soup is never hot enough! No matter what you do! The soup could be coming from a nuclear reactor and it would still not be hot enough. My dad will always send it back. 'You call this hot?!' Hell would not be hot enough for my father. He'd be sitting there going, 'You've been to the Catskills in August? Hey, you with the tail! Where's the goddam thermostat around here?' "

—DYAN POLLACK

The mix is _____ and _____.

"It's hard being a flight attendant because you have to be nice all the time. I would like to be Xena—warrior flight attendant. 'You, stow your luggage up your ass! Your seat cushion can be used as a flotation device; however, the lard-ass in 22C, don't even bother. There are six exits on this aircraft, two in the back, two in the front, and two on the wing. If the plane should be going down you'll see my ass going out this exit here.' "

—MARCY PECK

The mix is _____ and _____.

Incorporating a Mix into Your Joke

Base the first act-out in reality. Then bring in a new idea based on an unreal "what if" premise, the mix. Do a second act-out based on this fantasy.

Keep the attitude going through the mix. If it's "scary" in the setup, in the act-out you'll need to act scared.

"What's scary is the guy who did the *X-Files* movie trailers. [*reality act-out*] 'On June nineteenth, take your deepest, darkest fear, your most paranoid suspicion, and your darkest nightmare, and multiply them by X.' This guy makes *everything* sound scary, even boring, harmless stuff—like picking up a cat at the pet shelter: [*mix act-out*] 'It was soft and furry . . . and they took it home as their very first pet . . . until something . . . went *horribly wrong* . . . Meooooowww!!! The Kitten, rated R. Starts Friday!' [*second mix act-out*] Can you imagine this guy having phone sex? 'I'm not wearing any underwear . . . Neither are you . . . and then something . . . went *horribly wrong!*' "

—CHRIS DUFFY

Here are two mixes on my topic "body piercing."

Premise	Act-out	Mix	Mix Act-out
What's scary is when your kids come home with their body pierced.	"Jimmie, that Batman pin is for your jacket, get it out of your eye!"	What are kids going to do next to rebel?	"Mom, I chopped off my arm. Isn't it cool! Look, I had my spleen taken out!"

It's scary when people in professional jobs show up with nose rings.	"We'll take your appendix out in a moment, Mr. Johnson; I just got to get the fishhook out of my ear. I wouldn't want to catch your spleen on it."	What if President Clinton had a pierced tongue? It would have kept him out of a lot of trouble.	"I want you to listen to me. I did not arrg, hummm, arrh, knoog!"

Look over your jokes to see which ones invite mixes. This works best when you're jamming with your comedy buddy. Get up and start asking, "What if?"—"What if Grandma got stoned at her bingo game?" Then act out the mix.

Premise	Act-out	Mix	Mix Act-out

Finishing Touches

Look through all your jokes that have attitude+topic+premise+act-out+mix+act-out and write a cue word for each joke on an index card. Congrats! You and your comedy buddy wrote some jokes! See how your jokes compare to those of professionals doing jokes about drugs. If you're wondering why some of these comics get paid millions for jokes that don't seem funny, it's because most comedy isn't meant to be read. It's meant to be performed. The laughs are in the execution of the act-outs. Check out the great premises and act-outs of these jokes, starting with Bill Cosby.

"[*Drugs are weird*] because people on pure air don't get so paranoid. When people start out, they say, 'Let's have fun,' and now they are paranoid." [*Cosby acts out someone very paranoid.*]

[*Stupid*] "The problem with drugs is that you have to inhale them, but your body doesn't want them." [*Cosby does an act-out of a person trying to hold a drug in and coughing.*]

"And the weird part about drugs is that when you are coughing, the person sitting next to you will say, 'Hey man, pass that over.' "

"I said to a guy, 'Tell me what is it about cocaine that makes it so wonderful?' And the guy said, 'Well, it intensifies your personality.' And I said, 'Yes, but what if you are an asshole?' "

Here are more drug jokes from the pros.

"Cocaine, what a weird drug. Anything that makes you paranoid and impotent. 'Hmm, give me more of that.' "

—ROBIN WILLIAMS

[*Weird*] "Only in America would they *invent* crack. Only in America would there be a guy that coke wasn't good enough for. One guy walking around New York City in 1985, going, [*act-out*] 'You know, that cocaine is pretty good, but I want something that makes my heart explode as soon as I smoke it, OK? I want to take one suck off that crack pipe and go, [*act-out*] Now I'm happy. I'm dead. The ultimate high!' "

—DENIS LEARY

"I think they should legalize crack. Legalize it. You know why I want them to legalize crack? Just so my friends' mothers can have something to brag about . . . 'You know, Ronald's got his own crack house now. Child, he's got his own crack house. And I drop by every day. I go, That's my baby's crack house right there.' "

—CHRIS ROCK

"Drug dealers don't sell drugs. Drugs sell themselves . . . You don't ever really got to try to sell crack. I never heard of crack dealers going, 'Man, how am I going to get rid of all this crack? It's just piled up in my house.' "

—CHRIS ROCK

Day 3 Action Checklist

By this point . . .

❑ You know how to write a joke using topic, attitude, premise, act-out, and mix.

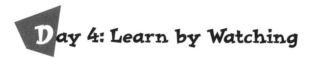

❏ You've jammed with a comedy buddy.
❏ You've written out some jokes about drugs on an index card.

Day 4: Learn by Watching

PRO TALK *with Rocky LaPorte*

"I learned a lot by doing it and watching Richard Jeni, Dennis Wolfberg, George Wallace, and Ellen DeGeneres when they were touring. There was such a difference from the A rooms to the B rooms. I think a lot of the young comics picked up bad habits watching B room comics."

Rocky LaPorte

Today you are going to put your own act aside and get some pointers from the pros—your favorite comics. A lot of beginning comics watch what other comics are doing and *copy them.* Instead, they should watch what other comics are doing and *learn from them.* Draw inspiration from your favorite comics but don't use any of their actual material.

Days 4 through 8 are going to be spent getting serious about comedy by studying what works and focusing on your favorite topic—you.

"But I thought you said that jokes are not supposed to focus on I, me, *or* my. *Why, then, is this section focusing on ourselves?"*

The topics you are going to joke about need to be *based* on personal things that are near and dear to you. That is your *starting* point. You are then going to be guided to craft those topics into the *joke* format, not *story* format, and get imaginative.

[*It's hard being a parent.*] "My kids like animals a lot so I took them to the track. They ratted on me. They go, 'Mommy, Daddy took us to the zoo and all the animals had numbers on them.'"

—ROCKY LAPORTE

Exercise: Honing Your Act

The first step to getting serious is to take all your index cards with "drug" jokes on them and toss them into a trash can.

"Why? I've got some killer jokes about drugs. Why did you make me do them if you were just going to tell me to throw them all away?"

Probably the biggest and hardest part of my job as a comedy coach is helping my students not settle for doing material that has already been extensively done by other comics. "Drugs" is a topic that has been done—a lot. Whether you're a comedy writer or a stand-up comic, your main goal as a creative funny person should be to create material that comes from who you are as an individual—your persona. The point of working with an assigned topic like "drugs" was to help you to concentrate on learning without being distracted by a topic that was personal. Now that you know the basics of structuring jokes, it's time to move on to more personal topics. So, unless you qualify to write about drugs because you were in rehab, or currently have a needle in your arm, lose the "drug" jokes or at least set them aside. It's time to find your own authentic, signature topics. Topics that aren't hack.

"What exactly is 'hack material'?"

Hack is . . .

- Choosing "this is something that will be funny" topics rather than "this is something that really scares me." When a comic picks topics such as "tampons," "toilets," or "penis enlargements," he is usually picking these hack topics because of the false assumption that the topic will get a laugh. Creativity is not about picking funny topics, it's about making ordinary topics funny.
- Bathroom topics like farting, pee, ka-ka, and poo-poo. Anything that comes *out* of a hole is hack. As Joan Rivers says, "Grow up!"
- "I eat so much roughage that I'm a human salad shooter . . ." Too much information!
- Topics that have already been done to death, such as Viagra, Asian drivers, traffic, drugs, anything about airplanes (food, bathrooms, flight attendants).

- Convenience stores, McDonald's, New-York-is-different-from-L.A., and "Have you ever noticed how cats and dogs are different?" Wow, there's a new one.

PRO TALK *with Andy Kindler, from "The Hack's Handbook: A Starter Kit," in the* National Lampoon

"Celebrity trashing, talk about not needing originality! Celebrity trashing proves it. It's the comedic equivalent of shooting fish in a barrel. 'Madonna—like a virgin? I don't think so.' Hack!

"What does Dr. Ruth know about sex? 'Stroke the penis, stroke the penis'—she can't even reach the penis.

"Commercials, better known as the Hack Happy Hunting Grounds. 'These tampon commercials say you can swim, horseback ride, and hike.' Who cares? Hack!"

Andy Kindler

If you know the punch line to a joke *before* the comic says it, chances are the material is hack.

"What are 'authentic topics'?"

To connect with an audience, comics and comedy writers need to find those topics that they are truly and deeply passionate about *and* that other people can relate to. These become their authentic topics. For stand-up comics, these topics form the core of their act and shape their *persona*. For writers, these topics form a point of view and shape their *voice*. All successful comedy writers started off their careers by finding a topic about themselves that is relatable and believable. Usually it was this easily identifiable personal chunk of material that catapulted them into a flourishing career.

> **PRO TALK** *with Michael Hanel, senior vice president of comedy development, 20th Century–Fox TV*
>
> "To do great writing, acting, and stand-up—reveal the things that you are most afraid to reveal to other people and, ultimately, probably most afraid to reveal to yourself. It makes you incredibly vulnerable and it makes people want to lean in and listen."

In an effort to have the audiences identify with them, a lot of beginning comedy writers pick their topics from magazines and newspapers, or use that clever observation about "men leaving that toilet seat up." If only it were that easy. The fact is, it's not enough for the topic to be relatable to the public. It also must resonate with *you*—deeply and emotionally. You're not qualified to joke about a topic unless you have extensive firsthand knowledge about it. Being obsessed with it is even better.

This emphasis on relatability and authenticity applies not only to stand-up comics but to all comedy writers. Each sitcom episode is based on a topic that must be *relatable,* and each line a character utters must be *authentic* to that character's persona. Even if you intend on writing custom material for other comics, you still need to understand these basic principles of writing from authenticity. And the best place to learn how to write for others is to first write an act for yourself.

> **PRO TALK** *with Bernie Brillstein, manager who oversaw the careers of John Belushi, Gilda Radner, Jim Henson, Dan Aykroyd, Lorne Michaels, Martin Short, and numerous others*
>
> "You can't do fake comedy today, you can't do mother-in-law jokes. If you do a mother-in-law joke it has to be *your* mother-in-law. You have to have lived it."

No matter how relatable your topic is, if it doesn't resonate with you, it probably won't resonate with your audience either. Passion about a topic can't be faked. The audience can sense if your topic is authentic for you or if it isn't. For a long time I did this routine about my biological clock running out and wanting to have children, and it always killed.

"Women in their thirties start thinking about *having* children, and men in their thirties start thinking about *dating* children."

Then all of a sudden this killer routine stopped getting laughs. It was nothing I did—I didn't change the language, the timing, or the attitude—but it just stopped working. Finally I realized this topic was no longer authentic to me. It was still a relatable topic, but it wasn't compelling to *me* anymore.

A woman in one of my workshops created her whole act around the following topic: *"When you're an older woman, it's hard to meet men."* She then went on to do some funny jokes about life without relationships. Showcase night, the audience didn't laugh, and I wasn't sure why until I found out that she has been happily married for twenty-five years and has two daughters. Her act was based on a lie, and on some level the audience knew it. She was dishing it out but they weren't buying. Cross out your fake topics now—you'll get more laughs later. Fake topics turn into hack jokes.

"What about comics who just do wild, kooky things with props?"

People can get their fifteen minutes of fame by eating lightbulbs, but it usually doesn't translate into a sustainable career. To achieve that requires digging deeper within yourself.

PRO TALK *with Richard Lewis*

"It's impossible to be as good as you can be if you hold back. If you start editing yourself, you might as well just stop, you won't be as pure as you can be, and why not go for the gold? You are only as authentic as you allow yourself to be. And if you start putting roadblocks up voluntarily, you are just headed toward mediocrity."

EXERCISE: How Much Do You Know About Comedy?

Match these stand-up comics with their signature topics.

Topics	Comics
alcoholic family	Tim Allen
Men are pigs.	Paul Reiser
being married	Brett Butler
being fat	Richard Lewis
being Jewish	Jeff Foxworthy
being a redneck	Roseanne Barr
low self-esteem	Paul Rodriguez
being Hispanic	Jackie Mason
GenXer	Kathy Griffen
sex crazed	Janeane Garofalo
being a wife/mother	Louie Anderson

Answers

Tim Allen—*Men are pigs.*

"Men are pigs. Right, ladies? Yeah. Yeah, right. Yeah, it's just too bad we own everything. Oink, Oink."

Paul Reiser

Paul Reiser—*being married.*

"No sooner do you become man and wife than everybody in the world starts giving you that annoying smile-with-a-head-nod that says, 'So? When are you taking the next step?' We constantly up the ante. We're a species that just can't leave well enough alone. Animals don't have this problem. You never hear snakes say, 'Ideally, we'd like two girls and a boy.'"

Brett Butler—*alcoholic family.*

"My mama would say, 'Y'all quit. Don't make me stop this car.' 'You're not in the car, Mama. You're in a hammock with a jelly glass of scotch in your hand.'"

Richard Lewis—*low self-esteem.*

"I have low self-esteem. When I'm in bed with someone, I fantasize that *I'm* someone else."

Jeff Foxworthy—*being a redneck.*

"Sophisticated people have retirement plans. Rednecks play the lottery. That's our plan. 'And when we hit the "pick six" we're going to add a room onto the trailer so we don't have to sleep with Jim's daddy no more.' "

Roseanne Barr—*being a wife/mother.*

"I've been married fourteen years and I have three kids. Obviously, I breed well in captivity."

Jeff Foxworthy

Paul Rodriguez—*being Hispanic.*

"Mexicans don't go camping in the woods, especially during hunting season. We'd be mistaken for a deer. Somebody would go, 'Your Honor, I saw brown skin and brown eyes. He had his hands up. I thought they were antlers. I shot his ass.' "

Jackie Mason—*being Jewish.*

"You can't find one Jewish kid with a Jewish name anymore. Every Jewish kid now is Tiffany Schwartz. Macadamia Ginsberg. Ashley Lipshitz. They try to out-gentile the gentiles. I know one kid, his name is Crucifix Finklestein. The only people left with Jewish names anymore are black people—Whoopi Goldberg."

Louie Anderson—*being fat.*

"I live out in California, where there are only three fat people. They have us on eight-hour shifts, so it works out. I tried to get into that California living. I tried the beach life. Every time I would lay down, people would push me back into the water. 'Hurry up, he's dying.' I was harpooned six times."

Janeane Garofalo

Janeane Garofalo—*GenXer.*

"Here would be my Valentine's card that I think I'm gonna send to my boyfriend. 'Things have been going so well thus far, I will find more ways to become unavailable to you.' "

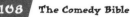

Kathy Griffen—*sex crazed.*

"It's too much trouble to get laid. 'Cause you have to go out with a guy, go to dinner with him, and listen to him talk about his opinions. And I don't have that kind of time."

Almost everything (and anything) in your life can be turned into a comedy topic if you care about it enough. The more painful or humiliating something is, the more likely it is to make an audience laugh. It's kind of a trade-off: *bad* for your life equates to *good* for your act.

Kathy Griffen

<u>PRO TALK</u> *with Chris Titus, stand-up comic and star of his own TV series, who found success from turning his problems about his dysfunctional family into punch lines*

"When I was being a happy comic, it was a lie. I found that my anger would work onstage and started experimenting with it. Then as much as the happy guy thing was bullshit, so was the angry thing. I finally found a place where I could just be myself and realized that I could do anything on-stage—if it's funny. I talk about my mom shooting and killing a guy, I talk about her suicide, and I make them laugh."

Christopher Titus

Funny people can find humor in even the most serious and sacred subjects and situations. Taking your problems seriously doesn't mean you have to take yourself too seriously.

• It's not just a bad childhood, it's material.

"What's hard about being a bad athlete is being picked last, especially when you're the only one standing there and no one is picking you! It's like, 'Dad! We're having a father-and-son catch!' "

—ANDREW LEAR

- It's not just an alcoholic mother, it's material.

"It's hard having an alcoholic mom. Like when your mom passes out on the front lawn and the kids in the neighborhood are like, 'Why is your mother lying on the front lawn?' ' 'Cause she's resting.' 'Well, why is she resting on *our* lawn?' "
—TRACEY ABBOTT

- It's not just a divorce, it's material.

"My parents' divorce settlement involved a bar tab. They had a big court battle on who got to keep me. Mom won. She made me live with Dad."
—CHRIS TITUS

"But I can do some killer impressions. How do I work them into my act?"

"Hey, what if Jack Nicholson and Michael Jackson took the same cab? It would sound something like this . . ." "And now for my next impression—can you imagine Arnold Schwarzenegger working in a 7-Eleven?" Hack attack!

Very often students have a certain talent that they want to work into their stand-up acts, such as impressions, mime, singing, magic, balloon animals, or birdcalls. Well, first of all, let's not consider all of these *talents.* With some of these so-called *talents* your career will probably peak headlining at a mini-mall opening. Impressions can be cheesy unless they are *set up in an authentic manner.* That means that the impression is an extension of the premise and not a "Hey, look at how I can do celebrity voices."

"My kid gets into a fight with his brother and I ask him, 'What's the matter?' and he sounds like Mike Tyson. [*act-out of his kid*] 'You know what I'm saying . . . if he's going to take my Power Ranger, I'm going to knock him out.' "
—DANA CARVEY

Here Janeane Garofalo does an impression of a waiflike young singer, Fiona Apple. It's not so much an impression as a long act-out with an opinion. Feel the venom.

[*Garofalo as Apple*] "Everybody out there that's watching this world. This world is bullshit and you shouldn't model your life about what you think we think is cool. Even though I have an eating disorder and I have somehow sold out to the patriarchy in this culture that says that lean is better. Even though I have done that and

have done a video wherein I wear underwear so that you young girls out there can covet and feel bad about what you have and how thin you're not. The point is, I have done it. I am lean. That's why I did succeed sooner than maybe other musicians that maybe were better songwriters."

Exercise: Study Comedy

Rent some stand-up comedy videos.

Collections such as *The Best of HBO* or *Comic Relief* are good starting points. A comic's first HBO special is the best because you are watching a one-hour presentation that probably took him five years to create. Don't bother studying comics after they become celebrities and host their own shows because they no longer need to do personal material since the audience already knows them. A rule of thumb: If the intimate details of your life aren't in the *National Enquirer,* you need to do personal topics until they are.

> **PRO TALK** *with Richard Jeni*
>
> "By the time I did my first HBO comedy special in 1989, I had a big backlog of stuff—it's like a band making their first album. Later when you do your next special you have some leftover stuff, but when I did my last HBO special, I hardly had anything left and I had to start from scratch."

Don't bother with older comedy tapes either. It is not that the people aren't good, but comedy has changed a lot in the past ten years and you want to study what's hip and happening now.

Make sure the people you watch are stand-up comics, not performance artists or actors doing a one-person show. Funny people who do one-person shows—for example, Lily Tomlin, Whoopi Goldberg, Billy Crystal, and Julia Sweeney—are all actors. Their work is great, but the structure of a one-person show is very different from that of a stand-up routine, and so it won't be of much use to you as a study tool right now. Later I'll show you how to turn a stand-up act into more of a theatrical experience, in the chapter "Creating Your Own One-Person Show."

As you watch a video of your favorite comic, write out a few of their jokes and answer these questions:

1. Is there attitude that is stated or implied? What is it?
2. Is there an act-out? A mix?
3. Where does the comic get the most laughs?
4. What personal details did you learn about the comic's life?
5. What did the comic *do* to get the laughs?
6. What topics did they use in their act?
7. What are the comic's signature topics?

Day 4 Action Checklist

By the end of this day you know

- ❑ to avoid hack material
- ❑ that act-outs are usually where comics get big laughs
- ❑ that all comics need to reveal things about themselves

If you watch enough comics you might get depressed, because it will seem like every topic has been done. Well, yes, they have. Except for one, that is: your life.

Day 5: Your Life Is a Joke—Finding Your Authentic Topics (Comedy Buddy Day)

Now for something *really* hard—being serious for a few days. If you try to be funny while searching for your topics, you'll end up sounding hack. But if you stay real and personal while finding your topics, you can discover material that will rock. An added benefit—it's better than therapy and a lot cheaper.

> **PRO TALK** *with Richard Lewis*
>
> "If you take yourself too seriously onstage, then it just screams of self-indulgence, but if you share pain in a humorous way and have some luck and some talent, then you are in good shape professionally."

What Are Your Authentic (Signature) Topics?

The questions in this section are designed to help you discover your authentic topics. When answering them, *be sincere instead of funny.* Later on you will turn these honest, authentic answers into killer comedy. But first you need to create a real, rock-solid foundation.

Doing that requires digging deep within yourself, then seeing where the issues that you discover lead. Always try to go deeper, to the next level. When asked what bugs them, most beginning comics and comedy writers mention things like traffic, bad drivers, airline food, waiting in line, and other overused, hack topics. Don't make the same mistake. Go beyond those topics to the more personal ones—being a loser, divorce, unemployment, or even being beaten as a child.

> [*It's hard when your parents are older.*] "Growing up I started realizing how much older my parents were getting. I remember my last ass-whooping my dad started. [*act-out of father whipping*] 'Didn't I tell you . . . Whew! My back hurts. Stay right there. I'm going to get your mother.' [*mother's voice*] 'Didn't I tell you . . . Whew, I'm tired. I'm going to get your father.' "
>
> —MIKE YOUNG

Mike's joke started with the topic of "relationships." The next step was to get *specific* about a topic. When asked which relationship in his life was the hardest for him, he said the one with his father. Continuing to get even more precise, what was hard about his parents was "having them be older" and "having them hit him." Then the premise emerged that they didn't have the energy for a good "ass whooping." He then added a mix, bringing in a surprise element:

> "Now when I go into the Gap and they ask me if I want a belt with that, I say, 'No! No! Help!' "

In our workshops, students can start with the same topic and all end up with completely different jokes. Topics tend to start out general and, after an intense investigation, get very specific. Throw the topic of "mothers" into a mind funnel and end up with a million particulars—foreign mothers, growing up poor, mothers who smoke, critical mothers, mothers who spit, Jewish mothers, coldhearted mothers . . .

> "We had a Jewish satellite dish. It picked up problems from other families."
>
> —RICHARD LEWIS

General Topics

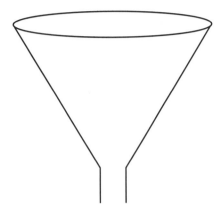

Specific Particulars of the Topic

[*What's scary is*] "My mother has no motherly instincts. I asked her how to get my newborn to stop crying. She said, 'I don't know. Did you try shaking it?' "

—CATHY CARLSON

Here Tricia Shore's topic was "parents," which funneled into "being adopted."

"It's hard being adopted. It has a lifetime effect on a person. In bed my boyfriend would go, 'Who's your daddy?' And I would say, 'I don't know.' "

The following exercises will help you discover your authentic topics, starting in childhood. I list the types of jokes that these topics can evolve into, but that's a subject we'll deal with later. For now, you don't need to know how these serious topics will eventually make people laugh. All of the example jokes started in the mundane, unfunny truth—so for now, don't try to be funny.

"I'm worried about joking about my parents. Won't it hurt their feelings?"

It depends on how you are joking about them. (See the second commandment, on page 57.) We comics have artist privilege to *all* the traumas of our life. Most of my students find that their parents love the attention of being the foil for fun. I asked comic and actor Chris Titus if he was worried about his family's reaction to his one-person show *Norman Rockwell Is Bleeding*, which was about his dysfunctional family. He said, "I never lied about what happened—it was all true. Still, I was tense about my father seeing my show, but when he saw the audience laughing, it made him feel OK about it. He said, 'You can use everything from my life, but after you get a TV show, you have to buy me a car.' "

"Dad collected things for me. Stepmothers."

—CHRIS TITUS

"Kids today can talk back to their parents. I could never do that. My parents used to chastise us. My mother used to drive us down to the cemetery. She'd say, 'This is your plot, right here—you can use it now or later if you be talkin' back to me.' "

—GEORGE WALLACE

Exercise: Childhood Writing

Stream of Consciousness Writing

Write free-form for fifteen minutes about your childhood. Write as quickly as you can without correcting spelling or grammar mistakes. Don't worry whether it's logical, funny, or even interesting. Just write whatever comes into your head.

Find Your Childhood Topics

Read what you wrote and pick out the topics—short phrases about your childhood problems, issues, and important experiences. While picking your topics, don't use the words *I, me,* or *my*—keep them general. Later, in the act-out, you will bring in specifics about you.

Examples: growing up poor, being a kid in New York, mom who had an accent, being Japanese, father who can't communicate, jealous sister, speech impediment, disabled parent, old parent, you were a bad girl, military father, uncommunicative father, hippie parents, lesbian mom, religious upbringing, foreign parents, mixed ethnicity, poor family, father in jail. (If any of these resonate with you, feel free to copy them.)

Write some childhood topics here:

1. _____

2. _____

3. _____

4. _____

5. _____

6. _____

7. _____

8. _____

9. _____

10. _____

Pick the *three* topics from the above list that resonate emotionally with you the most. Write premises for them using attitude words—*hard, weird, stupid, scary*—the same way you did for the topic "drugs." Premises are statements of truth. Remember—*don't* tell a story. For example, if one of your topics is "alcoholic mom," your premise could be: "I thought every mother was like that." How do you write it out?

Wrong way (story):

"My mother used to come home drunk and I thought that every mother was just like her. And I went over to my friend's house and her mother wasn't sleeping at 2 P.M."

This has no attitude, it uses the word *my,* and it tells a story.

Right way:

"What's *weird* about growing up with a mother who is a drunk is that you think everyone's mother is like yours."

There's an attitude—"weird"—and it cuts right to the chase. I know the compulsion to tell "what really happened" can be very strong, but for the sake of learning the craft, be even stronger.

Here are more premises on the topic of "growing up with an alcoholic mom." Notice that *I, my,* or *me* is not used in the premise and that the premise answers the question of *exactly* what is hard, weird, stupid, or scary.

> What's *hard* about growing up with an alcoholic mother is that you're just a little kid but you think you have to take care of the family.
> What's *scary* about it is that they always wait until you are in public to blow up.
> What's *weird* is that you end up eating dinner in bars during happy hours.
> What's *hard* about growing up with an alcoholic mother is that she doesn't do a good job helping with homework.

Write your most authentic and insightful premises below. Remember, this is not where you are funny . . . yet. Write ten premises about your mother or your father below and leave ten lines blank. You do not have to do this all in one sitting, and it's better if you fill in a few premises at a time. These should not be at all funny, but insightful.

Fill in some of your own, but leave ten blank for your comedy buddy to fill in. Sometimes it's easier to write premises on someone else's topics.

Your ten premises on your childhood topics:

_____
_____
_____
_____
_____
_____
_____
_____
_____
_____

Your *comedy buddy* adds ten more premises on your topics:

_____
_____
_____
_____
_____
_____
_____
_____
_____
_____

Exercise: Authentic Topics About Love Relationships

1. What is your relationship status now? Are you single, married, divorced, or separated? Write it here: _____.
2. Write ten things that are hard, weird, stupid, and scary about your relationship status without using the words, *me, I,* or *my.*

Examples, "single and dating" topic:

> *It's hard when you like someone and they don't like you.*
> *People get weird about saying the word* love.
> *It's hard to come back to dating after you've been married.*
> *It's scary that if you're over thirty-five and unmarried people assume that you're gay.*

Examples, "marriage" topic:

> *It's hard to keep romance going after you've been married for five years.*
> *It's stupid to ask someone to "love, honor, and obey."*
> *It's weird meeting your fiancée's parents for the first time.*
> *It's scary that you're not allowed to go out with anyone who isn't a couple.*

Fill in some of your relationship premises and, again, leave ten lines blank. *What's hard about being* _____ *is . . .*

_____

_____

_____

_____

_____

_____

_____

_____

_____

_____

Your comedy buddy's premises on *your* topic:

_____

_____

_____

_____

_____

_____

_____

_____

_____

_____

Day 5 Action Checklist

- ☐ You have written at least five premises on childhood relationships.
- ☐ You have five premises on your romantic relationships.
- ☐ You realize that your life is a joke.

Put this book by your bed and set your alarm fifteen minutes earlier than usual, because tomorrow you are going to write premises first thing in the morning, before you even make coffee. If that's too much to bear, then put the coffee in a thermos by the bed before you go to sleep. Then in the morning, before you really wake up, finish filling in your premises about childhood and relationships. You want to have ten good ones for each topic. If you are like most creative people, you'll find that this is an ideal time to write.

"But I'm brain dead when I wake up."

Exactly! Brains are good for finding where you put your keys or installing a software program, but they tend to get in the way of free-form creativity by analyzing and criticizing before ideas have a chance to blossom. Most beginners find that if they don't do this exercise first thing in the morning, they pull a Scarlett O'Hara: "I'll think about that tomorrow." So, do yourself a favor and do it before you get out of bed.

Day 6: Writing More Authentic Premises

Exercise: Morning Ideas

Before you get out of bed, write five more premises on "childhood" and "relationships."

Exercise: Capturing Your Ideas As They Happen

Ideas don't usually appear on demand. Instead you are in your car, at dinner, or on the ski slopes and suddenly it hits you, "I know why relationships *really* scare me." You don't write it down because you're sure you'll remember it. But you never do. And if you ask your friends, "What was that funny thing I said last night?" they don't remember because they were drunk. So that great routine is gone. How do you prevent that tragedy from occurring again? Carry either a notepad or a small tape recorder with you at all times. (Go to my Web site to see recommended gadgets for comics.)

As you go through the day, capture any additional authentic premises on "childhood" or "relationships" as you think of them.

PRO TALK *with Carol Leifer, stand-up comic, writer/producer on* Seinfeld

"I always have a comedy notebook since I started. I write more when inspiration strikes, as opposed to Jerry Seinfeld, who would be like, 'I'm going to write for an hour every day.' And everybody was like, 'Oh my God, is he crazy?' I find being in certain situations sparks some kind of humor—like the first time you go to a new place."

Day 6 Action Checklist

- ❏ You've written five more premises in the morning.
- ❏ You've gotten a notebook and pen or voice recorder and made it your Siamese twin.
- ❏ You've thought of five additional premises during the day and saved them on a notepad or voice recorder.

Day 7: More Authentic Topics (Comedy Buddy Day)

By today you have come up with some unfunny but truthful premises about "childhood" or "growing up" *and* "relationships." Hoping to be funny today? Not yet. Let's continue exploring your life for more authentic topics. If you take time to find your authentic topics now, making them funny later will be a piece of cake.

Exercise: Authentic Topics—Your Special Challenges

Have you had a special challenge in your life? You know: being gay, disabled, obese (size 12 doesn't count, ladies), middle aged (thirty years old doesn't count, even if *you* feel you're old), being from a different culture (except for coming to L.A. from New York because it's been done to death), and so on. If nothing strikes a chord here, that's OK. You can still be a comic. Maybe *that* can be your special challenge.

Kathy Buckley

"I was in a school for the retarded for two years before they found out I was hearing impaired. And they called *me* slow!"
—Kathy Buckley

"I was the only Jew growing up in an Irish Catholic neighborhood. If my parents didn't move in time I would have been the first bat mitzvah girl at Saint Thomas the Apostle. 'In the name of the father, the son that broke your heart, the daughter who never calls, *dayanu.*' "
—Phyllis Heller

"Oh my mom, she's so weird. She goes, 'But Vickie, are you a lesbian because it's fashionable?' Oh right, Mom, lesbians have always been known for their fashion sense. You're thinking of gay men. Gay men have the fashion sense, lesbians build the runways."
—Vickie Shaw

"It's hard being older. I used to take acid and now I'm taking antacid."
—Judy Carter

Write special challenge topics here:

_____

_____

_____

_____

_____

Write ten premises—things that are *hard, weird, stupid,* or *scary* about one of your special challenges. Fill in as many or as few as you can, and once again, *do not be funny;* instead, be truthful and sincere.

Your ten premises on a special challenge:

_____

_____

_____

_____

_____

_____

_____
_____
_____
_____

Your comedy buddy's premises on *your* topic:

_____
_____
_____
_____
_____
_____
_____
_____
_____
_____

Your Day Job

Many jokes are based on things that oppress us, and one thing that tends to demoralize a lot of people is their day job. Thus it's very relatable when a comic talks about stupid bosses, customers, and jobs.

List all of the day jobs you've ever had: waitress, lawyer, doctor, stripper, auctioneer, temp, unemployed . . .

_____
_____
_____
_____
_____
_____
_____

Circle the ones that you and others would consider the most stressful or the most oppressive. For instance, it might have really been a nightmare being a boss and having a bad secretary. But chances are the audience would be rooting more for your secretary no matter how bad she was and less for you because it is an accepted belief that it's secretaries and *not* bosses who are oppressed.

Now think of that awful job as a topic by itself and write premises about it. Keep the focus on the occupation without going into a personal story. For instance, if your day (or night) job was stripping, here's what *not* to do.

Wrong way:

"It's hard being a stripper when you have to drive so far to get to your job."

That's a faulty premise because that might have been particular to you and you alone, and it's not a detail about the profession. Premises are a combination of being truthful and relatable.

Wrong way:

"I was a stripper and even though I had the flu I had to go on. I really didn't feel like it and then I was doing a lap dance and I sneezed on this guy."

This doesn't qualify as a premise because it is a *story* about what happened to *you* and not about *stripping*. Here's a better way.

Right way:

"It's hard being a stripper because you have to be sexy when you don't feel like it."

The audience will know exactly what you are talking about.

If your job was being a waitress . . .

Wrong way (story):

"I had this job at this café and there was this woman who always asked me what she should eat."

Right way (cut to the chase):

"It's stupid that customers ask waitresses what they think they should order."

"Customers say some of the stupidest things. 'This steak, it's too tough.' It's too tough? Well, what do you want for $3.99? Filet mignon? This is Sizzler, you fool, not Spago. You're lucky it's mooing and not neighing! God!"

—VICKIE RABJOHN

Write premises for all the ways that your jobs were *hard, weird,* or *scary* without using the words *I* or *my.* Examples:

> *It's weird that in L.A. all waitresses are unemployed actresses.*
> *It's scary being a lawyer when your clients tell lawyer jokes.*
> *What's hard about being a janitor is that it's not exactly a babe magnet.*

Write ten premises on your day job (or jobs):

_____
_____
_____
_____
_____
_____
_____
_____
_____
_____

Have your comedy buddy write ten more premises on *your* topic:

_____
_____
_____
_____
_____
_____
_____
_____
_____
_____

Authentic Topic: Your Current Issue

Many successful comics and comedy writers base their material, or a portion of it, on a current issue. For example: this is a time in my life when I am dealing with being gay and coming out; being pregnant; going through middle age; being a student; getting sober; being a foreigner. For some of you, these issues might be the same thing as your special challenge, and that's OK. Topics based on a personal issue that is also a universal condition can lead to great jokes and later become the basis for sitcom scripts, humor essays, and motivational speeches.

A special challenge might be something in your life that's permanent, and a current issue might be a temporary event. Robin Williams's current issue was his wife having a baby.

> "You're saying, 'Let's breathe, honey, let's breathe,' because you have this myth that you're sharing the birth experience. Nope. Unless you're passing a bowling

ball, I don't think so. Unless you're gonna circumcise yourself with a chain saw, I don't think so. Unless you're opening an umbrella up your ass, I don't think so. You're not doing diddly squat, you're along for the ride."

—ROBIN WILLIAMS

Complete this statement: This is a time in my life when the number one thing that's on my mind is _____ _____.

Examples from my students:

> "going through a divorce"
> "being unemployed"
> "having cancer"
> "being a sober alcoholic"
> "breaking up a relationship"
> "being unemployed"

And once again write ten premises about your current situation here:

_____
_____
_____
_____
_____
_____
_____
_____
_____
_____

Stop here and have your comedy buddy fill in premises based on *your* situation here:

_____
_____
_____
_____
_____
_____
_____
_____
_____
_____

Day 7 Action Checklist

You have ten premises each about your

- ❑ childhood
- ❑ relationships
- ❑ day job
- ❑ special challenges
- ❑ current issues

Day 8: Fine-Tuning Your Topics— Relatable Topics

Finally the moment you've been waiting for—how to turn your authentic topics into stand-up comedy material. But before you start to learn the process, let's do a reality check on your topics. Sometimes topics are so personal or unique that they actually prevent the comic from connecting to an audience. It can be a real shock to find out onstage that your experiences are particular *only* to you and to you alone, and are totally unrelatable to most other human beings. There is a big difference between authentic topics that work in a nightclub setting and personal stories that sound like they should be revealed only in a therapy session.

Wrong way (unrelatable topic):

"I'm hypoglycemic and I have to eat small meals six times a day, and it's hard because sometimes I forget!"

Well, thank you for sharing. Self-absorbed topics such as this don't work because it's about the comic's personality and not about the topic.

"It's hard when you get a bee sting and it makes you talk dirty."

Well, just you. A topic needs to be something that most people can relate to. Unless you are a celebrity, no one cares. Topics based on *your* hypoglycemia, *your* procrastination, *your* eating disorder, and other personal idiosyncrasies are rooted in narcissism rather than in worldly interests.

Right way:

Having a "cheap father" is something a lot of people can relate to.

"My dad's so cheap. He's always yelling at me for spending money. 'Look at you, spending money, you're such a big shot.' Oh yeah, buying food, paying rent. I'm just showing off."

—CATHY LADMAN

PRO TALK *with Richard Jeni*

"I always start out with something that happened to me or something I've lived. The second criterion is how much of the audience has had the same experience and is going to relate to this. The most powerful thing you can do in comedy is to have the audience relate to the material."

Authentic topics that are also relatable

- are interesting not just to you, but also to total strangers
- occur in a similar fashion in other people's worlds (It's not just an idea about *your* mother, but about *all* mothers; it's not just about *you* losing your job, but it is about *everyone's* fear of unemployment.)

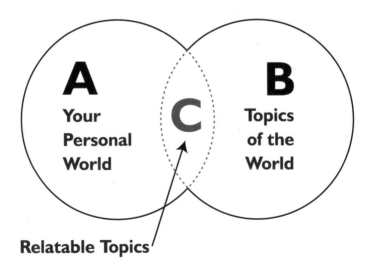

Relatable Topics

"A" is your authentic topics.
"B" is the *buzz* topics going around, authentic topics for a large number of people.
"C" is the overlap between you and the world.

Fame happens when a skilled comic hits on an authentic topic that is also hot with the audience on an emotional level. For example, Yakov Smirnoff was washing dishes at the Comedy Store in 1980 when he suddenly hit it big because his Russian jokes became interesting to the world. When Communism died, so did Yakov's jokes—good for America, bad for Yakov.

Tim Allen knocked around for years until he developed his routine about "men using tools."

> "I decided to rewire that weird little sprayer thing on the sink. It works really good with a paint compressor wired to it. I can clean my neighbor's siding from across the street."
>
> —TIM ALLEN

Tim Allen's stand-up was always funny, but focusing on the topic of "home improvement" created stand-up material that made TV executives take notice. "Men trying to be Mr. Fix-it" was a very relatable topic. His new focus led to a sitcom *(Home Improvement),* which led to starring in films, which even led to a line of Tim Allen tools, which are sold in Kmarts everywhere. Go figure.

San Francisco comic Rob Becker always did well as a stand-up comic. But it wasn't until he developed material based on his insightful observations that men are hunters and women are gatherers that he started really getting attention. He said, "When people started coming backstage and wanting to meet me, I knew that I had hit on a nerve with this topic." His act based on the topic eventually became the long-running Broadway hit *Defending the Caveman.*

Hot topics are things that are on everyone's minds, not just your own. Stories about your life that are inaccessible to others are called journal writing, topics only a therapist could love or musings for a captive bartender. All topics need to be relatable.

In this joke, when Jonathan Katz jokes about *his* father, he is tapping into *everyone's* fears about their parents growing old:

> "My dad's hearing is gone and he won't admit it. When he reads, he goes, 'What?' The mind is slowly following. He called me up the other night, very excited. He says, 'Jonathan, when I get up to go to the bathroom in the middle of the night, I don't have to turn on the light, the light goes on automatically. When I'm done, the light goes off automatically.' I said, 'Dad, you're peeing in the fridge, and it's got to stop.' "
>
> —JONATHAN KATZ

PRO TALK *with Johnny Carson, quoted from* The Great Comedians, *by Larry Wilde (1972)*

"The greatest thing that a performer can have if he is going to be successful is an empathy with the audience. They have to like him . . . if they resent you or if they don't feel any empathy with you or they can't relate to you as a human being, it gets awfully difficult to get laughs."

Relatable Topics

Pop Quiz

Which of the following topics would be *relatable* topics?

1. your bald spot
2. your alcoholic mother
3. your name

Choice #1—bingo for "your bald spot," a relatable topic! It has the chance of making an audience laugh because it's automatically authentic, especially if everyone can *see* your bald spot.

> "I guess I'm sensitive about my hair loss. I think everybody's making fun of it. I went to buy a VCR, the guy said, 'Four-head?'—and I beat the hell out of him."
>
> —DAN WILSON

The topic of "men's baldness" is also relatable, especially because audiences see TV ads for hair loss drugs. Although women don't often have to deal with this issue themselves, they have feelings about bald men. And all men can relate because they either worry about losing their hair or are losing it. It's something that is visual *and* is on the minds of the public. But to really work, the topic must not be so much *your* bald head, but rather the topic of "baldness" in general and what that means—getting old, vulnerability, lack of desirability, and so on.

> "It's really hard for a black man to cover up his baldness. We can't comb our hair forward, we can't comb our hair to the side. Somebody told me, 'Let it grow out!' What, and look like Homey the clown? I don't think so!"
>
> —WOODY WOODBURNER

Any joke based on something physically obvious is an authentic topic. Many comics turn their physical defects into their ticket to fame and fortune.

> [*Joking about his weight*] "I can't get into that California lifestyle. I was at the beach and every time I would lie down, people would push me back into the water. 'Hurry up, he's dying.'"
>
> —LOUIE ANDERSON

> "You women ever look at men's bodies like they are meat? Are you ever alone with your girlfriends, like, 'Look at that baby. USDA choice prime cut. Hmmmm.' My body is the part they make hot dogs out of."
>
> —DREW CAREY

> "I asked the clothing store clerk if she had anything to make me look thinner, and she said, 'How about a week in Bangladesh?'"
>
> —ROSEANNE BARR

Choice #2—"your alcoholic mother"—another relatable topic! Bad news is—you had a rotten childhood. Good news is—it's comedy material! Audiences can relate even if their mothers didn't have a drinking problem because we all know mothers who can be out of control and inappropriate. It's a relatable topic.

> "Drunks forget things. My mom got drunk and would forget little things like where her keys are, where her kids are . . . [*act-out of drunk mom*] 'Go to your room, you're grounded for a week.' 'Mom, we're at Denny's.'"
>
> —TRACEY ABBOTT

Choice #3—"your name"—hack! *Not* a relatable topic. Many beginning comics who have an odd or unusual name will pick their name as an authentic topic. It usually does not work because it's not what the public thinks about or cares about. After all, they just heard your name for the first time—if they heard it at all. A lot of neophyte comics have a hard time believing that the audience doesn't automatically care about them. Believe it. Sure, the joke you told about your name at a party might get laughs, but that's because your friends know you, or because they're being polite. A club audience is never polite. To make an audience of strangers laugh, you will need to pick topics that the audience cares about as much as you do.

Wrong way:

"It's weird having a name like mine—Yule Dansa. When I meet people they think I'm asking them to dance!"

Who cares! It's a topic that, yes, is weird and irritating to you, but not to us. And sometimes a heckler will be happy to tell you. Next!

Here are some examples of unrelatable premises.

"It's hard getting old."

You're thirty years old, get over it! Those of us over forty would give anything to have a three in front of our age. You don't really know anything about this topic.

"It's hard being fat."

Women, if you are a size 12 or under, *you are not fat!* Knock it off. You might be full of self-loathing, but you are not full of fat.

Exercise: Give Your Topics a Reality Test

"So how do you find out if your topics are relatable?"

One way is to test them out in public. Try this exercise with five people, but don't tell people you're testing out stand-up comedy material. They will expect jokes, and right now you just want to see if you're in the reality zone.

Testing your topics on the public is easy. You just ask them what they know about a topic. Ask friends, neighbors, coworkers: *What do you know about [your topic]?*

If you're met with a blank stare, then it's not a relatable topic.

If someone asked me what I know about "their boyfriend Sam," "their flat feet," or "being a compulsive vomiter," I'd say, "Nothing," or, "I don't care."

But if they asked me what I know about "failed relationships," "being sick," "dominating fathers," "wimpy mothers," or "growing up poor," I'd say, "A lot." Not because they are my topics, but because they are topics that almost anyone can talk about. And in some regards, that's what stand-up is—a conversation with an audience. Remember—the audience must care about what you are talking about in order to laugh about it.

So, take your topics out for a test run. Ask people at work, at school, even ask strangers. Here are some additional questions to ask people, and when you ask them, tell people to be honest, or ask only people who you know will be honest. Write down what they say—and don't defend yourself! Reality-check questions will tell how an audience sees you. If one of your special challenges was "having a big nose," and when looking at you, nobody said, "Big nose," you might want to cross that topic off your list.

What do you see when you look at me?

_____

_____

_____

_____

_____

If you were a casting director, what type of roles would you see me in?

_____

_____

_____

_____

_____

Exercise: Narrow Down Your Topics

After spending your day reality-checking your topics, find the winners and cross out the ones that didn't elicit any enthusiasm.

Day 8 Action Checklist

❑ You have reality-tested your topics with at least five people.
❑ You've asked people what they see when they look at you.
❑ You have crossed off all unrelatable topics.
❑ You've arranged for three consecutive jam sessions with your comedy buddy.
❑ You have an appointment with a plastic surgeon.

Days 9, 10, 11: Getting It Funny (3-Day Jam Session with Your Comedy Buddy)

You and your comedy buddy are going to spend the next three sessions jamming on your premises. In each session you and your buddy are going to focus on certain topics:

> First jam session: "special challenges" and "current issue" premises
> Second jam session: "childhood" and "current relationship" premises
> Third jam session: "job" premises

Tape-record each session. Sometimes material will flow out of you perfectly and you will need to know *exactly* how you said it. Also, you might find, when listening back to these tapes, that you've recorded not only ideas that will work as jokes but ideas that can be transformed into sitcom scripts, humor essays, or even bumper stickers. Save these tapes.

How to Get It Funny

Step 1: Write Premises for Your Buddy

By now, both you and your buddy should have written down ten premises for each of your authentic topics. Today, go back to the pages where you wrote your ten premises. You're going to switch pages, and each of you will write ten premises for the other person's topics. If you can't come up with any premises for one of your buddy's topics (or vice versa), chances are that it's not a relatable topic. Maybe the topic is too story-based—like "What happened with *my* boyfriend"—and needs to be made more general, like "mean boyfriends." Don't try to save a topic by rationalizing that it's hard to come up with premises on someone else's topics—I've found that most people actually find it easier.

Step 2: Walking and Ranting

It's time to shift from thinking about premises to having fun by creating the act-out. You don't want to be structured about this, but then again, don't get so comfortable with your comedy buddy that you just sit at a table with a pitcher of beer and *think* about coming up with act-outs.

Act-outs need to be created spontaneously and under the gun. Here's one way to do that.

Put each of your premises on an index card. Grab your tape recorder and cards and go outside for a walk. Pick a card and go to a corner, then walk quickly to the next corner while ranting about that premise into a tape recorder. The comedy buddy will just listen. You *have to* come up with a complete joke by the time you get to the next corner. It doesn't have to be a great joke, but it has to be an attempt at coming up with an act-out or a mix, or both. If you didn't come up with anything, throw that premise away. Take turns working while walking. Keep score and see who gets the most act-outs per block—it makes this fun.

Don't expect every joke to come out perfectly. I would say that on average a half-hour rant produces maybe two good jokes. Most beginners expect jokes to fall out of their mouths perfectly formed, and when that doesn't happen they give up in frustration. You and your comedy buddy should help each other work through any blocks, but if some topics keep hitting dead ends, then toss them.

Write down the winners on separate index cards. And yes, this time you can keep them.

Tips on Creating Act-outs

- *Don't use the words* I, me, *or* my *in the premise.* When you start a joke with "Let me tell you a little bit about myself," you're assuming the audience cares about you. They don't. Get personal in the act-out.
- *Make the premise general and then get specific.* You can't act out "people" or general concepts. Reduce your act-out to something very specific.

> "*[General premise]* When you're in a bad relationship, it's hard to ignore that wise little voice in the back of your head. You know, the one that's saying, 'Run, run for your life! He's the devil!' *[personal and specific]* I used to think that was just my fear of commitment talking. Turns out, it was his ex-wife leaving messages on my answering machine."
>
> —SHARON HALLINGDAL

- *Make sure you are in fact doing an act-out and not explaining.* Remember—the point of acting something out is to become the type of person you are joking about rather than describing that person.

" 'Love handles.' Who came up with that name? When was the last time I was with a woman and I stripped off my shirt and she said, [*act-out*] 'Oooh, are those handles, I love those'?!"

—Tom Allen

- *Keep away from stories.* If "so then I" is in your joke, you have left the world of stand-up. Also, stay in the present—use "I am" rather than "I was." Stand-up is not about *what happened.* It's insights about the important and relatable topics in your life.
- *Remember when creating act-outs that each joke needs to have a turn, a surprise, or a twist.* Start in reality with a grounded setup and then let yourself get wild on the act-out, bringing in new elements to the joke. The act-out is usually not "what really happened" but made-up, exaggerated reality, a major flight of imagination. Let your mind go wild and freely associate.

Tips on Adding Mixes—Comparison Jokes

Look over your jokes and add mixes to some of them. One way to do this is to use comparisons. For example, compare yourself to your parents. If you do an act-out of your cheap father, you could follow up with, "I'm worried I'm becoming him," and do another mix. You can compare the past to the present, such as, "Before I got married I was like [*act-out*] . . . and after I was like [*act-out*]." In this joke Carol Leifer compares what she was looking for when she was first single to how she felt six months later, when she was desperate:

> *"When you're first single* you're so optimistic. At the beginning, you're like, [*first act-out*] 'I want to meet a guy who's really smart, really sweet, really good looking, has a really great career . . .' *Six months later* you're like, [*second act-out*] 'Lord, any mammal with a day job.' "
>
> —Carol Leifer

You can compare any two things—"president of the United States" and "your grandfather":

> *"Ronald Reagan* was seventy-seven years old at the end of his presidency, and he had access to the button. The button! *My grandfather's* seventy-seven, and we won't let him use the remote control to the TV set."
>
> —Dennis Miller

"Sophisticated people" and "rednecks":

"Sophisticated people go to art auctions. Rednecks . . . we have yard sales. And the difference is . . . at art auctions the sale price is slowly working its way up. Not at a yard sale. In fact, if you've got enough patience, you can get a house full of furniture for a buck twenty-five."

—JEFF FOXWORTHY

In comparison jokes, notice how the setup and the payoff are all in the same rhythm and the same length:

"Articles about celebrities always exaggerate their lives, try to make them seem so amazing. 'He worked three years as a dishwasher before he made it big.' Hey, I worked three years as a dishwasher before I became a busboy."

—NICK GRIFFIN

Another way to do a mix is to change the environment in the mix. For instance, if the topic is "your self-absorbed mother," put her in a different occupation.

"Can you imagine my mother working for a suicide hot line? 'You want to jump? So jump! I've got enough problems of my own.' "

Here, comic Harland Williams puts his penny-pinching father in a different situation—the afterlife:

"When my father dies, he'll see the light, make his way toward it, and then flip it off to save electricity."

Get a feel of this mix exercise by performing act-outs of the following.

Character	New Situation
Negative Mother	as therapist
Hippie Mom	as president giving State of the Union address
Drunk Dad	as airline pilot
Religious Mom	as sex education teacher
Marine Dad	as Boy Scout leader

Exercise: Add Mixes

By now you should have a cast of characters in your act, such as your mother, your roommate, your boss. Make a list of them and play with them. Find new situations to put these characters into and act out the scene. However, in the joke you have to establish them by acting them out *before* doing the mix.

> "Driving with my controlling mom in the backseat is such a pleasure. [*act-out of controlling mom*] 'Oh my God, take a left. Oh my God, not that left. Right! Right! Stop! Stop!' [*retort*] 'Okay Mom, we're just in the driveway.' [*mix*] Can you imagine my mom as an air traffic controller? [*mix act-out*] 'Okay, four-oh-niner, you need to take a right. Oh no, not that right. Oh God, you need to take a left. Oh no, a quick left. Bye-bye, four-oh-niner.' "
>
> —Rebecca O'Brien

Character (e.g., Mom)	Characteristic (e.g., Alcoholic)	Situation (e.g., Performing Surgery)

Days 9, 10, 11 Action Checklist

❑ You got together for three days of comedy jam sessions.
❑ You and your comedy buddy exchanged premise lists and rounded off the total of your premises to twenty each.
❑ You jammed your premises on "childhood," "love relationships," "jobs," and "special challenges" and have added act-outs and mixes.
❑ You found some jokes that work and wrote them on index cards.
❑ You have at least six minutes of material (or eighteen premise+act-outs).

Day 12: Organizing Your Set List

"I have jokes now on all different topics. How do I put them together?"

To figure out the order of your jokes, think of your act as a first date with someone (the audience you want to like you). You don't talk about your pubic hair on a first date if you want a second one. The idea is to start with topics that are the most immediate and obvious—such as the way you look and sound, something that just happened, or something on everyone's mind—and end with more personal topics. Always put anything about sex at the end of your act; by then the audience should know you better (and is more drunk). You don't want your audience peaking too soon. If you use this structure, your topic chunks would be arranged like this:

1. special challenge/current issue
2. childhood
3. job
4. love relationship

For example, an Englishwoman might start with the special challenge of "being from England and living in L.A." and the stupid things that people say when you have an accent. For her "childhood" she'd talk about her British mother and growing up poor in England. Her "job" topic could be about stupid things that customers say to a waitress in L.A. She'd end with "love relationships"—differences between L.A. men and London men.

For sitcom writers, this skill of pacing material is called *creating the story arch,* and it will be discussed in the chapter on writing sitcoms. But whether you're a comic or a comedy writer, it's important to know the best way to arrange your material to keep any audience's attention.

"How do I get from one topic to the next?"

Just do it. Being off the wall is a good thing. Let's look at what *off the wall* means. Throw a ball against a wall and it hits the wall and abruptly changes directions. It's human to change directions quickly and sometimes you can get an extra laugh from it.

Hack Attack Warning: Segues

There is a natural tendency to want to bridge each joke or topic with a segue. Don't do it. Most segues are hack, especially these:

> *"And speaking of . . ."* Don't try to bridge one joke to the next.
> *"That reminds me of . . ."* Hack, hack, hack.

There is no need for anything in between jokes. If a sentence is not part of a joke, then it's part of a problem. If you feel the need to use words in between jokes, then use an attitude word to segue:

> *"And you know what else is* stupid . . . *?"* (Insert new topic.)
> *"Another thing that is* weird *is . . ."* (Insert new topic.)

Set Lists

Set lists are bulleted lists of your act—cue words that help you to organize and remember your act. They can look like this:

- fat
- Mom
- Kansas
- husband
- orgasm

Exercise: Your Set List

Arrange your set list. Put an attitude word next to each cue to remind yourself to plug into the emotion.

Your Opening

A good opening gets the audience's attention, defines your persona, and let's them know that *a pro is onstage*. Audiences will decide very quickly if you're worth their attention. That's why the first thirty seconds of your act, the first three pages of your script, the first paragraph of your essay has to rock.

George Wallace

PRO TALK *with comic George Wallace*

"Take command as you walk onstage. Your attitude should say, 'This is *my* show. I don't know what happened before, but I'm here and this is what I do and I hope you like it.' I'm making a sales call, that's all it is. Just as a salesperson, you have an opening, then you present the item, you hope they buy it, they laugh, and then you sell the second joke."

Opening Tips

- *Start with the obvious.* As I mentioned before, if there is anything really obvious about you, joke about it right up front. The audience is already thinking about it, so get on their wavelength. I had a little person in my workshop and she didn't want to talk about her lack of height. I convinced her that in order to take control she would have to joke about it right up front, because her audience would be whispering about it when she walked on the stage. The idea is to joke about yourself before the audience does.

"I used to be a waitress. Not only did I get paid 'under the table,' I worked there too."

—KATHY FOWLER

PRO TALK *with Phyllis Diller*

"The first word, that first sentence is one of the most important things you're gonna do. I found that I must joke about something that they can look at and relate to. For example—I had a dress that was, well, it looked like upholstery, and I said something about how I shot my couch. Right away that's a laugh."

Here is Louie Anderson's opening line from his HBO special with Rodney Dangerfield:

"Listen, I can't stay long, I'm in between meals. So bear with me on this. Let me move this [mike stand] so you can see me. Let's face it, if I didn't do these fat jokes you guys would sit out there going, 'Do you think he knows he's that big?' Like I woke up one morning, 'Oh no.' "

PRO TALK *with Albert Brooks*

"Comics make fun of themselves so it gives them permission to make fun of the audience. If you're fat, you do fat jokes. If you're Irish, you do Irish jokes. If you're Jewish, you do Jewish jokes."

Be sure you know what's obvious about you by completing the "Give Your Topics a Reality Test" exercise on page 130. You might be self-conscious about something, but the audience might not notice it. On the other hand, you might also think it's no big deal that you're missing half your teeth, but the audience might not agree. Also, make sure that this obvious aspect of yourself is clearly visible. That means jokes about your big feet are out.

[*Indian comic*] "My name is Malik Sooch and I'm sure you can tell by my name and the way that I look that I come from a culture that's a lot different than this one . . . I'm from Indiana. This racial tension in New York has gone way too far . . . even *I* can't get a taxi driver to pick me up!"

PRO TALK *with comic Greg Proops*

"Do ten or fifteen minutes up front of likable material and then go to your vile self."

■ *Open with something that is obvious about the room.* Sometimes I dump the opening I planned and start riffing about something that just happened. Things you could play off are the comic before you, the waitress who dropped a tray during your introduction, the curtain behind you that is covered with stains.

Whatever you decide to open with, be willing to toss it if it conflicts with the mood of the room. Get on the same wavelength as the audience. If every comic before you opened with, "How are you all doing?"—start with a joke about that. If there is something really obvious about the audience, do a joke about that. For instance, maybe there was a traffic jam in front of the club that night. Or perhaps the entire audience is there to see one comic and it's not you. Or there's a bus tour from a certain group in the audience. One time when I was playing the Improv, there was a group of fifty high school students in the audience, so I opened with something about that.

PRO TALK *with Richard Lewis*

"I usually open up with what's going on environmentally on the stage, or I spot someone, or if something happened to me moments before I went on or if something very newsworthy happened that day. It would be impossible for me to not talk about something that really happened."

- *Get to your first joke in a natural way.* Audiences take time to warm up to someone. Don't throw them a joke at the beginning that comes out of the clear blue sky. You want it to come from something real and immediate, something the audience is already a part of. For instance, one of my students wanted to start her act with, "It's hard being the middle child." The audience is sitting there drinking and "growing up as a middle kid" is not on the top of their minds. Imagine that you meet someone and the first thing that they say to you is, "It's hard being a middle child." It's too forced. So I coached her to get to her opening jokes in a more natural, real way:

"A lot of the other comics have relatives here. Yeah? [*audience responds*] I didn't invite mine because they would heckle. 'Get off the stage, you were never the funny one.' And that was my grandmother. [*laugh*] Growing up it was hard being the middle child . . ."

With this opening she *(a)* acknowledged what was going on in the room at that moment (the audience was packed with other comics' relatives) and *(b)* quickly got to an act-out (acted out her grandmother).

Only then did she introduce her topic. By that time the audience was engaged and easily became interested in her topic.

- *Make sure your opening sets a tone that you can sustain.* Don't open with a dirty joke if the rest of your act is full of cute observations about dating. The tone of your opening tells the audience what to expect, and you've got to deliver those goods consistently. George Wallace lets the audience know right up front what they're in for . . . and not.

> **"I'm different from the other entertainers you've seen, who try to establish a rapport with you and ask you questions, like, 'How are you doing? Where are you from?' I could give a shit where you're from. We're just here tonight to have a good time, right? Who's having a birthday? Did they sing 'Happy Birthday' to you yet? No? Well, I guess you sure are out of luck because I'm not going to be doing it neither."**
> **—GEORGE WALLACE**

- *Make your opening fit the circumstances.* Different rooms, different audiences, different nights of the week all demand different openings. If it's a big showcase room and a packed crowd, I go right for a big laugh up front. But that can be too heavy-handed for a smaller audience. In that case I usually engage the audience in conversation and *then* slide naturally into my first big laugh.

  Remember, that fantasy audience that howls at all of your jokes when you rehearse your act in the shower is *not* the audience you'll be facing onstage. Not only does every audience have a distinctive personality, but whoever precedes you can change the audience's mood in just moments. For that reason you must be *flexible* about changing your opening.

  I once followed an offensive comic who talked about a certain part of a woman's body smelling like fish. (He's now working at his father's dry cleaning business. *Smirk, smirk.*) I had to acknowledge what had been going on in the room, and I had to *speak it,* or as comics say, *call it.* I opened my show, "Oh, and now the fish is going to do some jokes." They laughed. I rearranged my set list and put the material about "It's hard being a woman" up front. It was very real. And it worked.

Hack Attack Warning—Openings

"So, let me tell you a little about myself."

Hack! Don't assume that the audience is interested in you. They are not. Matter of fact, club audiences are known to be none too caring and supportive. And if your family is in the audience, they already know all they want to know about you.

"I know what you are thinking . . ."

Hack! Yes, it worked for the first two hundred fat comics, who then said, "Anorexic." And for the Asian comic, who then said, "I hope he didn't hit my car." But it's been done to death now, and has become an opening cliché.

"How are you all doing?"

Hack! Cliché. "I'm doing the same as I was when the last eight comics asked me." This opening is hack because *(a)* it shows right away that the comic has nothing original to say and *(b)* it is totally inauthentic, because the audience knows that the comic doesn't really care about how they're doing.

"So, this is really true . . ."

Does that mean everything else you talk about is a lie?

"So raise your hands if you are . . ."

After paying a cover charge and ten bucks for a beer, the audience feels like they've done plenty. They don't want to have to come up with the comic's opening.

Calling the Moment

Calling the moment is a skill that takes many years of performing to do. It's saying out loud what everyone else is thinking to themselves—verbalizing the communal consciousness, which is basically the job of a stand-up comic. For instance, I once went to see some of my workshop graduates at an open mike. It was a very informal setting. A small crowd sat in a little room. The stage was just a raised platform. I watched in horror as each comic performed the exact same act that they did on their showcase night at the Improv. Their performances were fine for a large showcase room but were way too showy and impersonal for an open mike. There was a tall, heavily made-up, big-haired woman in a sequined gown sitting in the front row. Nobody was sure if she was really a she or a he. Hearing her order drinks in a low husky voice heightened the mystery. Not one comic addressed this situation. By the time I went onstage the audience had stopped laughing, or even listening to the comics. I threw away my planned opening and instead I entered into a dialogue with the lady in question instead. I started with, "What a fabulous outfit!" "What do you think about my outfit?" "Could you take me home and dress me?" As "she" answered it became clear that she was a transvestite. I then launched into some jokes about being a bad dresser. "I'm not a femme fatale, but a femme fatality." Big laughs now. I didn't put her down but I knew the audience was focused on her and I had to *call* the reality of the room.

An audience will judge very quickly whether you are an original with something fresh to say or a hack. So even when your jokes are rehearsed, they have to sound spontaneous to sound real.

Day 12 Action Checklist

❑   written out your set list on index cards
❑   decided on an opening

Day 13: Honing Your Material (Comedy Buddy Day)

Get to the Funny

Although the audience where you'll be performing has left their TV remote controls at home, they still have a channel-surfing mind-set. You've got to get to the funny (the act-out) in just a few lines, before the audience mentally changes channels.

Exercise: Taking Out the Trash

Today you are going to spend time honing each joke and wringing out more laughs.

1.   Write out your jokes, then underline the funny part. If there are more than three lines before the funny part, you're taking too long to get there. Cross out all the stuff you don't need—including any and *all* hack segues. Bottom line: if it's not part of the joke, it's part of the problem.

Practice by fixing this joke, taking out all the extra words and finding a way to get to an act-out as quickly as possible.

Wrong way:

"I got married last year and things have really changed. All my other friends changed when they got married, and I never thought I would change when I got married, but you do. In the sixties I was a political activist. I protested, marched, got arrested, and just the other day I caught myself reading *Martha Stewart Living.* I used to be interesting and go, "Hell no, we won't *go!*" Yesterday I started wallpapering the bedroom and I realized that now I'm thinking about Martha Stewart, thinking, 'Oh no, that won't go.' Or, 'Oh no, I'm going to miss her *show.'* "

Right way (same joke without story and extra words):

"It's weird how when you get married, you change. I *used* to be a political activist, *now* I subscribe to *Martha Stewart Living.* Instead of 'Hell no, we won't go,' it's, 'Oh no, that won't go!' 'What time is it? I'll miss her show!' "

—LEE ROSE

2. Make sure all your jokes are in the present tense: "I am" rather than "I was."

   Wrong way:

   "The other morning I woke up and although it was hot, I was cold, and I wanted to put on a coat and I thought, 'Oh no, it happened! I'm old.' And I was thinking, 'When is it that you are old?' Because it was four P.M. and I wanted to go to an early bird special."

   Right way:
   Fix the above joke by putting it into the present tense and giving it an attitude, topic, and act-out.

   _____
   _____
   _____
   _____
   _____

3. Check again, with as critical an eye as possible, that all your premises make sense to a group of strangers. Cross out all the premises that relate only to you and your little world.

4. Make sure every joke has one and *only one* attitude. Don't switch attitudes in midjoke, and toss any jokes that have no attitude.

   "My mother is *weird*. It *scares* me that she . . ."

5. Cross out any jokes that are illogical. What's wrong with this setup?

   "It's weird that everyone in Los Angeles has plastic surgery. This guy comes up to me and shows me that he waxed his chest. 'Feel this man, so smooth!' "

   This is an illogical setup because chest hair waxes are not plastic surgery. Your setup has to make sense. The setup should be:

   "It's weird that men in Los Angeles wax their chest hair."

6. Break up jokes that have more than one topic per joke. Count the number of topics in the following setup.

   Wrong way (too many topics):

   "You know what's weird? I'm from *Kansas* and I grew up on a *farm* with a *large Catholic* family."

   In the setup, the audience needs to know what the joke is about. Separate each topic into separate setups—"Kansas," "growing up on a farm," "being from a large family," and "growing up Catholic."
   You can have great jokes and still have a lousy act. Your entire act needs to make sense; otherwise you will have a comedy disconnect.

Comedy Disconnect

A comedy disconnect happens when the comic *tries to be funny* rather than *communicate* ideas. Reality is sacrificed in a desperate attempt to get laughs at all costs. Some examples:

- The comic starts out talking about how he "can't meet any women," and then later on jokes about how "hard it is being in a relationship." Huh?
- I once had a student whose primary topic was how "hard it is to find Ms. Right." He went on and on about all the nightmare women he dated. Then, in the last thirty seconds of his act, he did a whole riff about "being gay." Huh? Comedy disconnect.

- A woman opens her act by talking about how stupid it is when "girls flirt to get what they want." Later on she does a series of jokes about how she wants to form a "flirting school." Huh? Comedy disconnect.

> **PRO TALK** *with Greg Proops*
>
> "You have to be sincere and talk about what's real for you. Don't be sexy and then talk about how you're not getting dates. Or if you seem smart, don't talk about nonsense. Don't be afraid to talk about what you really think. They're not going to put you in jail."

The same principles apply when writing scripts or writing jokes for other comics. Never sacrifice a character's reality for the sake of a laugh. It creates a comedy disconnect.

Exercise: Comedy Disconnects

With your comedy buddy, do a reality check on your act and make sure that everything makes sense—and be on the lookout for comedy disconnects.

Cutting Jokes That Will Make the Audience Turn on You

This is a comic's worse nightmare—being despised by everyone in the room. I've seen it happen at our showcases—a comic is killing, and then there's that one hostile joke, and the audience turns, and no matter what the comic does, he cannot bring them back.

This applies to stand-up comics and comedy writers. One racist, sexist, or offensive joke in your writer's sample package can be the rotten apple that spoils the entire package.

Joke Fairly

Audiences generally turn if they feel that a joke is unfair. Audiences have a communal sense of fair play. They will laugh at whoever you are trashing as long as they feel that it is *deserved*. They will turn on *you* if you are not fair. For instance, what is wrong with these jokes?

"I was going out with this stupid woman. This woman was so stupid that she had to study for a Pap smear."

What's wrong with this joke—besides being hack—is that the audience thinks, "If *she* is so stupid, then why are *you* going out with her? She agreed to go out with you, so shut up!" The number one rule about trashing something or someone is that you need to prove in your setup that they deserve it.

Wrong way:

"My wife is such a bitch."

The audience will hate you.

Better way:

"My wife ran off with my best friend. What a bitch!"

Right way:

"My wife ran off with my best friend. How could I be so stupid? I should have known!"

Why is this the right way? Because the best person to poke fun at is *you*. That's how to get the audience's sympathy. Make your premises reflect the ultimate insight that the reason your life is screwed up is that *you* are the one who screwed it up. And what do *you* know—it's probably even true.

This premise can create more jokes, such as:

"My wife ran off with my best friend. How could I be so stupid? I should have known the relationship was over when she told me, 'You're a worthless piece of scum and I never, never want to see you ever again.' But no, I thought she was playing hard to get."

And you can get more jokes out of it by going:

"I should have known when she gave me a restraining order."

Now fill in the rest to get the feel of this.

"My wife ran off with my best friend. How could I be so stupid! I should have known when . . ."

1. _____
2. _____
3. _____
4. _____
5. _____

This technique of lighthearted self-mocking is a skill that will increase your likability whether you're performing at a club or pitching your script ideas at a meeting.

Don't Trash the Oppressed

PRO TALK *with Tom Dreeson*

"There is no such thing as a victimless joke. Each joke has a target and you have to make sure that whoever or whatever that target is—they deserve it."

Never further oppress someone who is already perceived as being oppressed. Make sure the butt of your joke deserves your barbs. This means getting out of your narrow little world and knowing who audiences perceive as being oppressed. For instance, you might be a boss and have the worst secretary in the world. Tempted to joke about how hard it is to get good help? Don't do it. First of all, you have the power to fire her and hire someone else, so what's the problem? But even more important, it's mean to make fun of people who get paid a lot less than you do. The audience will not take your side.

Only trash a minority if you are a member of that group. Chris Rock can talk about things he doesn't like about black people and he sounds hip and cutting edge. If you're white and you do it, you sound like an ignorant, ugly bigot. That goes for all minority groups—religious, sexual, racial.

Hack Attack Warning—Gender Bashing

If you think the problem with your relationships is that the gender you date is flawed—hack! Listen to gay men and women complain about their relationships and you will understand how bogus this notion is. "Women are impossible." "Men are clueless about relationships!" Hello! It's not just men or women who are horrible in relationships, it's *all* human beings.

The truth of the matter is that the reason your relationships don't work out is *you!* Take some personal responsibility and stop gender bashing in comedy clubs. It's hack!

My job as a comedy coach is to help my students get to a deeper level of truth, because there is a direct correlation between the level of insight and the volume of laughter. Underneath *hostility* is *fear*. Try it on for size. Change "I hate men (or women)" to "Men (or women) scare me." It will make a huge improvement in your work.

Gender Bashing

Wrong way:

"Women just want men for their money. Last time I had sex, my girlfriend said, 'Wait a second, I need to run your credit card.' "

This premise is hack because the last time the comic's thinking was even remotely insightful was in 1950, maybe. But now women have well-paying jobs and marry for reasons other than financial security. Here is the same joke reworked to be a bit hipper by making the comic look like the idiot.

"Women just want me for my money. I mean, I'm making $15,000 a year now. Hey! So, I was with this woman and she ran my TRW and I said, 'See, women just want me for my money,' and she said, 'No, I'm a prostitute and you can't afford me.' "

—DON ASKEW

Exercise: Cutting the Hostility

Identify who or what is the victim in each joke. Take the jokes that make fun of other people or groups and rework them so that you are the butt of the joke instead. If you do decide to trash someone, make sure you're justified doing it and that the audience will agree. Here black comic Paul Mooney trashes shock-radio DJ Howard Stern for a good reason.

[*Referring to a news item that a black man found the cure to AIDS*] "Howard Stern said, 'No black man discovered no cure. They can't even discover something

to keep their hair straight.' And I said, 'You go back and you tell that motherf**ker I said, "Oh no? Niggers have a cure for that, too. We will f**k all the white women and make sure all our kids have straight hair." ' "

—PAUL MOONEY

Paul Mooney

"What about using props?"

Props usually aren't worth the schlepp and can ruin your timing when you go looking for them. They also create a disconnection from the audience. Rather than *showing* the audience the big stupid hat your mother wore, *describe* and mime it. You'll most likely get a bigger laugh if you leave the prop to the audience's imagination.

"What about doing blue material?"

In case you haven't heard, blue material consists of swearwords, graphic sexual descriptions, and other things generally not found on *Sesame Street.* Many beginning comics will use blue material because certain words and graphic images will often get a sort of nervous, knee-jerk laugh because of the shock value, even if the joke is not displaying any skill, talent, or originality. Although HBO is filled with comics doing very graphic material, they usually got there by being able to also work clean. Generally speaking, working clean opens the door to more opportunities. And then by the time you get your own HBO special, you can do whatever the f**k you want.

The topics you choose to joke about can make the difference between a career as a TV comic and one as a "May I take your order, please?" comic. Beginning comics often pick topics such as body parts, body functions, and sex because they think that they're funny. Yeah, funny if you can find a paying audience of thirteen-year-olds. Many talented comics get passed over for jobs because all their jokes are X-rated. I once saw a comic at an open mike who was brilliant. I'll never forget him—each of his jokes was beautifully crafted with magnificent imagery. Besides being hysterically funny, his insights were extraordinarily perceptive. But his sole topic for his entire thirty-minute act was oral sex. Five years later I ran into him again. He was appearing nightly at the House of Pancakes—an international gig! Jerry Seinfeld, on the other hand, is famous for always doing squeaky-clean material, and look at his career. It's your choice.

JUDY'S BLUE MATERIAL RULE

If your topic is something that comes *out* of a hole—forget it, too graphic. That includes solids, liquids, and gas—that's right, no fart jokes. Going *into* a hole—OK.

Another thing to consider when doing graphic material—it may be very funny, but it might not fit with the rest of your act. For instance, I saw a clean-cut college guy who did some very funny lighthearted material about living with his girlfriend, then threw in an oral sex joke. It got a big laugh, but he couldn't get a laugh *after* that. The reason—the audience had thought he was a wholesome guy and didn't want to see him as a sexual predator. He sacrificed his likability for the sake of that one joke.

Having a naturally dirty mouth, I found it an interesting challenge to clean up my act for the corporate market. It took a lot more work to get killer laughs when I couldn't use the "seven dirty words." However, *clean* material is not necessarily *good* material. A lot of people, myself included, are far more disgusted by so-called clean comics who tell sexist, racist, and homophobic jokes than by brilliant comics who use colorful language. In the end, what matters most is being truthful to who you are and using the language that is most natural for you.

Exercise: Getting an R Rating

Insecurity is the most typical reason that comics use the f-word in their acts. (I'm calling it the f-word because I want my book to be in the library.) Go through your act and see if you can replace those four-letter words with more attitude in your delivery. Unless you're committed to a sleazy, scatological persona, cut all graphic sexual material.

For Women Only

When I first started doing stand-up, there were only a handful of us funny gals out there—Joan Rivers, Totie Fields, Phyllis Diller, and others. And our premises basically consisted of

"My husband is an idiot."

"Men are idiots."

"I can't get a guy."

"I'm fat and ugly."

Traditionally, women stand-ups have limited themselves to doing material about their relationships or about their bodies, making their defects the butt of the joke.

The new crop of female stand-ups is broadening the scope of what women talk about.

"The Second Amendment gave us the right to bear arms in order to have a ready militia. It's not for traffic incidents."

—PAULA POUNDSTONE

" 'Human cloning would not lead to identical souls, because only God can create a soul,' a panel set up by Pope John Paul has concluded. They also took care of a couple other things that were burning issues: apparently, Trix are indeed for kids."

—JANEANE GAROFALO

Hack Attack!

"I'm so fat . . ." PMS. "My breasts are so small."

In this millennium, if you want to do jokes about your body and be hip, you can't make yourself the victim of narrow, traditional thinking. Want to talk about being fat? Then approach it from a fresh new angle—such as the advantages of being fat. "Hey, if I'm going down on the *Titanic* I'm going to float. Grab hold of this, Leonardo!"

PRO TALK *with Judi Brown, manager and talent coordinator for the U.S. Comedy Arts Festival in Aspen*

"Everyone is looking for women who have a unique voice and are truly funny. A lot of the female comics fall into stereotypes. For some reason, it's hard for them to embrace doing something completely different. Be original and embrace your own voice. The payoff is huge because there are so few females that actually succeed at it. If you can hang tough and keep your own voice, you'll definitely rise to the top."

Day 13 Action Checklist

Double-check your act for the following:

- ❏ excess words
- ❏ attitude for each joke
- ❏ present-tense verbs
- ❏ relatable premises
- ❏ comedy disconnects
- ❏ excess hostility (making sure the butt of your joke deserves it)
- ❏ gender bashing
- ❏ blue material
- ❏ hack material

Day 14: Getting Ready to Perform (Comedy Buddy Day)

When doing stand-up comedy, calling a rehearsal doesn't take a lot of organization—it's just you. Wherever you are, you can rehearse. But it's helpful to prepare with your comedy buddy.

"How do I memorize my act?"

Break your act into chunks that make sense, such as the four categories—*special challenges, childhood, current issue,* and *relationship.* Rehearse one chunk at a time, keeping the following in mind:

- Never rehearse your act without emotion.
- Always picture what you are talking about. Visualizing who and what you are talking about makes material more dynamic and immediate.
- Don't practice in front of a mirror or a video camera. You won't be looking at yourself when you perform, so don't do it while you rehearse.

I practice while walking in an alley. Nobody sees me, and even if they do, I just look like another ranting bag lady wildly gesticulating and talking out loud to myself. I go through my act one joke at a time, asking myself after each one, "Do I like what I'm saying? Is this material comfortable?" When a joke feels awkward and I just can't memorize it, I toss it.

There comes a time when you know your act but keep rehearsing it out of fear of forgetting material. Don't overrehearse your act. It's OK not to know it perfectly. No one is going to say, "Well, you were real funny, but you left out a joke." Your act will never go the way that you imagined it anyway, so memorize it well enough not to have to struggle to remember it—but also know how to let go of it so you can swing with the moments.

"What do I wear?"

Hack attack warning!

Funny clothes—hack! If your clothes are funnier than you are, then you've got a big problem. Wear something that makes you feel good—it doesn't always have to be the same thing.

Having said that, do make sure your clothes match your persona. If one of your topics is about being an accountant, a conservative outfit would fit. However, if you're talking about being a poor student, don't come to the club in your Armani suit.

Also, have your clothes match the club. You'll look hack if you walk onstage at Bubba's House of Ribs dressed in a sequin-studded, Cher-type gown—unless, of course, you're a guy.

If your clothes stand out, you have to do a joke about them. I once saw a comic wear tight spandex workout pants onstage. He didn't get many laughs, mostly because the audience was distracted by what seemed to be quite a large package of malted milk balls in his pants. The big laugh went to the comic after him, who said, "How many of you think that was a sock in there?"

PRO TALK *with Beth Lapides*

"Wear what you feel comfortable in. Some comics feel good in tight clothes. Some in loose. Bobcat wears hats, which is saying, 'I see myself as a clown.' I bring changes of clothes with me because I don't know how I will feel when I get to the club. Although, I find that white is very unfunny."

"What if I forget my act?"

What's the number one fear of doing stand-up? Survey says—forgetting your act. Everyone who has ever contemplated doing stand-up has imagined the horror of going blank, standing there drenched in flop sweat as the audience stares pitifully at you. The easiest way to deal with this fear is to change the way you look at it. The fact is, memory loss and the humiliation that goes along with it can be funny. All comics forget their acts at some time or another. Comics who have a healthy sense of humor about themselves not only can survive forgetting their acts, they can make it work for them by joking about it. Rob Becker turned his stand-up act into the hit one-person show *Defending the Caveman.* He blanked out during one performance at Dallas's Majestic Theater and got laughs from the way he handled it. He simply announced, "I forgot my next line." He then walked to the side of the stage, where he consulted with someone behind the curtain. He came back out and said, "It just came to me! A lot of times you go for a walk, and it comes to you." The audience roared because, actually, everyone loves mistakes.

Look at it this way. What are most of your jokes about? How imperfect and stupid we human beings are, right? Forgetting your act is just another example of that. Ironically, it's often the comics who do their acts *perfectly* who *don't* score the *big* laughs—they're too slick.

Generally speaking, the reason a comic forgets his act is that he is disconnected from his material. Fear causes this disconnection. The moment he admits that he is a screwup is the most real moment of his act, and makes him likable, human, and funny.

Tips on forgetting your act:

- Let go of your obsession with being perfect. Make your inner critic accept that you might go blank. Being perfect might get you an A in high school math but it will only get you an A-nal retentive in stand-up.
- If you do go blank onstage, have a sense of humor about it. Use the moment to joke about what a jerk you are. It's a great way to get the audience's sympathy.
- Take in a deep breath, and then let it all out. If you give yourself a moment to breathe, your act will generally come back to you.
- If you leave out material when performing, it's probably a good thing. When comics skip material, it means that it wasn't right for that crowd. Trust your instincts.

PRO TALK *with David Brenner*

"When you get on that stage, you really got to feel that you own it. People have to know that they are in *your* domain."

Day 14 Action Checklist

❑ got your set list together
❑ rehearsed your act
❑ decided what to wear

Day 15: Dress Rehearsal (Comedy Buddy Day)

This is the day you and your comedy buddy do your dress rehearsal. You'll be performing your act just as if it were the real show, down to wearing the outfit you selected. This is not a time to be adding new material to your act, but rather a chance to get comfortable with what you already have.

Timing Your Act

Most open mikes give new comics between three and ten minutes to do their stuff. Whatever you do—*don't* go over. Because if you do, no matter how funny you were, you will always be remembered as the comic who screwed up the schedule. Get in, get out, and nobody gets hurt.

It's better to come in short than to go too long. Don't try to cram too much material into too little time. This is not the only time you will perform. If you are supposed to do five minutes, come in at four minutes in order to leave time for laughs and riffing. And if there are no laughs, you'll want to get off the stage at four minutes anyway.

Exercise: Timing Your Act

Have your comedy buddy time your entire act. Then time your last piece and practice getting to it from any point in the act. Let's say your last bit is thirty seconds. When you get to the club, before you go on, ask the room manager to cue you when you have one minute left. When you get the light, you'll have thirty seconds to finish the joke you are on, and move on to your last joke. The formula for figuring out when the room manager should cue you is the time of your last joke plus thirty seconds.

"How do I end my act?"

Put your most physical and/or sexual joke (or what you think is your biggest laugh) at the end of your act. But if you get a big laugh and you are anywhere near the end of your act, say, "Thank you, good night!" and quit while you're ahead. The goal is not to get in all your material, but to get out while the getting is good. Always make it clear that you are finished by saying, "That's it!" or, "Thank you." It's unprofessional to just walk off the stage without signaling to the audience for applause.

Hack Attack Warning!—Hack Closings to Avoid

> "Well, that's my time!"
> "Thank you and God bless."
> "I'm out of here."
> "There's the light!"
> "You guys have been great!"

"How do I deal with hecklers?"

Most novice comics are afraid of hecklers—they imagine that some drunken stranger is just waiting to humiliate them while they just stand onstage tongue-tied. The truth is, this particular nightmare rarely occurs. Most audiences are too shy to speak up even when asked a question, let alone to shout insults at the comic. During the few times that someone has talked to me, I've actually found it fun to take a break from doing my material and improv with them.

Here are just a few of the reasons why you shouldn't be afraid of hecklers:

- You've got a mike and are louder than them.
- They're drunk and hopefully you're not.
- You usually have the audience on your side.

The best way to handle a heckler is to let him or her dig their own grave. They don't need much help to make themselves look stupid. One technique is to repeat what they said and comment on it by applying the basic stand-up techniques of premise, act-out, and mix. Here's an example.

> [*Heckler*] "That really sucked." [*Comic*] " 'That really sucked.' Thank you for such an astute review of that joke. 'That really sucked.' Very good, sir. [*premise*] With commentary like that you could be working for *Meet the Press*. [*act-out*] 'What do you think of the new federal budget?' 'Well, that really sucked.' "

If you get stuck, a "Thank you for sharing" or "Oh, stop it, Mom" can be enough. It's a little hacky, but will work until you get confident in coming up with your own. If the person is really intent on ruining your show, signal the room manager to throw them out. It's not good business if one person ruins the show for everyone.

PRO TALK *with George Wallace*

"If someone has time to yell at you during your act, there is a reason for that. It usually means that there is a hole in your act. Notice that comics who don't have hecklers are coming up with good material. But sometimes there is one idiot in the audience. There are many ways to do it, but it depends on the moment whether you do it with kindness or embarrass the heckler. You can say, 'Hey, people are coming here and paying to see me, not you.' Or say, 'The people next to you are thinking:—'Three thousand people in this room, and I had to sit next to the asshole.' ' "

Hack Attack Warning!—Heckler Put-downs

- Keep away from the cliché comic put-downs—"This is what happens when the fetus doesn't get any oxygen." "You are two tacos short of a combo plate." These lines should have rim shots after them, they are so old.
- Keep your integrity intact by not going for a racial or gay put-down.
- Male comics—don't bash a woman even if she is drunk, ugly, and stupid. It will make you look even worse.
- Don't get sucked down to the heckler's level. They might be mean, but you need to be clever.

Exercise: Handling Hecklers (Buddy Exercise)

You'll feel even more confident if you have some of your own heckler stoppers in your hip pocket. Practice doing your act while your comedy buddy heckles you, and come up with some responses you like. Even if you are quick witted, take your time before responding so you don't say something so mean that it turns the room against you. Breathe.

Exercise: Practice Being in the Moment

The best responses to a heckler are thought of in the moment. They are funny because they are spontaneous. Here is a way to train with your comedy buddy to be quick on your feet.

Complete this list, adding ten of your own scenarios:

1. *Crash!* The waitress drops a drink tray.
2. It's really hot in the club.
3. Your fly is open.
4. The MC mispronounces your name.
5. Nobody laughs at your jokes.
6. The microphone breaks.
7. No one in the front row speaks English.
8. A waitress stands right in front of you.
9. A woman drops her purse and all the coins fall out.
10. Someone gets a call on a cell phone.

Now write down ten other things that you would hate to have happen.

1. _____
2. _____
3. _____
4. _____
5. _____
6. _____
7. _____
8. _____
9. _____
10. _____

Have your comedy buddy shout out each one of these scenarios while you do your act. React in the moment.

COMEDY BUDDY: It's really hot in the club.
COMIC: Isn't it great to have a comedy show *and* a sauna!

Then switch places and you heckle your buddy. This exercise is also very helpful to writers when preparing to pitch story ideas, because in a way, producers can be like drunk hecklers, and anticipating things going wrong can help you to be prepared for the worst. ("We've already done that story, what else do you have?")

Day 15 Action Checklist

❑ You timed your act, allowing time for laughs and riffing.

❑ You figured out when to tell the room manager to cue you so you have time to get to your last joke, do it, and get offstage without going over your allotted time.

❑ You practiced responding to hecklers and different situations.

Day 16: Your Gig

This is the big day, but not big enough to call in sick at work so you can practice your five minutes for eight straight hours. One run-through this morning is enough. Otherwise you'll end up sounding like RoboComic.

"Can I bring my set list up onstage?"

Try not to—it will stop you from connecting with the audience. If you simply can't go onstage without it, then stick it in your pocket or write it on the side of a water bottle. But don't pull it out unless you get hopelessly stuck. And if you refer to it, be sure to make a joke about it.

> [*Looking at her set list, which was written on her hand*] "This is my Palm Pilot."
> —BRANDY NIGHTINGALE, FIRST TIME ONSTAGE

I wouldn't suggest writing your list on the palm of your hand—especially if you tend to sweat. Suddenly your set list looks like abstract art.

"Do I need to watch the comic that's on before me?"

Yes, because you have to make sure they are not doing any of your jokes. Nothing is more embarrassing than to see a comic hit on a topic that's just been done and done and done. No matter how great your take on it is, the audience is tired of the subject and you're setting yourself up for comparison.

There are some pros who do not like to go near the room before they go on. Andy Kaufman was like that. He would stay clear of the room until the moment he walked onstage because he didn't want the audience's mood to dictate, or even influence, his act. However, the likelihood of the comic before him playing the conga drums and lip-synching the *Mighty Mouse* theme was pretty much nil. Personally, I like to take the temperature of the room before I go onstage.

"What do I look for when checking out the room?"

Check for:

- Burned-out topics. If the past three comics all joked about the same current-event topic and you're planning on opening with that, do yourself a favor and drop it. The audience is probably burnt out on that topic.
- Something that is happening in the room that you can riff off.
- How drunk the audience is.
- What kind of act went on before you. The worst thing is going after someone who stole your material. If you didn't watch their act, *you* look like the thief when you do *your* act. This really happened to me. Hello, Judge Judy.

PRO TALK with *Johnny Carson, quoted from* The Great Comedians, *by Larry Wilde (1972)*

"Your delivery can save you if the material isn't up to par. It always amazes me when I see guys working in front of an audience and they are not going—they don't seem to realize it. They plunge right on doing the routine, like, 'I'm going to do this folks, come hell or high water,' rather than change it and going into different areas."

"Is there a way to prevent my material from being stolen?"

Unfortunately, material gets stolen all the time because there is no way to register it and it's too expensive to sue someone. Also, a lot of times jokes aren't stolen, it is just that several comics came up with the same joke. This has happened to me. A woman once accused me of stealing her material, so I mailed her a video of me doing the joke on TV, way before she thought of it. That's one reason why it's good to save dated videotapes of your performances—they come in real handy if there's a disputed joke. If you catch another comic doing your material and you're sure there's no way they could have come up with the joke independently, ask them to stop, or if that doesn't work, get a Mike Tyson look-alike to ask them to stop. If you discover that several people are doing your material, then it's more likely that your material isn't very original.

"Should I riff off the comic before me?"

Yes, as long as you don't say anything derogatory about their act or their talent. Riffing off their topics, clothes, or anything that happened is a bonding experience. Dissing your brothers and sisters, however, is stupid. Five years from now you might need to suck up to them in order to guest on their talk show. So be nice.

Some additional tips for tonight:

- Tape-record your act.
- Stay out of the way of the business. You're not playing Carnegie Hall. The club makes its money by selling coffee, beer, or liquor, not by helping comics. Stay out of the waitresses' way and don't be a pest.
- DO NOT DRINK ALCOHOL before you go on. It will ruin your edge. It's OK to be nervous. As a matter of fact, having an edge is absolutely essential if you're going to be funny. That nervousness will translate into excitement when you hit the stage. Yes, it feels uncomfortable until then, and getting wasted may seem like a great idea, but just one beer can ruin your timing. *Don't do it.*
- Breathe. If you have the confidence to take one full inhale and exhale in between a joke, consider yourself successful. Breathing helps with timing and can prevent a comedy disconnect.
- Don't go over your time. If you have a three-minute slot, don't do four minutes. As I mentioned before, it doesn't matter how well you do. Go over your allotted time and you will be forever known as the person who messed up the lineup.
- After your show, drink as much as you possibly can.

"How do I stop from being so nervous?"

Rather than trying to stop yourself from being nervous, change your attitude about it. Being nervous can be funny, while being calm, together, confident, and perfect can be a bore. Richard Lewis, funny—the pope, not funny. Being nervous might *feel* uncomfortable, but nobody has ever died from it. If you are worried about dry mouth, then take water onstage with you. Also, pinching your cheek creates saliva, but do it *before* you go onstage.

Sometimes you'll have to wait hours before you go on and you might find yourself getting really nervous. One way to center yourself is to get still, close your eyes, breathe deeply, and focus on trying to hear your heartbeat. Do this for at least two minutes when you find yourself getting bent out of shape.

A word of warning—don't let your fear turn into hostility as a defense mechanism. The audience shouldn't be punished just because you're nervous.

"Should I stand still, or move? Hold the mike, or keep it in the stand?"

If you have to ask, keep the mike in the stand. This will keep you from pacing, which can make you look nervous—not good if you are being videotaped. It also frees up both your hands to gesture during the act-outs. I usually keep the mike in the stand except when I'm doing a big act-out.

> **PRO TALK** *with comic Greg Proops*
>
> "When doing short sets, have brief setups, leave the mike in the stand, and let your whole personality come out in the jokes."

"I'm too nervous. I'm a writer, not a performer. I'm going to skip doing a show."

Sorry, but you need to perform even if you are a writer because writers need to know how to engage an audience. Let's face it—show business is all about putting on a *show*, whether it's in front of a nightclub audience or network executives. It's all about selling your goods—your act, your sitcom script, or your talking toilet paper invention. All the same rules apply—be yourself, have fun, and connect.

> **PRO TALK** *with Cindy Chupack, co–executive producer of* Everybody Loves Raymond *and* Sex in the City, *executive producer and creator of* Madigan Men
>
> "Writing sitcoms is a collaborative effort with eight writers around the table pitching funny ideas, many of them ex–stand-ups or actors. It was hard to get used to the thought of just throwing out my ideas without fine-tuning them on a computer. Stand-up helped me get comfortable with that, because after being in front of an audience of strangers, being in a room with eight writers that I knew didn't seem so scary."

Day 16 Action Checklist

- ❑ Didn't get drunk.
- ❑ Checked out room.
- ❑ Didn't get drunk.
- ❑ Did gig.
- ❑ Got drunk.

Day 17: Celebrate

Congratulations! No matter whether you killed, bombed, or (more likely) somewhere in between, you did it! Spend a day being proud of yourself. No matter what happened, you deserve it. E-mail me and let me know how your first time went. And go to the Web page *(www.comedywork shopS.com)* and see stories and tips from other comics.

Day 18: Performance Review— Reworking Material

> **PRO TALK** *with Christopher Titus*
>
> "When I first started, I wrote and wrote and I had fifteen minutes of material that turned out to be six. My first set killed and in the next eight sets—I ate it."

OK, party time is over. Back to work. Whether you bombed or killed at your open mike, reviewing and reworking your act is absolutely essential. This is what separates the pros from the wanna-bes—a thorough scrutiny of your performance. Doing stand-up well requires constantly reworking jokes. One word can sometimes make the difference between silence and the big guffaws.

Professional comics want to know *why* a joke didn't work and *how* to fix it. They're willing to expend the time and energy necessary to perfect their craft and solve the problem. Comic wanna-bes, on the other hand, generally go, "I hate myself, let's get drunk," when a joke doesn't work. Pros don't take bad jokes all that personally—it's about the material. Amateurs take it all *too* seriously and make it about themselves or about the audience—"They really sucked."

PRO TALK *with Phyllis Diller*

"I never, ever come off and blame the audience. I have the same reaction whether I had a good show or a bad show. After a bad show I want to know what I did wrong, or after a good show, why was it so good?"

Becoming a successful stand-up is like becoming successful at anything else—you must be professional and learn your craft. There *is* a reason why jokes don't work. Let's figure it out together.

PRO TALK *with Richard Jeni*

"It was really a matter of going out to clubs every single night and trying stuff out and taping it and honing and refining it over a couple of years. If you took the time that you spent sitting around during the day thinking about it, and the time that you spent trying it out, and the time you spent listening to the tape, and what the attrition rate is and what actually makes the cut, it came out to twenty-two hours for every one minute that made it into the show."

Exercise: Reworking Your Act

Listen to your tape with your index cards in hand. Separate your cards into the Got Big Laughs pile and the Needs Work pile. Take the jokes that worked and put them aside. Now let's focus on the clunkers. But before we play Can This Joke Be Saved? let's go over the basics.

Pre-show

- ❑ Did you center yourself?
- ❑ Did you check out the room?
- ❑ Did you drink alcohol?

The Opening

Did you:

- ❑ open with something interesting to the audience?
- ❑ riff off the comic before you?
- ❑ call the moment?
- ❑ mention the obvious?
- ❑ say something that alienated the audience right at the start?
- ❑ connect to the audience?
- ❑ have a clear attitude for your first joke?
- ❑ take the time to breathe?
- ❑ get hostile to the audience? (If so, was it because you were nervous?)

Your Material

Now let's turn to the jokes themselves. Go through this checklist with all those in your clunker pile to find out why they didn't get a laugh.

- ❑ Did the joke have attitude? Remember, no attitude means no laugh. Did the attitude continue through the whole joke? Jokes without consistent, continuous attitude are usually stories, not jokes, and should be tossed.
- ❑ Was the topic relatable? Maybe that topic was wrong for that particular audience but could work with a different crowd. As you gain more experience you will find that each audience has its own personality, and sometimes that personality clashes with yours. No matter how much you dish it out, they're not going to be buying.

❑ Was there an act-out? That's what gets the big laughs, so make sure most of your jokes have them.

❑ Was there an element of surprise in the joke? Did you do more than just a funny story? Was there a mix that no one expected?

❑ Were your jokes based on stories, or on premises?

❑ Did you take more than three lines to get to the funny part?

❑ Did you pause after the joke, giving time for the audience to get it?

Eliminate Stories

Hack attack warning—stories suck.

Despite my many warnings, there's a good chance that a story has snuck into your act. Many beginning comics have this conviction that their life is just so damn funny, and like them, you've probably been saving up all these hilarious stories for years, just waiting for the time you actually *do* stand-up. I know it's hard to give them up. I have sympathy—really. But that doesn't change the fact that hysterical stories that kill at a party usually die at a comedy club. Save those stories to put in a one-person show, a humorous essay, or a novel, but get them out of your act.

Pop Quiz

Which of the following are not *topics for stand-up?*

1. airlines
2. cancer/AIDS/death
3. a funny story about your breakup

Answer: "airlines" and "funny stories" are *not* good topics for stand-up. Choice #1—"airlines"—hack, done-to-death topic.

Choice #2—"cancer/AIDS/death"—funny. Steve Moore, a comic living with AIDS, built his HBO special around this topic.

> "When I got AIDS I put a bumper sticker on my car. It says, 'Lose weight now, ask me how.' "
>
> —STEVE MOORE

> "I am a writer/producer/director/breast cancer survivor. Don't feel sorry for me. Cancer was easy—turning forty in Hollywood, now that's a fatal disease!"
>
> —DEVO

"It's time for me to get a drink of water. I figure this stuff is safe. Actually, I don't care if it's safe or not, I'd drink it anyway. You know why? Because I'm an American and I expect a little cancer in my food and water. I'm a loyal American and I'm not happy until I let government industry poison me a little bit every day. Let me have a few hundred thousand carcinogens here. [*drinks the water*] Ah, a little cancer never hurt anybody. Everybody needs a little cancer, I think. It's good for you. Keeps you on your toes. I ain't afraid of cancer. I had broccoli for lunch."

—GEORGE CARLIN

Choice #3—"funny story about your breakup"—*not funny.*

Although the topic "relationship breakups" is a good topic, a *story* about it most likely won't work in a club setting. One problem beginning comedy writers sometimes have is telling *stories* about their families, rather than molding their family stories into *premises* that others can relate to. If your material is dependent on an audience having to spend Thanksgiving dinner with you to understand your jokes—keep your day job.

Joke writing is *topic* based, not *story* based. If you have a funny story about, let's say, your grandmother, you will have only one hit on that topic. If your topic is "grandmothers" you will not be limited by "what really happened." Still, it is through our stories we can find topics to feature in our act.

Exercise: Stories

This exercise will illustrate the difference between a story and a premise. Stories can be converted into stand-up topics if you are willing to throw away the plot of the story (what really *happened)* and concentrate on finding the premise (the point of the spiel).

Look at this story and see if you can find the topic.

"I was watching a football game with my wife and she doesn't really understand the game because she said to me, 'Why does number 78 keep patting number 22 on the butt?' And she thinks that it's a gay thing, and I said, 'It means *good job.'* And she said, 'Nooo! There's something going on, and I think number 88 is jealous!' "

This topic is _____.
Do you notice the following?

- It takes a long time to get to the funny part.
- There is no way to do another hit on a story.

- Stories lack attitude.
- Stories use past-tense verbs.
- The words *I* and *me* are in the setup.

The topic of that story is not really "football" but "how women see things differently." The premise of that story could be "Women think in terms of relationships. To them everything is a relationship."

Here is the same story put into stand-up comedy format.

> "Women think in terms of relationships. I'm watching football and my wife sees a player pat another player's butt, and she thinks they're in love. [*act-out of wife*] 'Number 22 and number 78 seem very close to each other.' Or I'm watching basketball. 'Do Shaq and Kobe get along with each other? They seem mad.' To women everything is a relationship. [*mix*] They could be watching a sunset, 'Oh, look how the sun is kissing the ocean.' "
>
> —THOMAS TALLARINO

Jokes need to be concentrated. Audiences don't care about what really happened in your life. They want you to get to the point, and stories take too long to get there.

"But a lot of comics tell stories."

Don't be misled. The brilliance of a Jerry Seinfeld, Bill Cosby, or Richard Pryor is that they make it appear as if it's a story coming off the top of their head, when it's actually a finely crafted series of jokes.

Here Jerry Seinfeld's topic is "bathrooms." Examine how he breaks down this topic into premises, not stories (premises are italic).

> "Don't like other people's showers because *you can never adjust the temperature right.* I don't know the ratio on the dials. Sometimes a sixteenth of an inch is a thousand degrees. Gotta get out of the way of the water.
>
> "*There's always that little hair stuck on the wall of somebody else's shower.* You wanna get rid of it but you don't want to touch it.
>
> "*I don't know how it got up that high in the first place.* Maybe it's got a life of its own, and I don't want to get involved. You got to aim the shower head at the hair but that never works. You got to get a pool of water from under the shower over to the hair. You get it down a foot at a time, like this. The hair is hanging on.
>
> "*But we have to fight these battles. We are all alone in the bathroom. Whatever goes wrong, you have to handle it.* Did you ever go to a big party, go in the

bathroom, flush the toilet, and the water starts coming up? This is the most frightening moment in the life of a human being right here. You will do anything to stop this. You lose your mind, start talking to the toilet. [*act-out*] 'No, please, don't do this to me. C'mon, you know this is not my fault. I'll get you the blue thing, the man in the boat, just let me off the hook this one time.' "

Cut all stories out of your act or break them down into jokes.

Day 18 Action Checklist

- ❑ You've listened to your tape.
- ❑ Reworked material.
- ❑ Tossed the unsalvageable.
- ❑ Tossed out all the stories.

If you have very little left after reworking your act, don't worry, because I'm going to show you how to add more material.

Day 19: Adding Current-Event Material (Comedy Buddy Day)

Hopefully doing the previous exercises provided you with twenty minutes of material based on personal stuff. Then, after taking out the stories, the hack, and the unfunny, it was condensed into three to five minutes. Once you performed it and took out everything that didn't work, you probably ended up with a good two minutes of material. Consider yourself lucky. It takes a lot of material to come up with a solid two minutes. Creating comedy is sometimes a matter of inspiration, but mostly it's a matter of perspiration—in the form of constantly creating new material. And one good source of new material is current events.

Writing Current-Events Jokes

Current-event jokes are about the topics that are in the communal consciousness—movies, politics, celebrities, trends, events. A joke has a better chance of working if it's about a topic that's already on people's mind, rather than one they have to be reminded of. That means your jokes on the feast of Lupercalia don't fit into the current-events category. Jay Leno chooses his topics for his nightly monologue right off the AP wire.

"In a test program, forty drugstores in Washington State will be dispensing morning-after birth control pills without prescription. In fact, men can buy them in special gift packs with cards that say, 'Thanks, maybe I'll call you sometime.' "

—JAY LENO

TV audiences will change channels if they're not interested in Jay's topics. So, popular topics equal higher ratings. Popular guests raise those all-important ratings points too, including many comics. And comics who joke about the topics that Americans care about and can relate to have a much better chance of getting on *The Tonight Show* than those who don't.

All comedy writers need to have their finger on the pulse of the culture. As part of your ongoing homework, you must read an assortment of newspapers and magazines, watch TV, go to movies, and eavesdrop.

How to Pick Current-Event Topics

When creating material based on nonpersonal topics, the usual rules apply.

Topic Rule #1: *Don't pick a current-event topic because you think it's funny.*

Professional comics don't pick a topic based on its humor quotient. They pick a topic because:

- They have an interesting opinion about it.
- They have personal experience with it.
- They have a passionate attitude about it.

There is no such thing as a funny topic. I can't tell you how many people come up to me and say, "I've got an idea for a comedy routine—'Girl Scout cookies—S'mores!' So, what do you think?"

I think, "I'd like to eat some."

There are no funny ideas. It's what you *do* with an idea that makes it funny.

PRO TALK *with Steven Wright*

"As an exercise I pick unfunny topics and see how I can make them funny."

When writing jokes for others or writing for TV, you won't have the luxury of even picking your topic. As a corporate speaker, I am given topics to *make* funny. The topics themselves are extremely unfunny. For instance:

- uses of titanium dioxide in paint pigmentation (Kerr-McGee Corp.).
- aerospace, Mir space station (Boeing)
- potatoes (National Potato Council)

Not a knee-slapper in the lot. But my job isn't talking about the things I find interesting. I'm paid to customize my humor to fit the needs of these companies *and* be clean at the same time. It's a real challenge for a trashy-mouthed woman like myself. Here are some examples of the jokes I came up with on those topics.

Topic: "uses of titanium dioxide," for Kerr-McGee Corp.

"It says in your newsletter that 'titanium dioxide has microscopic hiding power.' Great! I'm going to put some on my ass! 'Hey, Judy, you look great! Jenny Craig?' 'No, titanium dioxide!' "

Topic: "Mir Russian space station," for Boeing.

"What's going on with that Mir space station crashing into the docking ship? It's weird because ground control said it was absolutely human error. The astronauts said it was absolutely mechanical failure. But one thing I know for sure—being a Russian space station, *Absolut* had something to do with it!"

Topic: "potatoes," for the National Potato Council, at Disney World.

"The potato needs more PR, maybe a theme park: Potato World with Spud Mountain . . . Potatoes of the Caribbean!"

Okay, they're not knee-slappers, but the farmers laughed and the check cleared.

Topic Rule #2: *Don't pick weird topics, but rather have unique opinions about ordinary topics.*

Novice comedy writers often pick the weirdest news items ("There is now an animal Prozac") to discuss.

Wrong way:

"Prozac is too expensive, so I'm taking animal Prozac. It's okay, but now I squeal like a pig!"

This open-miker created a *false* premise because she wanted to work her "funny" impression of a pig into her act. But it didn't work, because even though the pig impression was sort of funny, the joke wasn't authentic.

Hack Attack!—Current-Event Topics

Hack topics—"penile implants," "masturbating monkeys," "tampon commercials." If your topics are funnier than you, you've got a problem.

> "Tobacco companies still can't admit that nicotine is addictive. Some moron from R. J. Reynolds said, 'It's all relative. I heard carrots were addictive.' Oh really? I'll tell you something right now. No matter how many carrots you've had, and no matter how bad your carrot habit becomes—you're never going to have to eat one through a hole in your neck."
>
> —HEATHER ROUNDY

Exercise: Finding the Hot Topics

1. Go to your neighborhood newsstand and make a list of the topics on magazine covers.
2. Eavesdrop on the conversations at your local coffee shop.
3. Write down the topics you talk about with your friends on the phone.
4. Subscribe to a national newspaper like *USA Today*.
5. Set up your Internet start page to show the day's top news stories.

Exercise: Writing Current-Event Material (with Comedy Buddy)

Both you and your comedy buddy take a sheet of paper and rip it up into ten small squares. On each one, write down a current news topic. All these topics must be happening now, they can't reflect last week's news. Your topics can be political, such as elections, politicians in trouble, or international conflicts. Or they can reflect lifestyle trends, such as a new fad diet, a unique fashion style, or the latest hot movie or band. But all of them have to be topics that most people have heard about—new advances in the field of ichthyology don't fit the bill.

Now, put your pieces of paper with their current-event topics in a bag, and have your comedy buddy do the same. Both of you will pick one topic from the other's bag and work with it for the rest of this exercise. You may feel that you can't find anything funny about the topic you have drawn, and may want to switch to another one. Don't. Commit to this topic for the length of this exercise. Neophyte comics tend to switch topics before they've even had a real chance to explore them because they're afraid they can't immediately come up with material. When you're a staff writer for *The Tonight Show,* you don't have the luxury of waiting for funny news or easy topics to come along. You have to produce every day and it has to be funny. This is an opportunity to stretch your creative muscles. Take it.

Write down your topic below:

_____

My current-event topic: "NASA space program".

Exercise: Topic Rants

Standing in front of your comedy buddy, rant about your topic, using attitude. When you rant, let yourself get angry—yell, talk fast, and pace. Don't give descriptions or, God forbid, tell a story. Rather than being funny, be emotional. Tape-record these sessions and listen back to see if there are some ideas you can use. With your comedy buddy, arrange your material into the attitude+topic+premise+act-out+mix structure.

Here are some more ideas on writing current-event jokes. Remember that the jokes won't just come out of you fully formed and perfect. It's a numbers game. The more you write, the better your chances are of scoring.

1. Add an attitude *(weird, stupid, scary,* or *hard),* and push your topic into an interesting premise (opinion).

    Wrong way:

    "What bugs me about the space program is that I was reading the newspaper and I saw that all the astronauts were men and . . ."

    Come up with a specific opinion.

    Right way:

    "What's weird is that the space program doesn't have many female astronauts."

Another way to come up with your premise is to react to other people's opinions. First repeat what you read or heard and then give your hit or opinion on it.

> "You've heard people say, 'All God's children are beautiful.' All God's children are not beautiful. Most of God's children are, in fact, barely presentable."
>
> —FRAN LEBOWITZ

> "Congress voted against a proposal to have a national seven-day waiting period to buy a gun. Is a week a long time to wait to see if a former mental patient is qualified to own an Uzi? Come on, it takes three weeks to get a phone!"
>
> —JIMMY TINGLE

2. Drive your premise to an act-out. Here's mine on the space program.

> "It's weird because any woman would give anything to be weightless. 'How much do you weigh, Judy?' 'Nothing!' "

Repeat this exercise two more times on the same topic, with a different attitude: "It's *stupid* because . . . ," or, "It's *hard* because . . ." Keep pushing to an opinion, and then drive it to an act-out.

> "What's weird about the space program is that they are sending old men into outer space. If they can't find their socks, how the hell are they going to find Mars?"

3. Find a mix by bringing in another element. With authentic jokes, the mix usually goes from the personal to the global. With current-event jokes it's the reverse—they often start off global and then get personal.

> "[*Global*] The *New York Times* said that another woman has revealed that she had sex with President Clinton. [*personal*] I'd never run for president. I'm scared no woman would come forward and say she had sex with me."
>
> —GARRY SHANDLING

4. Comic Steve Marmel supplied this excellent current-event exercise:

Read *USA Today.* Pick one story from it and break it down into bullet points. For instance, if the story is about "The President has been found to have illegal campaign contributions," the bullet list might be:

- when they found it out
- who is accusing him
- who the illegal contributions were from
- how the president is responding to it

Take each bullet point, turn it into a premise, and create a payoff.

Do this exercise with the rest of your buddy's topics. Out of all these rantings, select three jokes you think will work and write each on a separate index card. I usually write down the setup but not the act-out because writing the act-out seems to diminish the joke's spontaneity. These index cards will stack up, and before you know it, you'll have a chunk of current-event material!

Day 19 Action Checklist

- ❏ You've done the "Topic Rants" exercise with all ten of your comedy buddy's topics.
- ❏ You have at least three solid topics with at least three good hits (premises) on each of them.
- ❏ You have written at least three jokes on separate index cards.
- ❏ You've created three minutes of current-event jokes.

Day 20: Creating Cutting-Edge Premises

The best way to stand out creating comedy material is to create soulful and insightful premises. To recap, a premise is an insight about your topic. It usually answers the question "what's *weird, hard, stupid,* or *scary*" about that subject. The way you answer that question is what separates a comic who gets laughs from a comic who gets laughs *and* gets jobs. To be a hip and happening comic or comedy writer, your premises need to express uniquely original insights. The following, on the other hand, are premises heard over and over at open mikes everywhere.

Hack Attack Warning!—Premises

- ❏ L.A. is very different from New York.
- ❏ I'm half Jewish and half Italian. That means . . .
- ❏ Dating is hard because men and women are different. (Duh!)

Rita Rudner

Hard to be more boring than that. These kinds of cliché premises are generally used as preambles to some "really funny" (not) story about something that "really happened" (who cares?). If being a successful stand-up was that easy, all the restaurants in L.A. and New York would be drive-throughs or cafeterias because there wouldn't be any waiters.

Let's look at the kind of premises that the pros come up with.

"They're trying to put warning labels on liquor saying, 'Caution, alcohol can be dangerous to pregnant women.' That's ironic. If it weren't for alcohol, most women wouldn't even be that way."

—RITA RUDNER

[*People say stupid things about homelessness.*] "Considering the harm people do when they work, laying on the sidewalk is not so bad."

—FRAN LEBOWITZ

"I honestly believe if you make the death penalty a little more entertaining and learn to market it correctly, you might just be able to raise enough money to balance the stupid, f**king budget."

—GEORGE CARLIN

"It doesn't matter what temperature a room is. It's always room temperature, right?"

—STEVEN WRIGHT

"Doctors are crooks. Why do you think they wear gloves? Not for sanitary reasons . . . Fingerprints."

—JACKIE MASON

"I don't think white women should be calling each other 'girlfriend.' Okay? Stop pretending to be black. And no matter what color you are, 'You go, girl!' should probably go. Right along with 'You the man, hey, you the man.' 'Oh yeah, well, you the f**king honky.' "

—GEORGE CARLIN

"You know, you're never more indignant in life than when you're shopping in a store that you feel is beneath you and one of the other customers mistakes you for an employee of that store."

—DENNIS MILLER

Having great premises will elevate your stand-up career from the dead-end "All the beer you can drink . . . and comedy too!" type of gigs into the realm of college, clubs, TV, and "This kid has a future" gigs. Later in this book, you writers will learn how basing sitcom scripts on cutting-edge premises is key to getting your scripts read and sold.

Working smart means taking risks because you have to give up "being funny." It means working close to the edge of where comedy meets tragedy. The closer you can get to that line without tripping and falling over, the more brilliant you will be. The danger of walking that tightrope is that you might bomb. There's no safety net with brilliance. But the best and brightest comics take that risk because they are more committed to their vision and their voice than they are to being liked by the audience.

> "Animals have two important functions in today's hectic society: to be delicious and to fit well. I can't get down on animals' rights because I've never met a person who likes people more than they like animals. You know what people are like. 'I'm going to step over this disgusting homeless person and pet this cute little kitten.' "
>
> —GREG PROOPS

Sometimes working on what you "truly believe in" takes you to the bottom before it lifts you to the top. Jimmy Tingle, a social and political humorist from Boston, got a shot on *The Tonight Show Starring Johnny Carson*. But he wasn't asked back because they told him he was "too political."

> "If Jesus Christ were here and running for office, would the Christian Coalition vote for him? 'Mr. Christ, we in the coalition would like to know your views on the death penalty.' "
>
> —JIMMY TINGLE

He didn't change his act. He stuck to his convictions, and in 1999 CBS gave him his big break—he's the new Andy Rooney on *60 Minutes II*.

If you want to have a career as a comedy writer or performer, being funny isn't enough. You have to have a unique point of view.

Taking a Stand Writing Comedy
Exercise: Smart Premises

Most brilliant insights occur spontaneously, while you're busy doing something else. You might have a crystal-clear realization of why all your relationships have failed while washing the dishes. You might get a complete understanding of the meaning of life while stuck in a traffic jam. You have to be ready to capture these gems when they come to you.

Carry your tape recorder or notebook with you *everywhere* and write or tape-record every single idea you have, no matter how weird, stupid, or inappropriate it might sound. Be alert to the possibility of a fantastic premise occurring at any moment. Start right now by jotting down five premises that could apply to people who read comedy books such as this.

Example: *People who want to perform or write jokes were not heard when they were children.*

_____

_____

_____

_____

_____

- Spend an entire day of looking at yourself and others in terms of premises.
- Throw away all premises in your act that are hack.
- Take your unfunny but insightful new premises and run them through the five-step process (attitude + topic + premise + act-out + mix).
- Don't throw away good premises just because they don't translate into good stand-up. They might come in handy later, when writing humor essays or a one-person show.

Day 20 Action Checklist

- ❑ You've come up with at least five new premises.
- ❑ You've come up with three new jokes.
- ❑ You've cut all hack premises out of your act.

Day 21: Topic Runs

People's attention spans are short. It's not easy to find a topic that really engages an audience, so once you do get a topic that clicks, get all the mileage you can out of it with a topic run—a chunk of material in which a comic gets a multitude of hits, or laughs, off one topic by using different premises on the same topic.

PRO TALK *with Phyllis Diller, who is listed in* The Guinness Book of World Records *as having gotten the most laughs per minute of any comic alive or dead*

"I actually got twelve laughs in one minute from an audience. It was Bob Hope who noticed. Of course he would, he is such a constructionist. He goes for six a minute and he realized I was getting twelve. But there is a secret to how you do it! Topper, topper, topper. Most comics do setup, payoff, setup, payoff, in other words six jokes per minute. In my case of twelve, *one* setup got *twelve* payoffs."

Here are the twelve jokes that put Phyllis Diller in *The Guinness Book of World Records.*

Setup: "Fang's mother is so fat that . . . How can I describe her—"

1. Jell-O with a belt.
2. When she sits down it takes the whole mess five minutes to settle.
3. When she takes her girdle off, her feet disappear.
4. In a bikini she looks like a bear in a jockstrap.
5. We didn't have a sunken living room till she arrived.
6. Now we have a Persian throw rug—she sat on the cat.
7. Her dress size is junior missile.
8. When she wears a white dress we show movies on it.
9. She ate my doormat—thought it was a Triscuit.
10. She puts her makeup on with a roller.
11. She blew her nose downtown, a construction crew broke for lunch.
12. She went on the Scarsdale diet—ate Scarsdale.

PRO TALK *with Richard Jeni*

"Once you get the audience fixated on a certain topic, why let 'em go? You want to be pounding and hammering on a topic and get that momentum going. If you do an act where each joke is a setup and then a punch and then another setup on a different topic and punch, then each one of those individual jokes better be really good. They each have to stand on their own and there are very few comics that can pull that off."

Jerry Seinfeld is a master of the topic run. He finds funny in the smallest detail of his topic. He notices and expands upon the minutiae of a subject that most people ignore. Good comics pay attention to the details of life, whether it's a person, an incident, or a moment—and then dissect them into microscopic particles. Jerry Seinfeld just doesn't tell a story about "going to a drugstore." Instead, he breaks down the topic "drugstores" into specific premises.

Exercise: Topic Runs

Examine this Seinfeld routine and underline his premises about the topic of "drugstores."

"I went into the drugstore last week for a cold medicine and I was totally over-whelmed by it. I'm trying to break it down. I mean there are six thousand products that are perfect for me. This one is quick-acting, but this one is long-lasting. When do I need to feel good, now or later?

"Ever catch yourself reading ingredients at the drugstore? 'Three-point-oh tetrahydrozaline. That's a good amount of that.' They know we don't know. They make up words. They always tell us on TV, 'Now with an extra drop of retzin.' Like we're all going, 'Well, finally we're getting some more retzin.'

"They always tell you how the medicine works on TV. You know, the commercials, that's my favorite part, where the guy says, 'Here is the human body.' It's always this guy, no face, mouth open. This is how drug companies see the public.

"Then they tell you about the pain-relieving ingredient. It's always extra-strength. There is no more 'strength' anymore, you can't even get 'strength.' 'Strength' is off the market, it's all extra-strength. 'I need extra.' 'What is extra?' 'Well, it's more. We're gonna throw a little extra your way. Don't say anything about it.'

"Some people aren't satisfied with extra, they want the maximum. 'Give me the maximum-strength. Give me the maximum allowable human dosage. That's the kind of pain I'm in. Figure out what will kill me and then back it off a little bit.'

"And why does that pharmacist have to be two-and-a-half-feet higher than everybody else? Who the hell is this guy? 'Clear out, everybody, I am working with pills up here. I can't be down on the floor with you people. I'm taking pills from this big bottle and then I'm gonna put 'em in a little bottle. And I'm gonna type out on a little piece of paper. It's really hard.' "

Having problems creating a topic run for one of your topics? It could be because

- Your material is story-based. After you finish telling the audience "what happened," there is nothing left to say.
- You don't have enough passion or attitude about the topic.
- The topic can sustain only one funny/cheesy gag, which means it's probably not a real topic.
- You've hit a creative wall.

Good news—if the last reason is the problem, there are ways to overcome the block. Two good ones are *mind mapping* and *list of ten.*

Mind Mapping Topics

Mind mapping helps you to generate a multitude of ideas by drawing a free-form diagram of the topic. Here's how it works.

Pick a topic that you have only one or two hits on, or that you don't know how to make funny. With mind mapping, it's OK not to have any ideas when you begin.

Write your topic in the middle of a page and draw a circle around it. Then quickly draw other balloons containing elements of this topic until your entire page is covered with words having to do with your topic. Then focus on each balloon and write offshoots containing the specifics of that topic. Don't judge, just draw as quickly as you can. Seinfeld's "drugstore" routine mind map might have looked something like the one on the following page.

Mind mapping a topic is a way to expand your ideas whether you are writing jokes, scripts, or essays.

Exercise: Mind Mapping

1. Examine the "drugstore" mind map and come up with three jokes on drugstores that Seinfeld didn't find.
2. Mind map a topic that's already in your act.
3. With your mind map in hand, do the "Topic Rants" exercise (page 175) while standing in front of your comedy buddy. The mind map will probably lead you to opinions, mixes, and other aspects of your topic that you couldn't come up with before.

Top Ten List

Another way to find more hits off a topic is to do a top ten list. This way you do one setup and keep adding *toppers.*

Mind Map of a "Drugstore"

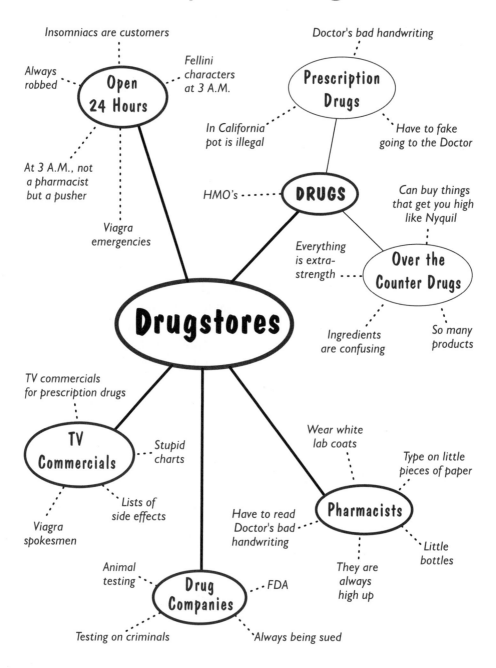

Insomniacs are customers

Doctor's bad handwriting

Always robbed

Fellini characters at 3 A.M.

Open 24 Hours

Prescription Drugs

In California pot is illegal

Have to fake going to the Doctor

At 3 A.M., not a pharmacist but a pusher

HMO's

DRUGS

Can buy things that get you high like Nyquil

Viagra emergencies

Everything is extra-strength

Over the Counter Drugs

Drugstores

Ingredients are confusing

So many products

TV commercials for prescription drugs

TV Commercials

Stupid charts

Wear white lab coats

Type on little pieces of paper

Lists of side effects

Viagra spokesmen

Have to read Doctor's bad handwriting

Pharmacists

Little bottles

Animal testing

Drug Companies

FDA

They are always high up

Testing on criminals

Always being sued

Student Trevor Green wanted to talk about being from Oklahoma. To get more ideas, he listed the top ten "stupid things people say about people living in Oklahoma."

These are the jokes he ended up with on showcase night:

"People from California have the weirdest stereotypes of people from Oklahoma.

" 'Have you ever slept with a cow?' 'Maybe an ugly girl or two, but I wouldn't call her a cow.'

" 'Have you ever been abducted by a UFO?' 'Yeah, how do you think I got here?'

" 'Have you slept with your sisters?' 'No way! They're lesbians!'

" 'Do you have homeless people in Oklahoma?' 'Yeah, we call them farmers.' "

Exercise: Top Ten List

Try doing a top ten list for one of your topics. Be sure to include one of the attitude words in the heading.

Next, add an act-out to each and every one. Cross off the losers and add at least a few new hits to every premise.

Day 21 Action Checklist

- ❑ mind mapped topics
- ❑ created jokes from a list of ten
- ❑ created topic runs on at least three topics

Day 22: Honing Material—"Take Two"

Creating great material is all about rewriting, cutting, and pruning. Here are four techniques to assist you in sculpting your act:

1. cutting out the attitude words
2. callbacks
3. list of three
4. runners

Cutting Out the Attitude Words

At this point you should still have an attitude phrase as the lead-in to every joke. "Do you know what's weird about . . . ?" Now that you have (hopefully) developed one solid attitude for each joke, it's time to cut the actual attitude phrase but keep the attitude in your performance so you don't sound stilted.

Exercise: Cutting the Attitude Words

Take one joke and stop *saying* the attitude, while continuing to *do* the attitude. Suppose your joke starts with, "What's stupid about the elections is that all of the candidates are lying." Change the opening to, "Oh boy, these elections!" Say it in such a way that you convey how stupid you think the elections are. Continue the attitude of "stupid" throughout the entire joke, using your voice, your gestures, your stance. Try this with all of your jokes to see which ones work best this way. You don't have to actually remove the attitude phrases from *all* of your material, just enough of them so you don't sound artificial or repetitive.

Vary how you set up your jokes. You don't want your setups to be repetitive by saying the attitude word on each joke as well as repeatedly saying your topic. For instance, if your topic is "elections," don't open each joke with, "What's stupid about these elections is . . . ," or, "Another thing that's stupid about the election is . . . ." After you set up the topic of "elections," get to the specific subtopic: "And aren't the way they count the votes stupid?"

Instead of depending on the words to convey your attitude, try rehearsing your entire act in gibberish and see if your comedy buddy can tell what the specific attitude of each joke is. Gibberish is speaking using nonwords such as "blah, blah, blah, blah." As you speak in gibberish, hold the attitude through the course of the jokes. If your comedy buddy can't tell what the attitude of a joke is, try it again really exaggerating the attitude.

Callbacks

A callback is when you *call back,* or mention again, something you brought up earlier in the act. The great thing about callbacks is that you're practically guaranteed to get a laugh. For me, callbacks usually occur spontaneously when I'm performing, and then I keep them in the act. Let's say, for instance, that in the beginning of my act I find out that a guy in the front row just got a divorce and his name is Mike. Later in the show, when I'm setting up a joke about "guys whose wives run off on them and they end up drunk and alone," I add, "like Mike here." Big laugh. Audiences love when a comic keeps track of what is going on and can tie things together.

In this example, comic Diane Forte calls back to a joke she made at the beginning of her act, using the phrase "Somebody's in here."

[*First joke*] "It's weird, when you're in a public rest room and someone knocks on your stall, that everyone always says the same thing, 'Somebody's in here!' Somebody? How come we don't say, 'I'm in here'? Are we too embarrassed that someone's going to guess who we are? 'I'm in here . . . Diane Forte!' "

[*A joke five minutes later in the act*] "The weirdest thing I've ever heard about cemetery plots is that in Paris, France, you can actually lease them. How's that work? What happens if you don't pay the rent on the first of the month? Do they dig you up and knock on your coffin lid? 'Somebody's in here.' "

—DIANE FORTE

Exercise: Callbacks

Look through your material and see what you can find that you can mention early in your act and then bring back later. For instance, if you joke about how disgusting it is when your father cleans his ears at the dinner table in the beginning of your act, you can do a callback later by saying, "So, I'm on a date and I'm cleaning out my ears and . . ."

List of Three

Three is a magic number in comedy—there's a rhythm that just naturally works. In the list of three the comic sets up a pattern on the first two ideas and then *turns* it on the third.

For instance:

"I like Florida. Everything is in the eighties: *the temperature, the ages, and the IQs.*"

—GEORGE CARLIN

> "Black people should get social security at twenty-nine. Black people don't live that long. *Hypertension, high blood pressure . . . NYPD.*"
>
> —CHRIS ROCK

"Hypertension" and "high blood pressure" set up a pattern and Rock turns the joke on the third—"NYPD."

Here Nick Griffin sets up a similar pattern:

> "The thing I hate about these [muscle-bound] guys is that they are predictable. You know, they're big, they gotta walk around in some ripped T-shirt with some tattoo skull and crossbones, barbed wire. OK, we get it. *'You're big, you're mean, Daddy didn't hug you.'* Whatever."
>
> —NICK GRIFFIN

See how the first two set up a pattern of expectancy and the third one is the surprise.

> "This is exciting. A woman recently had a baby from an embryo that had been frozen for seven years. She said, 'I had no idea if I was having *a little boy, a little girl . . . or fish sticks.'* "
>
> —CONAN O'BRIEN

Exercise: List of Three

Practice creating lists of three by filling in the turns of these unfinished lists.

"You have to break up when he (or she) . . ."

1. has an affair
2. doesn't respect you
3. issues a restraining order (or _____)

"You know you're not going to get that promotion when . . ."

1. you lose a big customer
2. they take away your secretary
3. _____

Go through your material and make sure anytime you start a list, the third item mentioned is a laugh. See if you can add a list of three to any of your jokes.

Runners

A *runner* is a catchphrase that runs through your act. It is based on your persona. Your persona is your character, your voice.

> Roseanne Barr: "I'm a domestic goddess."
> Rodney Dangerfield: "I don't get no respect."
> Dennis Miller: "I don't want to get off on a rant but . . ."
> Joan Rivers: "Can we talk?"

I have purposely not mentioned persona until now because one of the biggest mistakes a beginning comic can make is to decide on a persona or a runner and then force her material to fit it. If you try to make your act fit into a predetermined box you'll end up limiting yourself. Instead, create the best material you can and let your persona evolve from that.

PRO TALK *with Woody Allen, quoted from* The Great Comedians, *by Larry Wilde (1972)*

"There was never any sense of image. I just wrote what I thought was funny and wanted to perform it. I found after a year or two of performing that some sort of image formed itself. The critics and the people would come away and agree on certain images they had of me . . . certain aspects. I think the worst thing I could do would be to believe the images of me I read in the newspapers. Whatever I feel is funny, I do, no matter what it is, without any regard to the subject matter, and if an image emerges, fine!"

Exercise: Creating a Runner

Go through your act and see if there is any through line that can be summed up in a sentence. It might be an overall emotion, such as "I'm bitter!" or a repeating phrase such as Judy Tenuta's "Well, it could happen!" If you can't come up with a runner right now, that is normal. Sometimes it takes years to find.

Day 22 Action Checklist

- ❑ cut out saying the attitude phrase before some jokes
- ❑ practiced my jokes in gibberish
- ❑ looked to see if you can add a callback to your act
- ❑ created a list of three
- ❑ created a runner (or at least gave it serious thought)

Day 23: Throwing Out the Clunkers

Gather up all your index cards that list your topics—both authentic and current events—and run your entire act for your comedy buddy. You will both be able to feel which jokes are clunkers. They are the bits that are:

- confusing
- obscure
- out of date
- long
- hack

Tear up the index cards with the clunkers and throw them away. What is left is your act. It will be up to an audience of strangers, however, to decide what actually works. The good news: you probably have at least three minutes of current-event jokes, plus even more material that is based on your personal issues. The bad news: in today's constantly changing social and political climate, current-event jokes become real old real fast. Don't be surprised if the current-event joke that got a big laugh on Monday gets no reaction by Friday.

Because the world changes so quickly, beginning comics should limit current-event jokes to no more than 20 percent of their act. Writers also don't want to submit sample jokes that are dated. At the time of this writing what's going on is:

> Bush is elected president in contested election.
> Holiday depression hits hard.
> Viagra is the best-selling drug.
> Teenagers are piercing a variety of body parts.
> The utility industry is deregulating.
> One-year-olds are taking IQ tests.
> Sony PlayStation 2 is sold out.

Notice how old these topics seem. Sometimes you can stockpile certain types of current-events jokes. For instance, you might have a holiday chunk you can use every December. However, most current-event topics have a very short shelf life, which is another reason why every comic and comedy writer has to learn to create jokes on a moment's notice. Even if you are a prolific joke writer, if you do only current-event jokes you'll end up competing with all the pros on TV. By the time the audience sees *your* current-event joke, they will have probably already heard it. That's why it's important to have the bulk of your act rooted in those authentic topics that can last for years: "childhood," "puberty," "parents," and so on.

Exercise: Honing Your Act

Go through all of your index cards.

1. On each card, circle one topic. (You should circle only *one* topic and *one* joke per card.)
2. Make sure the topic is relatable.
3. Write an attitude word on each card. (You don't have to *say* it, but you must *act* it.)
4. Is that attitude expressed by any of the following words: *stupid, weird, hard, bugs me, scary?*
5. Does each topic have a premise that is written out?
6. Does that premise answer the attitude-topic question? ("Do you know what's weird?")
7. Do most topics lead to an act-out?
8. Does the act-out have the same cast of characters as the setup?
9. Does the act-out exaggerate the attitude?
10. After some act-outs, do you have a mix?
11. Do you follow the mix with another act-out?
12. Do you have a lot of hits on most topics (topic run)?
13. If you have a list of three items, is the third one a turn?

Day 23 Action Checklist

❑ You've tossed the clunkers.
❑ You've gone through the keepers to make sure that they meet all the good joke requirements.

Day 24: Getting Ready for Your Second Performance

For your second performance you will be adding no more than two minutes of current-event material and *repeating* the reworked material based on your life.

Repeating Old Material

Stand-up is about constantly reworking material until it falls into the "just right" groove. Once material lands in that perfect groove, *stop* fussing with it. Sometimes changing one word in a joke is the difference between hearing laughs and hearing a pin drop. So if a joke ain't broke, don't fix it.

The challenge for all comics is making old material sound fresh—like we just thought of it that moment. Material becomes stale when the comic is no longer in touch with the emotions (attitude) that drove the joke initially to a laugh. Have you ever told a funny story at a party and got a laugh and then told the same story again to utter silence? The first time people tell a story, they picture it as they tell it, putting themselves inside the story. The second time they tell a funny story, they usually go for the laughs, the reaction to the story, and this puts them outside the story. When this happens with stand-up material, there are only two things to do:

> Cut it.
> *or*
> Get back into it.

Exercise: Picturing It

To get the spontaneity back into your material, picture what you are talking about and feel the attitude as if the event just happened and this is the first time you're mentioning it.

Working New Material into Your Act

PRO TALK *with Phyllis Diller*

"Placement of jokes in your set list is very crucial. I put new jokes in a line at a time or a bit at a time, someplace I think it would be OK. I have taken a line out from a place it has been for five years because it wasn't getting the laugh that I thought it should. I play with my material, but once you get it set it's like Mozart—you don't even change a rest."

Sandwich the new material between material that you know is solid. This is the best way to find out if your new stuff works. If the old joke gets its usual laugh and the new joke that follows it bombs, you'll know the problem was the joke and not the audience. The old joke after the new one will rescue you, get the audience back on track if the new joke falls flat.

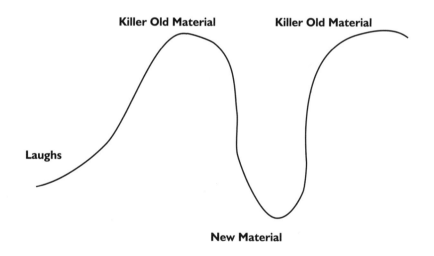

PRO TALK *with Greg Proops*

"Stand-up is like jazz—you're not going to do the same material every day but you're going to weave in and out of the scene. You can make it sound just like the album or you can take off."

Exercise: Sandwiching In New Material

Create a set list with your new material in between jokes that you feel confident about.

Timing

One of the most important aspects of performing comedy is timing. Unfortunately, it's not something you can learn from a book, try to do right, or even think about. In fact, if you *are* thinking about your timing, you can be sure it's off. Ever try to dance with someone who is counting out loud? Enough said.

Attitude creates timing. If you are really into the attitude of each joke, then you don't have to worry about timing. Here is a tip that can also help keep you from stepping on the toes of your jokes: *Don't talk while the audience is laughing.*

Stand-up is not a monologue—it's a dialogue with the audience. You talk, then the audience talks (by laughing, hopefully), and then you respond to the audience. You wouldn't talk while someone also was speaking during a conversation, so shut up after each joke to give the audience time to laugh—or otherwise they might not.

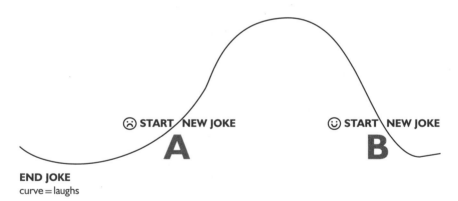

☹ START / NEW JOKE   ☺ START \ NEW JOKE

A   B

END JOKE
curve = laughs

Look at the laugh graph above. When you end a joke, it takes a few seconds for the audience to laugh, which sometimes seems like an eternity. Amateur comics will start their next joke at *A,* cutting off the laughs. A pro will put off starting the next joke until *B,* letting the audience laugh.

Exercise: Holding for the Laughs

Perform your act for your comedy buddy and practice sustaining the attitude and holding for the laughs.

Time your acts and limit yourself to do no more than five minutes for this performance.

"What do I do while I'm letting the audience laugh? Just stand there?"

Adding Tags

You never "just stand there"—*always* convey an attitude. So while the audience laughs, you add a *tag* to the joke by repeating the attitude. For instance, if the joke starts off, "It's weird . . . ," at the end of the joke, tag it by repeating, "It's weird." This tag can be said quickly, as if to yourself, or you can shout it. It can even be unspoken, perhaps shown by a shaking of your head. But one thing the tag should never be is absent. There should never be even one moment when you are onstage and attitude-free. It's the kiss of death because audiences respond to emotions, not words.

"What about talking to the audience? Asking them, 'Where are you from? How are you all doing?' "

Talking to the Audience

In the old days comics didn't talk to the audience because it took away from their act. But these days, with TV talk shows, live chat on the Internet, and everyone out for their fifteen minutes of fame, there is less of a division between the show and the audience. Now, comics need to know not just how to talk to the audience but also how to respond to what they say with humor. Since you are only doing five-minute sets at the moment, this isn't really a big concern for you yet. But as your career grows it will be a challenge you'll face. Even TV writers need to hone this skill because producers can often sound like hecklers. And if you can handle hecklers as a stand-up comic, it will make all future hostile situations easier. Here are some tips from veteran Texas comic Dean Lewis.

- The majority of hecklers are men. Women tend to be hecklers only when drunk. Men usually heckle because they want to challenge you and gain control. Drunk women heckle because they want attention. If either gets what they want (control or attention), they will keep coming back for more. Do not give it to them.

- Men heckle if they sense weakness. Take control of the stage as soon as possible. Do this by having good microphone technique, having strong material, making eye contact with audience members, being energetic, and getting onstage quickly. Avoid looking meek.

- The way you give the audience opportunities to heckle is by taking too long to get to the funny. The sooner you get laughs onstage, the less likely you are to get heckled.

- If you get heckled, always ignore it at first. The heckler just wants to get some attention. If you stop your show and slam the heckler, he got what he wanted. In other words, he won. It is better to ignore the heckler because this prevents him from getting what he wants.

- If the heckler is with somebody, ask her or him to make the jerk shut up. The heckler may be trying to impress their date and if you make their date feel uncomfortable, then the heckler will probably not want to continue with the situation.

- If a heckler persists in challenging you, try getting the audience to shut them up for you. Ask the audience if this person is bothering them. They will usually respond with a loud "Yes!" Or applause. Usually this will embarrass or appease the heckler so he will shut up.

- Never hit a heckler harder than they hit you. For example, if the heckler makes a comment about your hair, and you respond by slamming the heckler's mother, you may shut them up but you will very likely lose the audience. You cannot come back too hard or you will appear to be a bully. If they heckle your hair, come back with something about their hair. If they slam your shirt, you can then say something about the way he is dressed.

- Try to distinguish between a heckler and somebody who is verbal and just having a good time. Some people will respond to your material by laughing and talking back to you. They will say things like, "I heard that," or, "I know that's right!" and so on. These are not heckles! This is the way this person responds. Stopping your show to deal with this type of interruption is a mistake. The verbal audience member doesn't realize he is a pest. If you make a big deal out of it, two things will most likely happen: (1) The verbal person will hate you for making them feel foolish. (2) The audience probably doesn't know that this person is bothering you, so if you stop your set to pick on this one person, the audience can turn on you. They didn't see a problem, so it appears as if you are just a jerk comic picking on a helpless audience member.

- It is almost always best to phrase a comeback to a heckler in the form of a question. The reason for this is twofold:

    1. Asking someone a question causes him to stop and think of an answer. This breaks any rhythm he may have. This pause gives you a chance to slam them with another comeback, make fun of how slow he is responding, or answer the question for him in a funny way. In other words, you've taken control of the situation.

    2. Phrasing the comeback so it has to be answered makes the situation no win for him. No matter how he responds, he will sound foolish. Once again, this gives you more control in this situation. Here is an example. A comeback to a heckle might be, "You, sir, are the reason why brothers and sisters shouldn't marry!" Very funny, but the problem is that the heckler can now slam you. Here is a better way to use the comeback in the form of a rhetorical question: "Sir, does it bother you knowing that you are the result of your father marrying his sister?" No matter what response he has, he will now sound stupid. If he says, "No," you can make fun of that. If he says, "Yes," then he has admitted that he is an interbred freak, and you can make fun of that. Either way, the heckler will realize that he is in a no-win situation and shut up.

- If you want to dialogue with the audience as a way of involving them more in your set by asking the audience a question, make it a simple rhetorical "yes" or "no" question. It is fun for the audience to get involved in your act, but this does it in a way that doesn't encourage them to yell out long answers. For instance . . .

Wrong way:

[*Talking to man in the audience*] "What did you think of the Super Bowl?"

This puts someone on the spot—he has to instantly come up with an opinion. It's also risky, because he might say something that's funnier than your next line.

Right way:

"Anybody watch the Super Bowl?"

This involves the audience without putting anyone on the spot and elicits a simple "yes" or "no" answer.

- If something happens in the room, respond to it. Saying anything immediately is more important than thinking for a few seconds and then saying something "funny." Respond to a disruption ASAP! This helps keep the audience focused on the show and not the disruption. You don't want to be a joke machine who just gets up and delivers material. You should comment when a waitress drops a tray of drinks, or five people get up and leave, or someone asks you a question. If you say, "I'm going to college," and someone asks, "What college?" you have to answer.

- When a mishap occurs, such as the mike stand breaks, the lights go out, or there is a puff of smoke from the grassy knoll, acknowledge it. When you *call* the situation, it puts the audience at ease. They see that you're not thrown by what happened, and they don't have to feel sorry or embarrassed for you. Make a joke about it and move on.

- If it's a small crowd, less than fifty people, talk to them because they'll tend to laugh more in their heads than out loud. That's especially true if they are spread out in a room. Involving the audience in a conversation reminds them that they aren't watching TV—you can hear them, and it's appropriate to laugh out loud.

- Talk to the audience in small increments rather than large chunks—otherwise it will seem like filler.

- Audience members can feel very uncomfortable when the comic talks to them. Most people in an audience do not want to be the center of attention. Therefore, try not to talk to one person immediately. Talk to the audience as a group, then maybe address a row, and then a table, and finally one person. This way you have slowly gained their trust as you worked your way down to one person.

There are certain occasions when you shouldn't talk to the audience:

- When your performance is also an audition. A producer wants to know that he can buy the act he is seeing. Even if your improv with the audience was really funny, it's something that can't be recreated.

- When a club manager tells you not to talk to them—don't.

- When you're doing only a five-minute set. And while we're on the subject: don't waste your time doing improv with the audience. The audience will sense that you're using them as filler and resent having to pay $10 for a beer *and* write your act. They don't mind being a *part* of the show, but they don't want to *be* the whole show.

- Don't start every setup with a question like "Anybody here on a date?" It gets redundant really fast. Space your questions out throughout your act, and ask them only if you have a good reason for doing so. In other words, you have a punch line for their response.

The biggest key to talking to the audience is *listening* to them. Relax, breathe, and listen. Remember, the audience is more scared to talk to you than you are to talk to them.

Keeping Your Energy Up and Out

Energy drives an act. Without energy there is no performance. The way that energy expresses itself can be anything, from the quiet concentration of Steven Wright to the intense ranting of Dennis Miller, but it *has* to be there in everything you do and say for every moment you're onstage.

Before I go on, I always feel a surge of energy inside me. Call it nerves, excitement, or incontinence—I'm bursting with it. It's not very comfortable, which is why some comics try to escape it with drugs or alcohol. Big mistake, because both of them will screw up the timing and connection to the audience. Being sober onstage enables me to be in control of my energy releases. When I set up my joke, I pull in the reins on my horses. During the act-out, I let them gallop at full speed. After the laughs I pull them back in again to set up the next joke. After a while you'll probably get a feel for this too and be able to pull in your energy and then release it again. Don't drink or do drugs to smooth out your nerves. Ride the wild horse and just stay out of your own way.

Exercise: Sustaining Energy

Perform your act for your comedy buddy so that she can make sure your energy level is controlled during the setups and up and out for the act-outs.

Day 24 Action Checklist

- ❑ reconnected yourself to your authentic material
- ❑ worked current-event material into your act
- ❑ practiced holding for the laughs
- ❑ carried the attitude of the joke into a tag
- ❑ had comedy buddy check to make sure you kept energy up in your act
- ❑ timed your act and cut it to five minutes or less

Day 25: Performance

Have fun and don't forget to tape your act.

Day 25 Action Checklist

❑ bought new batteries for tape recorder

Day 26: About Last Night . . . How Good Were You?

PRO TALK *with Greg Proops*

"If you don't mean what you are saying or if you don't care about what you are saying, you're just up there being funny. Utter attention must be paid to *what* you are saying and *how* you are saying it. All the great comics, Bill Hicks, Richard Pryor, and George Carlin, are absolutely about what they are saying. George Carlin started very square, in a suit and a tie, playing Vegas. He had an epiphany onstage. When yelling at a crowd he realized that his act didn't reflect his life and he had to stop doing it. He threw it all out and started developing authentic material, playing in the Village in New York."

Once again, stand-up is about reworking your act. It's not about being great, it's about getting better. Listen to your tape and repeat the "Reworking Your Act" exercise on page 167.

"How do I know if I should cut a joke that didn't work or if it was just a bad audience?"

You should try out a joke for several performances. If it doesn't work three times, then cut it. However, if it's something you really love, keep fussing with it. In some *rare* cases, if you have a really unique persona, rather than change your material, change your audience. You might be doing niche material that works only for a certain kind of audience. Later in this book I will show you how to market your act. But the general rule is—if the joke doesn't get laughs, it isn't funny.

PRO TALK *with comic Andy Kindler*

[To the audience] "I know you think I'm having a bad set. I'm not, *you're* having a bad set. Go home, read a book, study, and in ten years you will be laughing at this stuff."

"My act went really well. Am I ready for the big time?"

More than any other creative field, stand-up comedy lets you know exactly how you are doing. The audience tells you instantly. When you can make an audience laugh constantly for one hour, you'll be making the big bucks.

Until the checks with lots of zeros start pouring in, here's a way to put your performance in perspective.

LPM (Laughs per Minute) Formula

(Courtesy of Davey DiGeorgio, staff writer on *Late Show with David Letterman* and former student.)

Listen to the tape of your set and *give yourself points at the end of each joke* according to this formula:

> LOUD laughter and EVERYONE applauds = 5 points
> LOUD laughter and a SMATTERING of applause = 4 points
> LOUD laughter from EVERYONE and NO applause = 3 points
> MEDIUM laughs = 2 points
> SMATTERING of laughs = 1 point

1. Add up your total laughter points. _____
2. How many minutes were you onstage? _____
3. Divide line 1 by line 2 and enter your LPM here. _____

> 12 to 20: You are rockin', baby, and if you aren't making the big bucks yet—you will.

9 to 12: You're doing well and are ready to get paid, but think about shortening your setups.

6 to 9: Not bad, but not ready for the big time.

Below 6: Something ain't working. Use the guidelines on page 167, "Reworking Your Act," to get better.

Congratulations, you've completed the joke writing/stand-up course. If you really loved being onstage, you might want to consider a career as a stand-up comic. If performing is not your thing but writing is, there are many opportunities for comedy writers. Whether you are a writer or a performer or both, you need material, and a lot of it. The next section provides exercises on creating more material on a daily basis.

Advanced Stand-up Exercises

Living Funny

Being a comedy writer or a stand-up comic is not a nine-to-five job. It means spending twenty-four hours seven days a week looking for the funny, writing the funny, and performing the funny. You are constantly documenting your perception of the world through your unique filter. This filter transforms the ordinary into the extraordinary—or at least into the funny. Civilians (what I call everyone not in the creative business) might be annoyed by a rude salesman, but the comic thinks, "How can I use this?" Life becomes a nonstop hunt for material. When civilians meet a strange character, they might think, "Weirdo. I'm getting out of here!" But we creative types enjoy engaging with the peculiar types because they can be rich fodder for material—an amusing character to act out in a joke or write into a sitcom. If you are serious about comedy, your whole life revolves around getting material.

Daily Exercises to Generate Comedy Material

A comic can never have enough material. Professional comics and comedy writers usually have a stockpile of two hours of *good* material. Working comics carry a Rolodex of jokes in their heads that has material right for *any* audience. College students—no problem. Senior citizens—no problem. Convicted felons—well, problem.

We all get stuck. The following exercises can inspire you and help keep new material flowing. Some might work better for you than others. Get in the habit of doing at least one exercise every day.

PRO TALK *with Chris Titus*

What does this stand-up comic and star of his own sitcom, *Titus,* do when he is stuck? "I sit down and write crap for forty minutes. Everybody thinks that they have to write funny, every line. All you have to do is pick a subject and write about that and then pick another subject and write about that. I guarantee you that at the end of forty minutes, you will crank out a funny line because it takes forty minutes for your brain to click over from the dealing-with-life side to the creative side. Then go back to what you wrote and fix it. And the more writing sessions you have, the quicker your creativity will click in."

Exercise 1: Using the Internet

One of the biggest misconceptions about writing comedy is that you start by coming up with funny ideas. If I had to wait for something funny to strike me before I wrote, I wouldn't be writing much material but I would be taking a lot more drugs. The "funny first" approach to creativity can be stifling and depressing when nothing seems funny. A more productive approach is starting with an unfunny topic and making it funny. And if you're having a hard time finding new topics, the Internet can steer you to the hot topics that are on everyone's mind. News sites and chat rooms are a good source for new topics, and search engines will help you learn more about them. When I worked for the National Potato Council (no joke), I did a search on potatoes and found out tons of information on topics like cross-hybridization, crop rotation, and potato diseases. "What's up with blight?"

Find three unfunny topics on the Internet that you don't cover in your act. Spend an hour researching them and come up with one good new joke. Starting today, if you come up with just one great new joke every day, you'll have an hour and a half of great material in a year.

Exercise 2: Go to a Newsstand

If you can't squeeze out any more jokes about that dysfunctional family of yours, get out of the house and hang out at a newsstand—it's a Mecca for premise seekers. Magazines entice you to buy them by putting catchy headlines on the cover. Comics need catchy setups to entice the audience to listen, and writers need to keep topical. The headlines on a *Cosmopolitan* cover are often the perfect setup for material chunks. ("Ten ways to attract a man." "How do you know when you need a therapist?" "Ways to break up a relationship." "What's hot in music today?") Magazines spend millions on market research in order to be hot, hip, and happening—why not benefit from what they've learned, for free?

Mine for comedy material by using the magazine headlines as a premise for a *list of ten,* a *mind map,* or a *rant.*

Exercise 3: Turn Stories into Comedy Topics

Ready to take a walk on the wild side? This exercise is potentially very dangerous—don't do it unless you promise to follow the directions to a tee. If I've said it once, I've said it a million times, stories are the kiss of death to joke writers. However, it is possible to turn these bombs to blow-away comedy.

First, in your idea book write out a funny story about something that happened to you.

Then circle any one- or two-worded topics and list them here:

_____

_____

_____

_____

_____

_____

Now give these topics an attitude and see where the emotion takes you. Forget the story reality, "what really happened" and so on. Instead let the attitude take you someplace you've never been before. Let yourself be surprised.

> **PRO TALK** *with comic Kathy Griffen*
>
> "When writing material I look to what happened to me that week. I'm in heaven if there is some horrible movie of the week on or if I had a crazy run-in with a celebrity. Or if some guy just dumped me—I'm golden. What's funny is anything tragic. We just had our Griffen family Easter and it was just a disaster where my sister-in-law got drunk and everything got hideous and ugly, and I thought—this could be good funny."

Another way to turn a story into comedy material is to write out a story and create a joke every four or five lines. Continue the same joke writing throughout the entire story.

Exercise 4: Talking on the Phone with Friends

When talking on the phone with friends, write down anything you (or they) say that gets a laugh. Write down all topics that you talked about and do attitude runs on them.

Exercise 5: Comedy from Characters

> **PRO TALK** *with George Wallace*
>
> "Most people write my material. People will come up to me and say something stupid. I was at the airport waiting for my luggage and a lady comes up to me and says, 'Mr. Wallace, mighty quiet today.' And I'm thinking, 'Well hell, I'm standing here by myself. Who'd I be talking to?' "

Spend the day noticing the people who cross your path. Make a list of these characters and find places in your act where you can act them out. Many times comics create jokes backwards—they start with the act-out and *then* find the setup.

Richard Jeni transformed an act-out of an NFL referee into a killer routine that he performed on *The Tonight Show with Jay Leno.* He started with a premise.

> "Referees stop the entire game so the referee can click a button on his belt, activate a giant sound system, and point the guy out in front of the whole country and humiliate him. It's so unnecessary. [*act-out*] 'Pssht. [*he clicks his belt*] The reason we stopped, the reason we're all hanging around out here not doing anything right now is because some people don't seem to know the *rules.* Isn't that right number [*pointing*] seventy-one? Seventy-one, I can't even look at you.' "

Then Jeni found another premise.

> "It's a human thing to want to be heard. [*he then acts out a mix of a sixty-two-year-old guy who just wants to talk*] 'Uh, there was no penalty. This has nothing to do with the game, the players, or the National Football League. I need to talk. I can't keep this up anymore. I feel like an idiot out here. I mean, sure I'm the ref, but who am I to judge these players? I mean, look at some of the choices I've made in my own life. I'm sixty-two years old and I'm a freaking referee. I'll be honest with you.' "

Jeni sat down on the stage and continued this act-out/mix of the referee.

> " 'My wife is getting fat as a house. I'm telling you . . . I don't know . . . I love my kids but if I had to do it again . . . Ooh, I'd wear a condom.' "

He took the act-out/mix even further.

> " 'You know what's really bothering me? I just kind of feel like I'm a woman trapped in a man's body. Do you ever dress up in your wife's panties when nobody's home? Give me a pair of panties and some perfume, I am one happy ref. The hell with football. I feel a lot better now. We better get back to the game. [*he stood up*] First down!' "

Writers especially will find that keeping a journal of characters will come in handy when writing not only jokes but comedy scripts.

Exercise 6: Stream of Consciousness Writing

In the morning, spend ten minutes writing stream of consciousness—whatever comes into your head—ignoring all rules of grammar, spelling, and even logic. It could look something like this:

> Woke up with a dream of dead goldfish and looked outside and it was another cloudy day. Dark, dark. My vegetable garden is a mess. I forgot when I planted seeds that something would grow—yeah, weeds. Oh, I've got to pick up my photos at one-hour photo which have been there for a week. Boy am I hungry. Breakfast and then there's lunch. That's what I want. But I have to get out of bed. A maid would be nice . . .

These stream of consciousness ramblings are the raw material of your unconscious mind, and there are probably some authentic topics in there that haven't surfaced yet. Circle any words that can be topics, maybe even freely associate to them, and then run them through the joke development process. For example, for the above list topics could be

- death
- goldfish as pets
- breakfast
- lunch
- maids
- vegetable gardens
- one-hour photo

A joke might come out of these topics:

"In L.A. relationships don't last. You go on vacation and break up by the time you come home. Thank God for *one-hour photo,* so you can see your vacation photos while you're still in the relationship. 'Honey, look how happy we are . . . [*looking around*] Honey?' "

"I don't understand why people say, 'I want to kill myself, I have nothing to look forward to.' How can anyone not have anything to look forward to when there is *lunch!*"

Exercise 7: Mixes

Write ten "what if's." For example, "What if dogs had thumbs? They could open the door for themselves. They could hitchhike instead of walk. They could give movie reviews—'*Gone With the Wind*. Good story, but not enough dogs. Thumbs down!' " (Don't steal that. Write your own.)

Exercise 8: Writing Opinions on Current Events

Write a list of the headlines off the Internet news sites or today's newspaper. Pick at least two current-event topics and write ten opinions about each of them.

Exercise 9: Rants and Raves

Tape-record yourself ranting out loud for ten minutes about one topic. Do not stop talking. Keep the energy up and the attitudes flying. Listen to the tape and write down any material that might have emerged.

Exercise 10: Comedy Buddy Exchange

Exchange topics with your comedy buddy and write jokes for each other.

Exercise 11: Characters

Make a list of the people who have had a big impact on your life. These should be people you actually know. (Don't put down the pope unless the two of you had some funny chats while you chauffeured the Popemobile.) This list could include husband, first love, ex-wife, Weight Watchers meeting coach, cell mate, current lesbian lover, and so on. Pretend to *be* them. Have your comedy buddy interview you as that character. Put these characters in different situations and find their opinions on different topics. See what material these characters generate and work backwards from your act-outs to find premises and setups.

Exercise 12: Detailing an Event

Write out the details of the first two hours of your day. Include the most minute details.

Wrong way:

Woke up, ate breakfast, and went to the beach.

Right way:

Woke up with my dog licking my face, wanting to be fed. I went to the bathroom, washed my hands, and went into the kitchen to face all the leftover dishes from last night. My dog licked the dishes as I put them into the dishwasher.

Underline every topic and, next to each, write other things about that topic. For example:

Dogs—I let my dogs lick my dishes, but when people are over I pretend to be shocked. "They've never done this before. This is disgusting!"

I washed my hands—Does everyone really wash their hands after they use the bathroom? Or do we just do it when other people are watching? What else do we do or not do when other people are watching?

Exercise 13: Buddy Up

Write twenty topics on separate pieces of paper. You can get these topics from the Internet, magazines, newspapers, TV, whatever. Then as quickly as possible, pick one out of a bag and put a "What's up with" in front of it and riff on it until you come up with an opinion. Then have your comedy buddy come up with an opinion on it. Then you come up with *another* opinion on it. Keep going until each of you has come up with three opinions on each topic.

Exercise 14: Stepping-Stones of Life

Make a list of the major stepping-stones of your life, keeping the descriptions brief. For instance: *puberty, going to college, getting married, your first bra, your first walker.*

Take a stepping-stone and mind map it. For instance, if the stepping-stone was college, then your circles might include *leaving home, parents being alone, dorm rooms, roommates, drinking, living for the first time without parents, early morning classes, cafeteria food, studying, drinking,* and *more drinking.*

This is a very powerful exercise. Mind map a different stepping-stone every day until you've done them all.

Need more exercises? Go to *www.comedyworkshopS.com* for new writing exercises.

Study and restudy the rules of comedy until they are second nature. Then cut loose and ride your talent. Technique can carry you only so far. Passion and soul have to take you the rest of the way.

Creating
Your Own
One-Person Show

Producers, development people, and network executives are scouring small theaters in search of the next break-out talent, so one-person shows have become a great way to be discovered. These shows are similar to a play, but all the parts are played by one person. One-person shows can be a collection of character vignettes, but usually they are fully developed, highly personal stories. A one-person show doesn't have to be humorous, although most of them are. Actually, the subject matter is often serious, but the story is often told in a funny way. Rather than reducing the emotional impact of the story, the humor in a good one-person show actually heightens it—sometimes to the point where the audience is actually laughing through their tears. These shows are generally written and performed by the comic but produced and directed by someone else.

PRO TALK *with Judi Brown, talent coordinator for the U.S. Comedy Arts Festival (Aspen)*

"We collect a number of one-person shows, and the performers range from newcomers to established actors. We look at the shows from a development standpoint. Do they tell a story, and is it a story that we can develop into a show?"

One-person shows were the path to success for such powerhouse comic actors as:

- Lily Tomlin
- Whoopi Goldberg
- Chazz Palminteri
- Spaulding Gray
- Chris Titus
- Pee-wee Herman (Paul Reubens)
- Julia Sweeney (the androgynous character Pat on *Saturday Night Live*)
- Rick Reynolds

What is the difference between stand-up and one-person shows?

When doing a one-person show . . .

- You don't have to make the audience laugh the whole time.
- You tell a *dramatic* story, using humor.
- The show is at least an hour with no opening act.
- You don't have to include the audience in your show.
- You usually act out a number of characters.
- Your audience is usually sober, but not necessarily—many comedy clubs present one-person shows.

PRO TALK *with Mark Travis, director of the one-person show* A Bronx Tale, *Dana Gould's* Insomnia, *and many TV shows*

"Stand-up consists of disconnected pieces or jokes. As a matter of fact, sometimes the more disconnected the jokes are from each other, the funnier the comic is. A one-person show has a story line. While a stand-up comic focuses on getting an immediate reaction from the audience after every joke, a person doing a solo show takes the audience on a journey."

When you perform at a club, you're obligated to fulfill the expectations of the owner, which is to make the audience laugh a lot. This means that any piece that goes longer than fifteen seconds without getting a laugh is thrown out. Any piece that is emotionally moving gets tossed too. Comedy club owners don't like it when their customers cry. Most audiences don't want to feel touched either—that's not why they came there. But if you shine at storytelling or doing characters, you might want to consider doing a one-person show in a theater.

"How do I know if I should put together a one-person show?"

Examine your motivation for doing it.

> Good reason—I want to express myself and connect with others.
> Bad reason—I want to get discovered and get my own TV show.

Of course, most performers would love to be famous stars with a Jacuzzi in their dressing rooms and personal masseuses on staff. However, if career advancement is your sole motivation for creating a one-person show, your cousin Harold, the one who ties cherries with his tongue, has a better chance of hitting the big time than you do. At least that is entertainment. Ego productions are a bore.

There is only one reason to do a one-person show—you have a burning desire to tell a particular story. And that story can be anything from a repertoire of different characters to a story that brings tears to people's eyes. In fact, most one-person shows are based on quite significant and serious themes.

Julia Sweeney's *And God Said, "Ha!"* was a comedy based on the true story of both her brother and herself getting cancer at the same time, and her whole family moving into her two-bedroom apartment. Her show sold out in L.A., went on to a Broadway run, was published as a book, was released as a movie by Miramax, and was rereleased as a rental video.

Rich Shydner's one-man show *True Love Confessions* was the story of his marriage and included insightful observations about relationships.

"I think being in love means that 90 percent of the time you look at the other person and think to yourself, 'I want to spend the rest of my life with you.' But 10 percent of the time you may think, 'How can I fake my death?' "

PRO TALK *with Rich Shydner*

"The show is much more personal than my act was. In stand-up, every other word is *you,* and everybody relates to your act based on how good your *you* is. With this [one-person show], I get down to the essentials and tell my story."

Claudia Shear's one-person show *Blown Sideways Through Life,* recounted sixty-four of her temporary jobs. Her sold-out off-Broadway run won the prestigious Obie and was job number sixty-five.

Whoopi Goldberg did a one-person show that included a repertoire of seventeen characters, including a blitzed-out junkie and a brainless Valley girl. It took her from the Comedy Store in Hollywood to Broadway to starring in movies.

PRO TALK *with Whoopi Goldberg*

"I did my [one-person] show because I wanted to make people laugh *and* think."

In Rick Reynolds's one-person show *Only the Truth Is Funny,* he starts out by saying, "I won't lie to you once tonight, not once." Reynolds found his highly successful one-person show from "throwing out all my comedy routines and writing the truth." His show is about his family from hell—a manic-depressive mom who brought home a succession of men with whom she had screaming fights; a stepfather who whacked the back of Rick's hand with a steak knife during dinner and made him sit at the table bleeding and crying; and another stepfather, who robbed banks and who, after he was caught, sent Rick ski masks he had crocheted in prison.

Reynolds's one-person show led to high-powered managers, a Showtime cable special, and finally a deal with NBC. He also appeared on *The Tonight Show* and Letterman and was written up in *People* magazine. Telling the truth (in a funny way) can bring rewards.

Chris Titus was a Star Search winner and a comedy club headliner who spent seven years on the road going nowhere. Then he wrote his one-person show *Norman Rockwell Is Bleeding,* about his mother stabbing his stepfather and attempting suicide, and his father's alcoholism and abuse. The result—his own network prime-time sitcom, *Titus.*

PRO TALK *with Christopher Titus*

"A one-person show is not just an hour of stand-up. It has to be dramatic *and* funny. I tossed my stand-up act and wrote forty minutes about my life—real stuff, scary stuff, true stuff, but always funny. I worked on my one-person show for two years. We did it in a theater. My wife produced it, my niece did the lights."

Bruce Smith, Titus's agent, says, "Chris's one-person show was the only way to demonstrate to the industry that his story was irrefutably funny to a crowd and not scary. A one-person show doesn't have to be laugh after laugh after laugh, but it always has to be interesting and entertaining."

One of the most successful one-person shows is Rob Becker's *Defending the Caveman,* which took Becker from comedy clubs to a Broadway hit. One night he got onstage in his stand-up act and said he was tired of all the politically correct male bashing. "I don't think we are bad, we're only different." And the caveman was born.

Rob Becker

PRO TALK *with Rob Becker*

"It's strange. The idea for this show simply flashed in my mind. But I knew then I wanted to do a show about relationships, something that had a beginning, a middle, and an end. That's when I knew I needed ninety minutes."

"Who should do a one-person show?"

Answer these questions:

❑ Do you prefer telling stories rather than jokes?
❑ Can you repeat a story and make it sound as fresh and spontaneous the tenth time as you did the first?

❑ Can you act?

❑ Do you find it stifling to have to make people constantly laugh?

❑ Do you have a burning desire to tell a particular story?

Then this might be for you.

A word of caution—doing a one-person show is not for novices. If it's something you want to do, you have to work up to it. When it's done well, it appears as if the performer is simply talking about themselves or portraying a character from their life. If it really was that easy, we'd all quit therapy and rent a theater. A one-person show is not just about sharing stories from your "oh-so-interesting" life. It's finding the themes in your life that are universal, the ones that overlap with other people's themes, and making them really funny. It's for experienced writers and performers, not for people starting out. You can't do a one-person show by the book—it's an extremely personal artistic experience. To do it well, you often break the rules—but you have to really know the rules and have played by them many times before you can successfully break them.

How to Put Together Your Own One-Person Show

The process of developing a one-person show is the same as creating new stand-up material. Don't start "funny"; start "deep." It's hard not to imagine the audience sitting stone-faced and silent while you explore serious topics, but thinking of them too soon can choke your creativity.

Exercise: Starting the Process—Picking a Story

Make a list of the turning points in your life—all the "aha!" moments and meaningful events. Go back to the "Stepping-Stones of Life" exercise on page 210 for help. Start with a life-changing event rather than a funny one, because it's a lot easier to make a dramatic story funny than to make something that's funny dramatic. Not sure if a particular event was really meaningful? Write it down anyway. Sometimes it's only by exploring the seemingly inconsequential details of our lives that we realize just how momentous they were.

Tim Bagley

PRO TALK *with Tim Bagley, winner of Aspen '99 Best One-Person Show for* Happy Hour

"After winning the Aspen award for my show about a best friend's death, I got the idea for my second show when I was reading a book about the Playboy mansion. One of the Playboy bunnies said, 'There were butlers all around and we did everything in front of them, but it was like they weren't really even there.' And I remember lying there in bed and reading that and thinking, 'Guess what, I was there and I saw . . . ' And in my mind, I thought, 'You know, I've got a show'—telling stories about my experiences as a butler at the Playboy mansion. *Clean Boy/Dirty Stories.*"

Exploring Your Events

Pick one of your key events and write out the details. Don't worry about your spelling or grammar or if you change directions and flow into another event that isn't even connected. Let your writing be as messy, disorganized, and disjointed as it needs to be. We all want our writing to come out perfectly the first time—write it on Monday and perform it on Friday. That may be possible with short stand-up pieces, but when creating a one-person show, probably everything you write during the first two months will never make it onstage—it's exploratory material.

PRO TALK *with Irene Penn, manager and director (Lily Tomlin, Reno, Kathy and Mo, Sandra Bernhard, Sherry Glaser)*

"Write from your gut, because if it doesn't move you, it's not going to move anyone else. Most of us go through very similar things, or we know people who have gone through similar things, and even if your show is deeply personal, you have to find a way to connect to the audience."

Here are some tips by renowned Los Angeles one-person coach and director Mark Travis.

- ❑ Don't worry about how the event you are writing about will fit with any other event you want to explore. If you are called to write the story, then write it. Worrying about "How does this fit with that?" just gets in the way of the process.
- ❑ Don't get distracted by wondering how you are going to perform the event, like, "I have a wedding scene with thirty characters. How will I do it?" I have yet to find a scene that can't be shaped so that it can be done by one person.
- ❑ Don't write in past tense, such as, "I *was standing* on the street corner and I *saw* this woman." It should be, *"I'm standing* on this street corner and I *see* this woman." When you write in the present tense, your whole emotional system shifts to the inside of the story. If you work in the past tense, not only do you distance yourself from the material, but you distance the audience from it as well.

In Tim Bagley's award-winning one-person show *Happy Hour* he played several cocktail-guzzling members of his dysfunctional family at a family reunion. The show was based on a painful event—a friend's death. "While I was writing it, I didn't have an outline. I didn't have any form. I was just kind of writing and trusting that at some point I would be able to piece it together."

PRO TALK *with Tim Bagley*

"I just started writing about the death of my friend—writing like a crazy person, sleeping during the day and writing at night. At that time, I didn't know what the theme was or how it all connected."

Detail Your Story

The story you've written so far is a starting point. Now expand it by focusing in on the details. For instance, in Julia Sweeney's show about getting cancer at the same time as her brother, the details for the day she found out she had cancer would include the trip to the doctor's office, what she wore that day, what the doctor's waiting room looked like, what his office looked like, the way the nurses behaved, what diplomas were on his walls, what the doctor wore, whether his nails were clean.

At one point in *Happy Hour*, Bagley goes into great detail about his attempt to organize his dysfunctional clan for a family photograph. He acts out each member of his family—directing his befuddled dad to stand next to a chair is harder than getting a hyper poodle to stop yapping. Waking up his Bible-thumping brother-in-law from a nap almost leads to a physical confrontation. Tim's streetwise brother agrees to pose, but only if Tim agrees to listen to the obscene song he wrote.

Most of the "funny" is in the details.

Back Story

You've written about a significant event in your life. Now write about the events that led to that experience, so that we know *why* this event is so significant. What background information should we know about the people in your story to better understand their behavior in the event?

Tim Bagley:

> I really try to get into what makes people behave the way they do and not some other way. You have to go deep into the characters; otherwise they come off one-dimensional. My brother talks nonstop. He'll talk about everything—his new barbecue grill or working out at the gym—except his wife dying and the pain that he's experiencing. So, when I'm in his character and chattering, I want to make sure that the audience sees what is at the root of his behavior—that he is hiding behind all the chatter.

Detail the Characters

A character's essence—the qualities that make him or her a unique individual—is shown in the details. Explore the different ways your characters express their true natures by noticing all the tiny behaviors and choices that reveal various aspects of their personalities. For instance, if your mother comes into the room in your story, notice every detail about her. How does she enter the room? Hesitantly? Shyly? Drunkenly? What is she wearing? What does she smell like? Who or what does she search out first? Second? What does she say? How does she stand when she talks? What does she do with her hands? In stand-up, you superficially sketch characters in the act-outs, but in a one-person show you will need to do finely detailed portraits of your characters so they come across as three-dimensional.

Exercise: Character Act-outs

Put each character on an index card—list their mannerisms, idiosyncrasies, and behavioral quirks—then practice them by acting them out. Act out all the people in each scene.

Tim Bagley: "I wrote two or three different monologues for each character in my story, and ended up using the one that I felt moved the story along."

Finding the Show

There are two aspects of your show that you need to find: (1) the *story* and (2) the *theme*.

Exercise: The Story

By now you might have a ton of pages of material about your event that shoot off in many different tangents. To help you find the through line, reduce your material to bullet points—the events that move your story along. Write each bullet point on a separate index card. For instance, for Tim Bagley's *Happy Hour* he wrote down on different cards: "Brother sings a song." "Mom's drunken confession." "Dad giving clues."

Consider each index card as a scene, and detail each scene by answering:

1. What characters are in the scene?
2. What is the location of the scene?
3. What happens in the scene?

Organize all your index cards into an order that tells your story. Then get up on your feet and rehearse your story, using the index cards. As you practice acting out the story, you will find that certain scenes feel out of place. Trust your gut feelings and keep rearranging your cards until you feel that the whole thing flows.

Finding the Theme

So far you've picked an event, written all you can about it, examined and explored every detail of it, found the characters, itemized all the details about each one, and arranged the scenes in an order. You might have a very interesting story, and a couple of hours of good material, but it is not a show—yet. You need to know the theme of your show.

A theme is a universal message, a point of view or a premise that permeates every aspect of the story. All the characters and events represent some facet of the theme.

Some performers know their theme right from the beginning. Others spend years finding it. Rob Becker did years of research, reading books and articles and talking with marriage and family experts, before coming up with his theme for *Defending the Caveman:* "We are not far removed from our prehistoric roles. Men remain hunters, women gatherers, and there will always be friction unless the two honor their differences and explore each other's 'worlds' without judgment." And that was his show.

Sometimes it's extremely difficult for the writer/performer to figure out what the theme of the show is. As director Mark Travis says, "You will be the last one to know where or what it is because you are the main character, and as the main character, you are not sufficiently removed from what's going on to know the true theme of your story."

Tim Bagley found the theme of *Happy Hour* in a moment of insight:

> Once I wrote everybody, I saw that, without realizing it, I had revealed how my siblings and my parents each have their own unique way of hiding. And then I thought, "I haven't written about how I hide because I've been hiding my friend's death from my family." And then it came to me—that's my theme. My friend's death brings truth into my menagerie of denial. I knew that I had to do a monologue that explains all that I have hidden, and that was my show.

Exercise: Finding the Theme

Learn about themes by examining the structure of a variety of movies, plays, and one-person shows. Answer these questions:

1. What is the plot of the story (in just a few sentences)?
2. What is the story *really* about?
3. Tell the through line of the story, using the main character. For example, *Gone With the Wind* is about Scarlett O'Hara, who through her stubborn optimism survives great tragedy. "Tomorrow is another day . . ."
4. How does the main character change during the course of the story?
5. Why is the story interesting to you?
6. What conflict or idea resonates through the story and drives this mate-

rial? (It's usually something much more profound than just the events of the story itself.)

Getting Perspective

To find out what your show is *really* about, you'll probably need to get a little distance from it. Put it away for a few weeks. When you come back to it, read it as if someone else wrote it and look for the theme. Even better, enlist the help of a director or a coach to help you to fine-tune the theme and the structure.

Tips on Structure

- The audience should always wonder, "What's going to happen?" That means that every element of the story should build up to the end, which contains some sort of revealing information.
- Hook the audience in the first five minutes by giving them a sense of what the story is about.
- Keep the show in present tense.
- Don't describe your characters, act them out.
- Pick a story that is emotionally meaningful to you because you are going to be telling it over and over again (if it's successful). If you're telling this story only to "be funny" or because you hope it will land you a job, you won't make it.
- Think of your one-person show as a play where you play all the characters.
- Get a director, coach, or comedy buddy to work on the show with you. Another option—work on your piece in a class. You need a fresh, emotionally detached pair of eyes to look at it and tell you how much of what is in your head is actually coming out onstage. Many universities have adult extension classes in the arts. See my Web site for one-person show coaches.
- Don't sermonize and tell the audience what the theme is and how they should respond. Your place is inside the story—reacting to what's going on as it's happening at that moment. Let the audience make their own judgment at the end as to what it's about and how they feel about you. Director Mark Travis sums it up by saying, "Your approach should be, 'I'm going to take you on an extraordinary journey. I went on it and I'm going to go on it with you.' "
- Know what the theme of your show is. It might be based on *your* life, but

it has to say something about *all* human beings in order to touch the audience. Just as with stand-up, it has to be *relatable.*

ounting a Production

Unlike a TV show or a film, a one-person show can be a work in progress for years. There's only so much you can learn about your show from writing it. You'll learn a lot more from performing it in a workshop and getting feedback. It can take years of performing, getting input, rewriting, reworking, and then performing it again to get it to the point where you can invite the public to your show.

Tips on producing your show:

- Don't spend a lot of money on mounting your show. No matter how good or ready you think it is, chances are it still needs work. Most one-person shows don't depend on sets, props, or costumes for success. The story is the star. Find a space where you can invite ten to twenty people to watch. Churches, temples, schools, and even some community centers have small theaters that they rent out for a minimal fee.
- Hold a discussion afterward so people can give feedback. Occasionally someone will say something that will help you make the production better. It's hard not to defend yourself when people give negative comments, but the best thing to do is just write down what they say. Then trust your instincts, use what you can, and toss the rest away.

Here are some tips from Leigh Fortier, a Los Angeles award-winning theater producer, on how to produce a one-person show in Los Angeles (or another big city).

- Hire a good director who specializes in doing the kind of show you want to do. Get the best person you can possibly afford—this is not an area to cut corners. Look at other projects they've developed and directed before making a decision.
- Do two or three performances for a select group of friends before inviting the public. Don't invite the press until the show is as good as you can possibly make it—all the rough spots polished and all the kinks worked out.
- Create a provocative press release. Target it to the newspaper and magazine arts editors who *specialize* in theater. Chris Titus in *Norman Rockwell*

Is Bleeding included in his press release that he watched his mother kill his stepfather. This was intriguing enough to get out a lot of the press and industry people.

Doing a one-person show is an act of passion and love—but it might not make you a cent, even if it's really good. If you break even doing a one-person show, consider yourself extremely lucky.

19 Days to Writing Your Sitcom Spec Script

Look at the staff of any TV sitcom and you will find writers who started as stand-up comics or who have had at least one open-mike experience. As I said before, *performing* comedy is key to *writing* comedy, in order to get a hands-on sense of all the elements of a joke—timing, attitude, and delivery. If you just want to be a stand-up and enjoy working the road, then skip this chapter and become the best stand-up you can be. Write jokes every day and find a place to perform every night. However, there are many stand-ups who do both—they work on a sitcom staff during the TV season and off-season they are on the road.

Top Ten Reasons for Writing Sitcoms

1. It's a way to get an agent or a manager. When presenting yourself to an agent, it's a plus to have things for them to sell other than just being a performer.
2. Greed. Generally writers make more money than stand-up comics, and if you are on staff, you get a steady paycheck and it's a big one.
3. If you write a good spec script, it can lead to a writing assignment.
4. You don't have to travel. Although fun at first, the road can be wearing.
5. It's an outlet for creative ideas that don't lend themselves to the stand-up format.

6. It's a nesting place for stories that don't fit into your act.
7. It's a good outlet for character comedy.
8. It gives you a chance to be part of a team rather than always working alone.
9. It's a great way to network to get more stand-up jobs. Garry Shandling, Jerry Seinfeld, Conan O'Brien, and David Letterman all worked as writers on TV.
10. Free doughnuts.

pec Scripts

Practically everyone who has ever produced or written on a sitcom started by writing many spec, or sample, scripts. *Spec* is short for *speculation* or *speculative.* A spec script is usually an episode of an existing TV show that you write for no pay, because you're speculating that it will get you a job. Spec scripts—don't try to get a job without one.

And it's not just neophyte writers who write spec scripts. After being co–executive producer for *Everybody Loves Raymond,* Cindy Chupack still had to submit relevant fresh material when she was up for HBO's *Sex in the City.*

"How much do spec scripts sell for?"

You have a better chance of winning the tristate lottery than you have of selling your spec scripts. Even if it's the funniest, most brilliant script ever, it might get you a writing assignment or a staff position, but producers rarely buy a spec script. It's strictly a way to get your talent noticed.

"My life would make a good sitcom. Wouldn't it be a good idea to write an original sitcom based on my wacky life?"

A lot of beginning comics write original sitcom scripts, hoping to star in them. These scripts are called pilots—original shows. As they get more sophisticated about the business, they realize that pilots are developed with extremely successful producers or stars and packaged by powerful agencies. Even if you write a really terrific pilot, unless you are a star, it is very unlikely that anyone will spend a million dollars producing your sitcom with *you* in it. And an original script won't get you a job writing on current sitcoms unless you have some spec scripts as well. There is really no way around it—if you want to get a job writing sitcoms, you have to have written some spec scripts.

Writing sitcoms is not so different from writing jokes. A joke has an attitude, topic, premise, act-out, and mix. Sitcoms incorporate the same elements.

Attitude. Each character has a specific attitude. The way they react to one another creates your story.

Topic. Each episode of a sitcom is usually about one or two topics. Like a stand-up topic, it's something very ordinary rather than unique or weird. Just like stand-up, it's not the topic that makes your work unique, it's what you do with the topic.

Premise. This is the log line, the one-sentence synopsis of the story. It is usually structured like this: When something happens to the hero, he tries something and gets into more trouble. For example: *(Seinfeld)* When the Internal Revenue Service seeks to audit Jerry, George arranges for his girlfriend, who once worked for the Internal Revenue Service, to help Jerry out. *(Frasier)* When Frasier falls for an attractive traffic cop, it turns out that she would rather date Martin.

Act-out is dialogue.

Mix creates the *situation* when you bring in an element that will create conflict with the characters. *(Ellen)* When Ellen meets an openly gay woman, it makes her confront her own sexuality.

Preparation for Writing a Spec Script— 2 to 8 Weeks

PRO TALK *with Abraham Lincoln, president of the United States*

"If I had eight hours to cut down a tree, I'd spend six hours sharpening my axe."

Before you begin the actual writing of your spec script, there is a lot of prep work to do. This can take anywhere from a few weeks to several months. Don't rush this prep work. Be thorough. When you build a house, most of the time is spent on the plans, because a house built with a faulty design will collapse. If you rush ahead and start writing your script without doing the necessary prep work, you will probably end up with a script that doesn't work.

"Should I write with someone?"

If you have a comedy buddy that you work well with, you might want to write a spec script together. There are advantages to writing with someone. Besides having someone to bounce ideas off, a lot of sitcoms hire writing teams. The downside is that you will have to split your salary and you will not be able to get a job as a solo writer with a jointly written spec script. But hey, half a salary is still going to be more than working at Sizzler.

PRO TALK *with Cindy Chupack, producer/writer*

"Pick a partner who has complimentary skills to you. My partner was much better at structure than I was when we first started out. I learned from her and our whole product became better than what we could have done individually."

Prep Step 1: Picking a Show

The first step is picking the sitcom you are going to write. Watch TV sitcoms intensively for two weeks. Then answer these questions:

1. Which show makes you laugh? Don't bother picking a show just because it's popular. You have to find it funny or you will get bored trying to write it.
2. Does the show have a character on it who has your voice? Is there someone like you on the show? If you have a day job as a secretary, you might want to pick a show that takes place in an office environment. Maybe a character on the show has a relationship similar to one you have. For instance, a show might center around the relationship of two brothers that resembles *your* relationship with *your* brother.
3. Does the show have legs? In other words, is this show going to be around

for a while? You can't use a spec script for a show that is off the air. So unless you want to keep writing new spec scripts every few weeks, pick one that's doing well enough in the ratings to be picked up for a few more seasons.

4. Is this show well liked and well respected by the industry? It's hard enough to get someone to read any spec script, let alone a script for a show they hate. And no matter how good your script is, if the show itself is thought to be bad writing, your script will suffer from guilt by association. Some shows don't get high ratings but are noted as well-written, hot shows. It doesn't matter if the show is a cable show, as long as it's generally regarded as a high-quality show.

5. Is this show too popular? If it is, you'll be one of a million writers doing spec scripts on it. Under these conditions, it's harder to come up with a story idea that's not already done, and harder to stand out and be compared to everyone else.

"My dream job would be getting a staff job on* Friends. *Should I write a* Friends *spec script?"

Writers rarely get hired on the show for which they did a spec script. Most producers won't even read a spec script for their show. In addition to the fact that they know the characters and the show better than you ever possibly could, they don't want to read something similar to something in development and get sued. The best way to be considered for a writing job on *Friends* is to submit a killer spec script of another sitcom that has a similar tone.

My spec script is for _____.

Prep Step 2: Get Scripts and VHS Copies of Your Show

This is the hardest part of the spec script section. You're going to have to find someone who can get you a script, and even harder, program your VCR to tape your show. AHHHHH!

Once you have picked your show, you'll need to get your paws on at least three scripts of the show and videotape at least six different episodes.

"How do I get my paws on a sitcom script?"

- Go on the Internet and search for places that sell sitcom studio scripts, such as *http://www.hollywoodbookcity.com*. Make sure that you are getting original studio scripts that have the original formatting, rather than scripts that have been transcribed.

- If you can't buy a copy of the sitcom you want to write, call the show directly. Many shows do sell scripts.

- If there is an episode you really liked, send a note to the writer (in care of the show). Tell them you are a beginning writer and are a great fan of their work. Ask them if they would please autograph a copy of their script for you. Most writers will be thrilled to have a fan. Be sure to send a self-addressed, stamped envelope with your note, but don't harass them.

- Rack your brains for a connection to someone who works on a show. You might figure out that your cousin Sally used to date this guy Fred who lives next door to Barney, the script assistant on your favorite show. Call him.

Prep Step 3: Dissect the Show

Each TV sitcom has its own structure, and you need to know what it is. The person reading your script needs to know that you can nail a character's voice, the tone of the show, and even the way it's laid out on the page. Each sitcom has its own quirks, and you need to know them inside out. Your script could be brilliant but no one will even know because they won't read past the first page if it's not formatted properly.

Exercise: Breaking Down the Sitcom Structure

Ellen Sandler, who was co–executive producer of the hit show *Everybody Loves Raymond* as well as having staff positions on many other sitcoms, offers advice on dissecting a show's structure.

You have to get at least three scripts of a series to figure out the show's basic structure. From watching the show, answer these questions:

- How many scenes are in the show?
- How many times does the lead actor appear?
- How many jokes are on a page?
- What are the main locations, and how many times are the characters in each one?
- How many scenes is each character in?

- How many pages is each scene?
- What is the style of the show—jokey, physical humor, irreverent?
- Is there a B-story (a subplot that's not the main focus of the show but still important)? Is there more than one B-story?
- How many pages are devoted to the B-stories?
- What is the relationship between the A-story and the B-story? Are they connected by a similar theme, as in HBO's *Sex in the City?* Does the B-story counterpoint the A-story? Do all the stories dovetail at the end? Or is there no connection between the stories?
- Is there a pattern in the dialogue? Does one character always have the final say?
- Is one character's humor physical?
- Who is the viewing audience?
- How racy does the dialogue get?
- Are there guest or recurring characters? How many in an episode? How many pages do they take up?
- Does the sitcom happen in two, or three, acts?
- Where are the act breaks? Where do the commercials come in?
- Can you find any other consistencies between the three episodes?

Do not skip any of the above questions, because these answers will become your template for writing an original episode. Wrong answers or incomplete information will lead to script problems later on. If you don't know an answer, reread or review the show until you do.

Exercise: Sitcom Structure

In order to truly understand the structure of the sitcom you selected, as you watch the six episodes you taped, write out *what* happens in each scene and *where* it happens. Later, when you write the spec script, you will use these notes as a road map to understand the structure of your show.

For example, an episode in *Everybody Loves Raymond* might look like this:

Scene 1—INT. [interior] Ray and Debra's kitchen
Amy is crying to Debra that she and Robert broke up again. She realizes that in the past she has been attracted to gay men and wonders if Robert might be gay.

Scene 2—INT. Ray and Debra's bedroom—night
Debra asks Ray if he thinks his brother Robert might be gay. This annoys

Ray. Debra gets angry at Ray for being so closed-minded and feels that Ray's family would not be very sympathetic or supportive if Robert were gay.

Prep Step 4: Understanding Sitcom Structure

Sitcom structure is very simple, according to Bill Idelson *(Get Smart, Andy Griffith, The Odd Couple, Happy Days, M*A*S*H,* author of *Writing for Dough).*

> All stories have these elements: a hero, the hero's goal, and the obstacle to the hero obtaining that goal. Someone wants something and there is something stopping him. Look at Jack and the Beanstalk. Jack (the hero) wants to help his poor mother (goal). He gets magic beans and climbs the beanstalk to the riches at the end, but there is a giant (obstacle).

Idelson is right. As basic as the structure of that old tale is, it is no different from that of modern-day sitcoms. A sitcom story is usually broken down into six beats:

1. Setup—there is a problem in paradise.
2. Complicates and escalates—the problem gets bigger.
3. Twist (act break)—things don't go the way the characters thought they would.
4. The characters plan what to do about what just happened.
5. The conflict gets bigger as they execute the plan—this is the big physical or emotional comedy scene.
6. The situation gets resolved—all the loose ends of the story are wrapped up, and usually the main character has a heartfelt moment and learns some kind of lesson about life.

Here is an example from an *Everybody Loves Raymond* episode broken down into the six story beats:

1. *Setup*—Amy breaks up with Robert, and both Debra and Amy consider if Robert is gay.
2. *Complicates*—Debra is pissed at Ray for being closed-minded about the possibility of his brother being gay.

3. *Twist* (act break)—Ray, wondering if Debra is right about his family being closed-minded about the gay issue, asks his parents how they would react if someone in the family were gay. Ray's parents think that he's telling them that Robert *is* gay—his father is horrified and his mother is surprisingly fine. When Robert comes in, his mother tells him that it's "OK to be gay." *Commercial.*

4. The *plan*—The family tries to accept that Robert is gay.

5. The *conflict escalates*—Robert is confused; if his whole family thinks he's gay, maybe he *is*. Ray comes over to apologize for starting this mess and starts to wonder if he also is gay. Then their father comes over angry from a fight with his wife and says, "Women. Who needs 'em?" Now Ray and Robert think that Frank might be gay. *Commercial.*

6. *Resolve*—Robert forgives Raymond for starting the mess. Ray makes peace with Debra by staying home with her and her friends rather than going out with the guys. He realizes that he's straight—but miserable.

The *goal* of the main character, Ray, is to make Debra happy by showing that he and his family are not homophobic.

The *obstacles* are his father's homophobia and his own homophobia.

Now write out the six beats of an episode of a sitcom according to the above template, then answer these questions:

- What happens in each step?
- How many pages is each step?
- Where are the commercial breaks?
- What is the goal of the main character?
- What are the obstacles?

Log Line

Look at the scene breakdown of the sitcom you are researching and write out the basic log line of the story in this format: "When something happens to the hero, he tries something and gets into more trouble."

The log line for the above story would be:

(Everybody Loves Raymond) When Robert and Amy break up again the family starts to wonder if he might be gay.

Log lines can be found in *TV Guide* or on the show's Internet sites.

(Sex in the City) When Carrie runs into Mr. Big's seemingly perfect Natasha, she wonders: Are there women in New York City who live for the sole purpose of making other women feel bad about themselves?

(Family Guy) When the trophy turns up missing that Peter and his neighbors won in the annual Harvest Festival Parade, the winners all suspect one another of stealing it.

Exercise: Log Line

Write out the log line from an episode of the sitcom you are researching.

Log line:

_____

_____

_____

Prep Step 5: Sitcom Formatting

Examine your sample scripts for their formatting. Each sitcom has different formatting. Some have long character descriptions, some none. Some have huge margins, some small. Some have parenthetical descriptions for the actors, such as "crying loudly" or "shouting," and some sitcoms hate them. You need to know the preferences of the sitcom you're writing for. Even if the producers of that show never read your script, the producers of other shows will know that show's format and it will make your script look more professional.

PRO TALK *with Ellen Sandler*

"Don't underestimate the importance of the page layout. When I have a huge stack of scripts to read, I'm looking for any reason to get out of reading them. So if a script isn't in the right form, or if a character's name is misspelled, I think, 'This writer is not up to speed,' and I don't read it. A good agent will never send out a script that is not formatted properly."

Although each show has a slightly different format, here's the template for the standard format. This is excerpted from Tony Pelzer's Web site *www.sitcom-net.com*.

SAMPLE SCRIPT

ACT ONE

SCENE A

Title goes here underlined.

FADE IN:

All scripts start with "FADE IN:" and end with a "FADE OUT."

INT. JERRY'S APARTMENT—NIGHT

This is a "slugline" and describes the scene. "INT" means interior and "EXT" stands for exterior.

THIS IS WHERE THE ACTION GOES. NOTICE IT'S ALL CAPITALIZED AND SHOULD BE DOUBLE SPACED.

Scripts begin with the title centered, capitalized, and underlined at the top of the page. Then the act number and scene letter follow below underlined. All scripts start with a left justified "FADE IN:" and end with a right justified "FADE OUT." The font is usually Courier, 12 point.

Each scene begins with a slugline that includes where and when the scene takes place. There are at least three parts to this slugline: whether the scene occurs indoors ("INT.") or outdoors ("EXT."), the location of the scene, and when it happens.

JERRY (CONT'D)

Indicates that Jerry "continues" speaking from the last page.

The dialogue is double-spaced and centered under the character's name.

GEORGE

(YELLING) Character's reactions are capitalized and enclosed in parentheses. Dialogue follows next to the reaction.

Indicates you're going to switch to a new scene and location.

CUT TO:

Action is ALL typed in CAPITALS and is single spaced and enclosed in parentheses. Double spacing makes the script longer because it adds lots of white space so figure each page is approximately 30 seconds.

Everything is capitalized except the dialogue; this includes set descriptions and the character's actions.

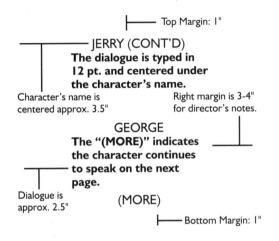

When writing dialogue, the character's name is centered at approximately 3.5" from the left. Dialogue is centered under the character's name at approximately 2.5". You must leave 3–4 inches on the right margin so the director can mark notes. If a character is going to continue speaking on the next page, then a centered "(MORE)" needs to be added at the bottom and a "(CONT'D)" needs to be added after the character's name on the following page.

NORM (CONT'D)

Norm continues speaking.

Each scene or act begins on a new page and pages are numbered in the upper right. New scenes are capitalized and underlined along with camera directions.

Set up your computer for sitcom writing. If you use Microsoft Word, you can download (for free) from my Web site sitcom writing templates with complete directions on how to use them. Go to *www.comedywork-shopS.com* for this download. There are also software programs for writing sitcoms and screenplays, but they are expensive and you can do the same thing with ordinary word processing programs by creating a sitcom template.

If you don't have a computer, don't fret. Emmy award–winner David E. Kelley writes on a legal pad and someone else types it up. There are

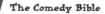

many services that will convert your chicken scratch into a formal sitcom script. Go to our Web site for recommendations for this service as well as professional scriptwriting software.

Prep Step 6: Starting at the End

When you go on a trip, the first decision you make is where you want to end up, and usually it's the same when you start to write something. Sometimes completing a script can seem like an overwhelming undertaking. That's why many anxious writers find that it's psychologically helpful to have a "pretend" finished project as a reminder that writing a sitcom is not brain surgery, it's about filling in forty-five pages. So, gather forty-six blank sheets of paper and create your title page on the top sheet. It should look something like this:

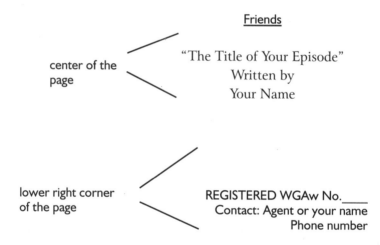

Friends

center of the page

"The Title of Your Episode"
Written by
Your Name

lower right corner of the page

REGISTERED WGAw No.____
Contact: Agent or your name
Phone number

You probably won't know your episode title until you're done, so for now just put a temporary title on it. "Reg. WGAw" means that you have registered your script with the Writers Guild of America West to protect yourself from illegal use (details on how to do this are in the Appendix). Punch three holes, fasten the pages together with brads (paper fasteners), and put this pretend script on your desk, by your bed, or wherever you can see it every day as a reminder that it's just about filling in forty-five pages.

Prep Step 7: Committing to Finishing

Just as expectant parents furnish the nursery *before* the baby is born, you need to prepare a nurturing environment for your spec script project too. That means setting up both a *place* and a *time* to write. My favorite time to write is in the morning, and my favorite place is in bed on my laptop. I have to write first thing in the morning; otherwise, if I check my e-mail, go on the Internet, or return calls, I never get to the writing. The time and place for you to write might be different from mine. I know of some writers who get up at 3 A.M. to write and then go back to sleep. Some writers need quiet and some prefer writing in the middle of hotel lobbies. It doesn't matter where or when you write, but what does matter is your commitment to it—every day until you are finished. Make that commitment now.

I commit to writing the sitcom until all forty-five pages are done. I will write every day at

_____.

The place I prefer writing is _____.

The real world operates on deadlines and so should you. If you were diligent doing the prep work, by following the instructions in the following section you will have a finished script nineteen days from now. Write that date down here. It's your deadline.

Date: _____

Action Checklist

- ❑ picked a show
- ❑ watched and outlined six episodes
- ❑ read at least three scripts of the show
- ❑ outlined each episode of the show
- ❑ set up my computer to conform to the formatting of the show
- ❑ committed to a finish date
- ❑ committed to a time and place to write

Common Mistake: Writing Too Soon

STOP! Don't go further until you have fully completed the prep work in this section. Otherwise, you're wasting time and paper. Save a tree by taking the time to do the prep work *before* starting to write your spec script. When you are finished, the next section will guide you through nineteen days of writing your sitcom episode.

Sitcom Day 1: Getting Sitcom Story Ideas

Sitcom writing utilizes many of the same principles as writing stand-up. When writing stand-up, you started with an authentic, relatable *topic*. When writing sitcoms, you start with an authentic, relatable *situation*.

> <u>PRO TALK</u> *with Emily Levine, producer/writer*
>
> "Build your story first and get your humor out of that rather than try to build a story out of different little things you think are funny."

Finding Your Situation

Good sitcom scripts are little morality plays. They aren't just a collection of jokes but rather tell a story where the main character learns something and is transformed in some small way. When creating a story, here are some things to avoid.

Ten No-No's of Sitcom Stories

1. Don't make the characters go through big changes. If the show is *Fresh Prince of Bel Air*, you don't want to write a script where they decide to move to Las Vegas. Or, "Frasier has a terminal illness." Not a good idea to knock off the lead character.
2. Don't give any main characters some back story that we haven't heard about, such as, "Ross and Monica in *Friends* find out they have a half sister."
3. Don't do anything different from what you learned by dissecting the show. For instance, if the show *always* takes place in the bedroom and the living room, don't put a sex store scene in your script. Keep to the format.

4. Don't make your story weird. Even with all their moments of exaggeration, sitcoms are pretty realistic. In the classic *All in the Family*, all the stories centered on the family members talking to one another and neighbors coming over—in other words, typical family life. There was never an episode where aliens landed and one-eyed creatures came over. Even if the show is based on an alien family, such as *Third Rock from the Sun*, the story lines involve relatively normal, mundane matters.

5. Don't force the characters into *your* story. Just because you have a great story that "really happened to you" doesn't mean that it should happen to the characters in the sitcom. Events should appear to happen because of the characters' personalities not because of the writer's imagination.

6. Don't have a character say anything that is out of character. Study the sitcom until you *know* their voices.

7. Don't create a story that has been done before. Go to the show's site on the Internet because most major shows have synopses of all episodes.

8. Don't add a lot of guest characters. Even better, don't have any, if possible, or if you do, make them characters with recurring roles. Keep the story focused on the main and secondary characters and show how much you can do with them.

9. Don't use gimmicks to create a story, such as one in which someone wins the lottery or goes on a game show. The story should be generated by the characters and not by an external event.

10. Even if your show occasionally adds new locations, stick to the usual sets.

Getting Your Story Started

PRO TALK *with John Truby, Truby's writers studio, story coach*

"The biggest mistake writers make when trying to break into sitcoms is to think they must have as many jokes in the script as possible. Not only does this belief keep many writers from even trying the form, it guarantees that even funny people will fail as sitcom writers. Rule number one about writing sitcoms: Sitcoms are not jokes. They are story."

You might already have some ideas for your story, and that's great. Sitcom ideas are similar to stand-up *mixes*—you mix in a situation that is uncomfortable for the lead character. Your main character has personality flaws. Put that character into a situation that will trigger his or her flaws. For instance, in *Everybody Loves Raymond,* Raymond's character flaw is that he feels responsible for the happiness of his entire family. Good situations would be ones where the solution for one family member's problem would cause another one's misery. On *Seinfeld,* George's character flaw is that he has an unrealistic sense of entitlement. So a situation that could flow out of that would be when George tries to go out with women who are out of his league.

Exercise: Character Flaws

What are your lead character's flaws?

_____

_____

_____

_____

In general terms, what situation would trigger his or her flaw?

_____

_____

_____

_____

Don't go with your first and only idea. *Create a list* of many ideas, both A-stories and B-stories.

Need some help coming up with story ideas?

- Start with a premise.
- Start with a story about something that happened to you.
- Start with a current-event topic.

Read on for the specifics . . .

Turning Stand-up Premises into Sitcom Stories

Stand-up premises often translate nicely into sitcom themes. Again, think in terms of insights rather than thinking funny. The entire premise of Christopher Titus's sitcom, *Titus,* was taken from his act.

Sixty-three percent of American families are now considered dysfunctional. That means that we're now the majority. We're the normal ones.

It's the people who have a mom and a dad and a white picket fence—those people are the freaks.

Some stand-up premises that could work as sitcom story lines:

(From a student) It's hard being a black woman in corporate America because you use a different personality with your boss than the one you use with your ghetto friends.

(From my act) It's weird falling in love on a vacation. When you have an affair on a vacation, don't mistake it for a real relationship, because your lover has on their "vacation personality." You are not in a *relation*ship, you are in a *vacation*ship.

Exercise: Picking Premises

Write down three of the strongest premises of your act that could also be an opinion of one of the lead characters in the sitcom you picked.

1. _____
   _____
2. _____
   _____
3. _____
   _____

Now write out how these premises could translate into sitcom plots. For example, my stand-up premise of "vacationships" in the example above could translate into a situation on the family sitcom *Everybody Loves Raymond*. The basic situation of that show is that Ray and his wife live across the street from his parents, so he is always caught between trying to please his parents and trying to keep his wife happy. Using my premise, the log line might be: *"When Ray and his wife invite over a madly-in-love couple they met on vacation, it makes them question their own relationship."* Taking this premise to the next level, perhaps watching the love-crazed couple gets Ray's wife to thinking that he is more attentive to his parents than to her. So Ray decides to make his wife happy by being more romantic *(goal)*. The *obstacles* to this could be *(a)* his mother has the flu and needs him to take care of her and *(b)* the difference between what men and women consider to be romantic.

1. Write out the story that your premise could inspire.
2. What is the goal of the main character and the obstacles in your story?
3. What is the log line of this story? (A log line is a one- or two-sentence description of a story, similar to the episode descriptions you see in *TV Guide.*)

1. _____
   _____
   _____

2. _____
   _____
   _____

3. _____
   _____
   _____

Sitcom Day 2: Turning Life Stories into Sitcom Plots

> **PRO TALK** *with Robin Schiff, co–executive producer of* Grosse Pointe.
>
> "When coming up with sitcom ideas, think what would entertain you rather than imitate what's already been done. When I have my antennae open, I see ideas everywhere—sometimes it's a magazine, a person, and sometimes it's something that happens in my life."

Stories don't work in stand-up, but they can inspire great plots. The stories, however, must be relatable to most people. The TV series *Seinfeld*, although supposedly about "nothing," was really about the topics that we all deal with on a daily basis—alienation, rejection, self-loathing, underemployment, indifference, and bad personal habits. On *Seinfeld* these topics transformed into plot lines such as

- getting lost in a parking lot
- pretending someone's ugly baby is cute

- forgetting a date's name
- trying to get a promotion
- trying to get rid of a bad smell in a car

PRO TALK *with Carol Leifer, writer/producer on* Seinfeld

"At the beginning of the season the writers pitched story ideas to Larry David [executive producer] and Jerry—and a lot of them were things that happened to us. I wrote an episode called 'The Beard.' It was where Elaine is a beard for a gay guy. That was inspired by a real event. I actually went on a date with a gay friend of mine who is closeted and asked me to go to the Hollywood Bowl with him and his boss. In real life we didn't pretend that I was his wife, but you take poetic license when writing a sitcom—you amp it up in other ways. In the script Elaine and the guy were all over each other."

Story ideas can come from stupid things. Sitcom writer/producer Ed Yeager got the story idea for his spec script from his baby-sitter. "She told me that somebody gave her a rat that they didn't even want. Then the rat got sick and had a tumor removed. I thought that that was funny and worked it into my spec script."

People who work on sitcoms become story collectors. Very often the producer will open a writers' meeting with, "What's going on with everyone today? What happened over the weekend?" And it's not because producers care about the writers' personal lives; they care about good stories. Sitcom writers pay attention to things that are problems or things that are frustrating or perplexing. This becomes the starting point for a story that is then shaped according to how the characters' world responds to that situation.

For instance, Rob Lotterstein and his partner Ellen Idelson went to pitch story ideas for *Will and Grace,* a sitcom about a straight woman who lives with a gay man. They took an incident from their own lives—an actor who visited their office and flirted with *both* of them—and turned it into a two-minute pitch. Will and Grace have an attractive guy flirt with them and they don't know which of them he is flirting with. They need to find out if he is gay *(goal).* They can't just ask him *(obstacles).* They make a plan to break into his house and go through his things, only to get in big trouble. The pitch got them a writing assignment.

Exercise: Writing Out Stories

Write out some of your favorite stories. You know, the ones you tell at parties that always get big laughs. Then plug these stories into your sitcom and come up with three different log lines.

Sitcom Day 3: Turning Current Events into Sitcom Stories

Sitcoms mirror the hot topics of the moment—a character thinks about getting a *tattoo;* a character feels that her husband is *addicted to the computer;* a character sucks up to someone to get into a *stock offering.* Stand-up/writer Steve Marmel has this joke about the *homeless:*

> "I was walking down the street and this guy asked me for a quarter. I try to have sympathy for the homeless, I really do. But I'm $25,000 in credit card debt so it's not going to happen . . . ever. 'Do you have a quarter? I'm broke.' 'F**k you, you're not broke, you're even. I'm broke. You work for food, I work for Visa. I'm working for food I bought in March . . . of 1989.'"

Steve then turned the topic of homelessness into a spec script for *Spin City.*

> *Log line:* When the mayor befriends the homeless he becomes homeless for the day.

Exercise: Turning Current Events into Sitcom Stories

Look at the current-event topics in your stand-up act and see which ones could translate into a story line. See if you can turn some of your current-event topics into simple sitcom log lines.

1. _____
   _____
   _____

2. _____
   _____
   _____

3. _____
   _____
   _____

$itcom Day 4: Honing In on Your $itcom Plot

The plot is the action of the story. It's the "what happens." In a sitcom, things happen because of conflict between the main characters, not because the writer thinks that they will be funny. If you have really done your prep, you will know everything there is to know about your characters. You will know their voices. Then, when you put the characters in a certain situation, the script will write itself as the characters talk to you.

PRO TALK *with Ed Yeager, producer/writer*

"Put your head around the main characters and get into the mind-set of the character—their problems, their family—and let the stories flow out of that."

Once you've picked a story, you might be tempted to start writing your script. Don't. First play with your ideas to milk them for all they're worth. Here are some exercises to help you get the most, and most *original,* mileage from your story.

Exercise: Improv Writing

Emmy Award–winning sitcom producer/writer Tracy Newman uses this improv writing exercise to get started:

Start with this sentence: "YOUR CHARACTER woke up this morning and . . ." And I just write what happens. It doesn't have to be interesting or funny; this is just a way to see how a story can develop from just one line.

Exercise: Write a Letter

Sitcom writer/producer Ellen Sandler suggests writing a letter from the main character to a close friend, telling the story. For instance, if *Everybody Loves Raymond* is the sitcom, and if the premise is that falling in love with someone you meet on a vacation is a bad idea, the letter from Raymond could be:

> Dear Bill,
>
> I thought things were going well with my wife, Debra. Then she invited over this couple, Gerry and Linda, we met on vacation in Hawaii. They had fallen in love while in Hawaii and were still all coo-coo eyes over each other. After they left, Debra started complaining about how little I do for her. Then the next day my mom's car broke down. I had to drive her home and so I missed meeting Debra for dinner. What could I do? I couldn't leave her stranded. Talk about a lose-lose situation. But Debra said that if I were really in love with her, I would treat her the way Gerry treats Linda. I said, "What do I have to do, give you flowers every day?" And she said, "Yeah." So we go out with this couple again and I'm doing everything I can to please her, but it backfires. Everything I do ends up being stupid and wrong. Next thing I know, Debra wants to go visit this guy she used to date in high school. So my brother, the cop, gives me this surefire plan for romance. Well, everything went wrong. I got all of these candles and accidentally set fire to the curtains and practically burned down the house. Debra stopped speaking to me because of that. Then Linda came over to return something and told us that Gerry dumped her. It ended up that it wasn't a relationship but a vacationship. She said she wishes she had someone like me, and did Debra know how lucky she was? All I can say is, thank God for Gerry making me look good.

Try this technique using a few of your log lines as inspiration. Don't try to be funny; you can make it funny later. Don't try to break the stories down. Just write the letters.

Exercise: Talking Out Your Story

Tell your stories to someone face-to-face and tape-record the conversation. By doing this, you will be able to see if and when the other person gets bored. Ideas will probably come to you as you tell the story, plus you'll discover which aspects you want to emphasize.

Sitcom Day 5: From Joke Structure to Story Structure

Sitcoms are character driven, which means the story should unfold due to the characters' conflicts with one another. Events don't happen because the writer wants them to or because they are funny. Instead, one character's needs collide with another character's needs and this creates the situation. Each story contains a lesson the character needs to learn or a problem they have to solve.

PRO TALK *with John Truby, writing coach/story consultant*

"It is important to come up with a unique desire line [goal] that gets the hero in trouble. This trouble will then escalate. The humor then comes from the situation that the hero himself has caused. Once you have established the hero's trouble, take it to the farthest extreme. Of course, none of this is easy. But if you think dense story, you've got a good shot at a script that will get you through the door."

Exercise: Reviewing Your Story

Listen to the tape where you told your story to a friend. Notice the ebb and flow of the story and ask yourself these questions:

1. Is there a place where the story became boring?
2. Is the story realistic? Would these characters really react the way you have them reacting?
3. Is the story character-driven? In other words, do the characters' personalities and desires create the story, or does something external happen to the characters?
4. Is the story too big or too weird? Don't create a life-changing (or show-changing) event for the main characters. For instance, don't have someone get breast implants. Instead, have them think about getting a breast job. Let the character explore the idea and how it would affect their relationships and life.
5. Does the main character have a strong goal that he or she is pursuing?

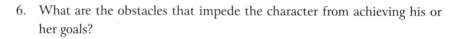

6.   What are the obstacles that impede the character from achieving his or her goals?

Goal/Obstacles

Conflict is the source of comedy and is created by obstacles, which can be physical or emotional. Humor is created from the gap between what the character wants to happen *(goal)* and the things that stand in the way of getting what he or she wants *(obstacles)*. And the stronger the goals and the bigger the obstacles, the bigger the laughs.

Exercise: Setting the Character's Goal

What is the main goal of the character in your A-story?

_____

What are the obstacles standing in the way of the character achieving that goal?

_____

What are five additional obstacles that come up when your character pursues his or her goal?

1.   _____
2.   _____
3.   _____
4.   _____
5.   _____

Break your story into the six beats I mentioned before:

1.   Setup
2.   Complicates and escalates
3.   Things don't go the way they thought it would go.
4.   Plan
5.   Big physical or emotional comedy scene when the plan doesn't work
6.   Resolve

Don't worry about the details, just get the six major beats of your story.

Sitcom Day 6: The Story Arc

PRO TALK *with Chuck Adams, vice president, Simon & Schuster*

"The story arc is the key to virtually any successful story-based writing. So often I see really well written novels that don't so much *arc* as they have a little *burp,* and it's on to the resolution. Without the arc, the viewer/reader loses interest. Relatability, story arc, and through line are the keys to successful storytelling of *any* kind."

Like stand-up jokes, sitcoms are highly structured pieces. One reason is that most of them (with the exception of commercial-free HBO and a few other cable networks) have commercials. Sitcoms generally have a cliffhanger at the act break—before each commercial—where it looks as if the hero is not going to achieve his goal. Theoretically, the viewer won't change the channel because he wants to see how the hero is going to overcome the obstacles and win in this seemingly losing situation. Conflict is what creates the momentum and leads to the obstacles and the cliffhanger. The escalation and subsequent resolution of this conflict creates the story arc.

The story arc charts the amount of tension or conflict in the story. The characters start out in peace, and very quickly something happens that disrupts that peace. The character then has a goal. The arc climbs higher and higher as the hero's attempts to achieve his goal are impeded by obstacles. The chart returns to a low point as the conflict gets resolved.

When working out the six beats of your story, you want to make sure that your arc works—that all the elements in your story build to the resolution.

Story Arc

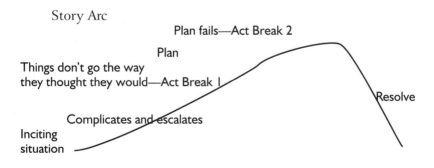

<u>PRO TALK</u> *with Emily Levine, writer/producer*

"Every beat should be working toward building the arc by pushing the conflict forward and then building toward the resolution. If you have an extraneous beat that's funny but does not serve the story—cut it. The biggest problem beginning writers have is they think, 'What would be funny?' rather than, 'What would make a good story?' "

Exercise: Story Arc

Break your story into obstacles and chart a detailed story arc.

1. What is the shape of your arc?
2. Does it peak too soon?
3. Is there a point where there is no conflict?
4. Is there a point where the conflict is not heading toward resolution?
5. Is the conflict always escalating?

The B-Story

Some sitcoms have just an A-story, but most sitcoms have a B-story and a few sitcoms have a C-story and even a D-story, such as HBO's *Sex in the City,* where all four characters each have their own story. The A-story is the main story of the sitcom and almost always involves your star.

"How do you deal with ensemble shows like **Friends** *that have more than one star?"*

In these shows the A-story alternates between the characters each week.

According to producer/writer Emily Levine, the substories can serve several different functions, depending on the sitcom.

- B-story fills out episode—In these situations the substories don't connect with the A-story or one another. This is the least complex form of storytelling.
- B-story counterpoints A-story—In these stories, what happens in one story affects the other. They dovetail at a certain point, or the payoff of

one might depend on the payoff of the other. The relationship between the A- and B-stories is both funny and surprising. *Seinfeld* had A-, B-, C-, and D-stories, which usually dovetailed, because the premise of *Seinfeld* involved the coincidences in life. An example of this was the "Chicken Roaster" episode. The inciting incident was that a Kenny Rogers Chicken Roaster goes up across from Jerry's building. In one story, Kramer protests trying to close the place down, while in another story Jerry's college buddy gets fired and starts working at the Chicken Roaster.

- Theme-related substories—Some ensemble shows have all the substories based on the same theme. For instance, in *Sex in the City* there is one theme and each of the four characters' stories illuminates an aspect of that theme. The star, Sarah Jessica Parker, always has the A-story, while the other three characters are in the B-, C-, and D-stories. For instance, in one episode the theme was "relationship deal breakers." Each substory had a character trying to answer the question "When do you stay with the person and compromise, and when do you dump him?"

Exercise: Substories

1. Review your preparation research on your sitcom and find out whether the structure of your sitcom includes substories.
2. What is the relationship of the substory (or stories) to the A-story?
3. Pick another log line for your B-story (and if necessary, C-story) and break it into goal, obstacles, and six beats.

- What are the goals of your characters in your B-story (stories)?

_____

- What are the main obstacles standing in the way of your character achieving his or her goal?

_____

- What are five additional obstacles that come up when your character goes for his or her goal?

1. _____
2. _____
3. _____
4. _____
5. _____

- Six beats of your substories:

1. _____
2. _____
3. _____
4. _____
5. _____
6. _____

Chart a story arc for all of your substories.

Sitcom Day 7: The Outline

Whether you are writing a spec script or writing on staff, everyone writes a story outline before writing the actual script. This outline is a very detailed "what happens where," scene-by-scene description of the story, which may even include snippets of dialogue.

Here is a sample—an outline of a produced episode of *Everybody Loves Raymond,* written by co–executive producer Cindy Chupack.

EVERYBODY LOVES RAYMOND [outline]

"What's With Robert?"

by Cindy Chupack

When Robert and Amy break up again the family starts to wonder if he might be gay.

TEASER—INT. RAY AND DEBRA'S KITCHEN—DAY (1)

Amy is crying to Debra about the fact that she and Robert broke up again. He's still not sure she's "the one," and he is not sure what he wants blah blah blah. It's the same old thing. He's never going to marry her, and she has nobody to blame but herself. She's always falling for the wrong guys. This is her pattern. Debra reminds her that her pattern before Robert was to be attracted to gay men, so at least Robert wasn't that. "As far as we know," Amy says. Debra laughs, but Amy is half serious. She never really considered it before, but maybe Robert could be gay. Amy: "Think about it. He likes show tunes, he can dance, he has a good sense of style, he didn't pressure me for a year when I didn't want to sleep with him, and he's very attached to his mother." Debra isn't ready to accept this theory. She points out that Robert was married and he seems to like women. Amy: "Sure, he started out straight. But I'm the spatula. I turn them."

SCENE A—INT. RAY AND DEBRA'S BEDROOM—NIGHT (1)

Ray was hoping to get lucky, but Debra's not in the mood. She's sad that Robert and Amy broke up, and she feels kind of responsible since she introduced them. This was a couple childbearing years off Amy's life, and it seems like Robert is never going to get it together to marry anyone. Ray: "Poor Robert. He'll never have a wife and kids. For the rest of his life he'll just have to go on date after date, looking for love with strangers." Debra doesn't appreciate Ray's jealous tone. Ray tries to cover by actually taking part in the conversation: "Why did they break up?" Debra: "I don't know. I think Robert has a fear of commitment." Ray: "Is that what Amy said?" Debra: "No, she thinks Robert's gay." Ray finds it amusing that women assume a guy is gay just because the guy rejected them. Debra rejects Ray all the time, and he doesn't call her a lesbian . . . every single time. Debra forces Ray to think for a minute—is it possible Robert might be gay? Ray is annoyed by the question. Robert obviously likes women. Why are they even talking about this? Debra: "Maybe he's gay and he doesn't know it yet." Ray: "I think that's something you know." Debra makes the case that some men can't face the possibility that they are gay because it would be too devastating to their families, so they never deal with it, and they end up alone and unhappy their whole lives. Wouldn't that be sad if that were the case with Robert? Ray: "Wouldn't it be sadder if he ends up with a closet full of leather chaps?" Debra is pissed at Ray for being so closed-minded, and his stupid comment proves her point that if Robert were gay, the Barone family would not be very sympathetic or supportive.

SCENE B—INT. MARIE AND FRANK'S KITCHEN—DAY (2)

Ray stops by Frank and Marie's to borrow something, but while he's there he starts to wonder if Debra might be right about his family. Are they too judgmental to accept alternative lifestyles? He asks Frank and Marie how would they react if someone they knew were gay. Frank doesn't want to hear this kind of talk while he's eating. Ray says he's just curious. Could they deal with it? Marie says of course. Her second cousin Freda is a lesbian. Frank never knew this. They get sidetracked with talk of Freda. Then Ray asks how they would feel if one of their sons were gay. Frank: "Holy crap! I knew it. Marie, didn't I tell you there was something funny about Michael?" After a frustrating moment of defending Michael's masculinity, Ray finally blurts out that he wasn't talking about Michael. He was talking about Robert. Marie and Frank are stunned. Marie: "Robert's not gay. He's a policeman." Frank: "One of those Village People was a policeman." Ray tries to explain that Robert isn't gay, he was just wondering how they would feel if he was, but Marie and Frank are already arguing about their gay son. Ray gets a glimpse of what it would be like to come out to his parents, and it's not very pleasant. Frank is horrified and completely ill-equipped to handle this, and Marie is surprisingly fine, saying that "the gays love their mothers." Before Ray can set the record straight (so to speak), Robert enters. Robert: "Hi, everybody." Marie hugs him and says, "It's fine with me if you're gay, dear."

END OF ACT ONE

Exercise: Writing an Outline

Now that you have the six major beats of your stories (A-story, B-story, and so forth) worked out, combine the stories and detail each one of them by writing a small paragraph about what happens and where it happens.

As Ellen Sandler suggests, "Figure out the best location for each scene to take place. Remember, you are limited. It is not a movie where they go away on location."

If you are writing with a partner, the best way to work on a story is to use a tape recorder. Sitcom writing team Rob Lotterstein and Ellen Idelson (*Grosse Pointe, Will and Grace, Ellen, Suddenly Susan*) tape-record sessions where they talk about the scene and improvise the different roles. "Only when we have acted out the whole story do we turn on the computer and transpose what made us laugh. That way you get natural dialogue—the way people really talk. If you just sit down at the computer, your dialogue can sound literary and stilted." Meaning—not funny.

Sitcom Day 8: Detailing Your Outline

By now you're probably chomping on the bit, ready to write your sitcom, but not yet. If your outline doesn't work, your script won't work. Better to find the mistakes now and save yourself time later.

Exercise: Making Your Outline Work

Compare your story outline with what you learned from dissecting the show in terms of numbers of scenes, theme of the story, locations,

B-story, and so on. Rewrite your outline so that it conforms to the show's structure.

> **Pro Talk** *with sitcom writer/producer Ed Yeager*
>
> "The more work you do writing your outline, the easier it's going to be to write the script."

Adding Dialogue

As you write and rewrite your outline (or talk it out into a tape recorder), you might think of snippets of dialogue. Add them to your outline. Remember that things don't have to be funny yet, but if you think of something funny, make a note of it.

> **Pro Talk** *with sitcom writer/producer Ed Yeager*
>
> "I get the drama of the story to work and then go back and fill in the jokes."

Exercise: Getting into Your Character's Head

Spend an hour as the lead character of your sitcom. How would she or he walk? Talk? Have breakfast? Answer the phone? Practice out loud how your characters speak to one another.

By today you should have an outline that is as detailed as possible. Go back over your outline and check for the arc of both the A-story and the B-story. The arc of the story is what will keep the viewer tuned in. Make sure that before each commercial break something suspenseful happens that will make the viewer want to stay tuned.

Sitcom Day 9: Writing the Burn Draft

A burn draft is an entire script you complete from start to finish in one sitting, not stopping to correct anything. You "burn" through it as fast as you can. It's not necessarily going to be good, funny, or tight, but this burn draft will lay the foundation for future drafts.

Exercise: Picture It

What the characters say and do, and how they react, must be *extremely* authentic: everything said must be in character. As in stand-up, if you write to be funny, you might sacrifice the authenticity and wind up with a script that loses the reader's interest on the first page.

Relax, close your eyes, and imagine the room in which you place your characters in the first scene. Somebody is doing something. What are they doing? What do they say? How does the other character react to this? What do they say?

Go through the entire story imagining the interplay between the characters—essentially, *watch* the show. Then open your eyes and write the entire script. Go for the realism first—in the next draft you can go for the funny. It's more important now to make sure the story works and is believable; you can punch it up later.

Then talk the script out into a tape recorder, acting out all the parts. Even if something isn't working, don't stop.

Write out the entire script. It's not important how many pages it is right now; just get the story out. If you don't have a joke where you want one, don't stop—just put something there as a "holding place" and keep going until the whole story is on paper.

Sitcom Day 10: The Story Pass— Trimming

For the next three days you are going to concentrate on the story structure. Any working writer will tell you that the key to good writing is rewriting. What often keeps a script from becoming great is that the writer is married to things that are just OK. Just as in writing stand-up, you must be willing to dump not only the things that don't work but also the things that are just adequate. Adequate won't get you a job. Only brilliance will.

If you truly want to be a working writer, you need to view your work with the same critical eye as a professional. That means cut out everything in your story that is phony, unreal, inauthentic, or hack (done before).

Exercise: Cutting Out What Doesn't Work

- Cut anything that is unauthentic or unreal, even if it is hilarious. It will break the reality of your story and distance the viewer (and the reader) from the story.
- If a scene is not about a main character (A-story) or a secondary character (B-story) striving for their goal, cut it.
- Is the story interesting? If the turns are predictable, then change them to something that is a surprise.

Sitcom Day 11: The Story Pass— Heighten the Obstacles

In a comedy, if anything can go wrong, it will. Robert McKee, writing teacher and author of *Story: Substance, Structure, Style, and the Principles of Screenwriting*, refers to this as the *comedy gap*—the gap between what is *supposed* to happen and what *actually* happens. For instance, in real life you walk up to your front door, put in a key, open it, and enter. In a comedy, you trip on the way to the door, hit your head on the doorknob, and then the doorknob comes off when you turn it. You reach into a pocket to get your keys, they get stuck in your pants. When you finally do yank them out, you rip your pants. Then the key gets stuck in the lock and, as you pull the door open, it comes off its hinges and knocks you over.

Exercise: Heightening the Obstacles

Look through your story and make it even harder for your characters to achieve their goals by putting more obstacles in the way or by heightening the obstacles already there. For example, in my "vacationship" story Raymond's wife wants his attention at the exact time when his mother's car breaks down. To heighten the obstacles, maybe the car doesn't break down in her driveway so that she needs a ride to the supermarket, but instead breaks down in the middle of rush-hour traffic and causes such a huge traffic jam that it's on the TV news. And instead of Raymond missing just an ordinary dinner with his wife, Debra, it could be he misses a dinner she spent hours preparing to celebrate the anniversary of the first time they said, "I love you," to each other.

Sitcom Day 12: The Story Pass—Structure

Spend one more day matching up the structure of your spec script to the structure of the produced scripts of the show. Go back to your prep work and make sure that your script follows the format of the show.

Sitcom Day 13: Punch-up Pass—Getting It Funny

Depending on the sitcom you're writing, the straight person gives the setup to a joke in dialogue and the funny person gives the retort. This is like in stand-up act-out, when one person says something and the other one reacts. Make sure the characters' lines are in reaction to each other or the situation, not just "funny" things. They have to be real.

Exercise: Punch-up

Put an asterisk next to every joke on the page. Then find five other possibilities for each joke. This is good practice even if you think that every joke is a laugh riot. If you do get a job writing sitcoms, you'll find that your opinion of what is funny doesn't count for much. It's what the producers, the stars, and the suits at the network think is funny that is important. Typically sitcom writers have to come up with new jokes at a moment's notice. Go back to the "mind mapping" stand-up exercise (page 183) to work out different retorts.

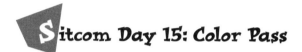 itcom Day 14: Getting It Funnier

Now that you made your funny jokes funnier, look at the straight lines in your script and turn those into jokes. For instance, instead of saying, "My father is an alcoholic," try, "Let's just say that my father's best friend was Jim—Jim Beam."

 itcom Day 15: Color Pass

Not every line can be a joke, but you can punch up even the straightest of lines doing what the pros call *adding color*. That means saying something in a clever way rather than a straightforward one. So, instead of, "Where were you? Getting a manicure?" your character would say, "Where were you? Getting those claws filed?" Adding color is an offbeat way of saying the same thing.

itcom Day 16: Read-through

One of the most painful but most helpful ways to find out what works and what doesn't work in your script is to have strangers read it out loud. Arrange a read-through with friends, or better yet, ask your local college or high school drama department if some of the students would do a read-through. Give the actors the script in advance so they have time to prepare. Be sure to tape-record the reading because you will probably be too nervous during the reading to remember what worked and didn't work. Plus, a comment or suggestion that slipped by you or that you dismissed at the time could be enormously helpful later. Listening to your work will give you a perspective on the flow, timing, dialogue, characters, and humor that reading it won't. Then ask the actors and listeners for feedback:

- Was there anything awkward or that didn't flow?
- Was there anything that felt unreal?
- Was there any time that the script became boring?
- Was there anything that really didn't work?

And don't defend your writing, no matter what comments people make. Just write everything down and review it the next day. There are always some people whose comments are totally worthless and who are just there to pee on your project. Still, don't defend yourself. Just keep the comments that make sense to you and toss the rest. From this process you will have a good idea of what flaws are in your script.

Sitcom Day 17: Rewrite

Gather up all your notes and the comments you've received. It's time to fix all the flaws and polish all the rough edges. If you did all the prep and story structure work, there's a good chance the basic structure of your script is solid. But if you didn't take the time to lay the groundwork, this is when you'll pay the price. It doesn't matter how funny your jokes are, because if there is a problem with the story, or the story doesn't fit that particular show or those characters, your script isn't going to fly and you will have to start over again.

"What do I do if the basic story is OK but I have one or two problems I don't know how to fix?"

Turn to your characters for help. Write a dialogue with the main character, or the character involved in your problem area, and ask her or him what to do. Be direct and to the point and, most important, don't think about or edit the character's response. Write down the first thing that comes to mind and continue the conversation until you get your solution.

Let's say that after doing the read-through, I discovered that my idea of having Debra make a dinner celebrating the anniversary of the first time they said, "I love you," didn't work, but I didn't know why or what to replace it with. The dialogue I would write out with Debra might go something like this:

JUDY: Why isn't this anniversary of when you first said, "I love you," to each other working?

DEBRA: Because the first time the L-word was said was a disaster. I said it to Ray, and Ray freaked out, and then I freaked out because *he* freaked out, and believe me, it wasn't anything to celebrate.

JUDY: OK, so what *would* be an anniversary worth celebrating in your relationship?

DEBRA: Our first big fight. We had been going out for almost a year. I don't even remember what the fight was about—it was something small and stupid that escalated into something big and stupid. And we were yelling at each other and all of a sudden Ray stopped and said, "Honey, this is our first fight." And we just stopped fighting, just like that, and started kissing, and, well, never mind what happened after that. But that's when I knew that I really loved him.

Having Debra prepare a special surprise dinner to celebrate the anniversary of their first fight is a great setup for the fight that occurs when Raymond misses the dinner to help his mom. Which sets up a call-back—Raymond tries to assuage Debra (once she tells him what anniversary she is celebrating) by saying, "Look, honey, this is our one millionth fight," which of course doesn't have the same impact as when he said it the first time. In fact, it makes her feel worse because they have fought a million times, which is very unromantic, and makes her think that maybe they're not compatible like Fred and Suzanne.

So if you have a script problem that you can't solve, put those characters to work and let them solve it for you!

Sitcom Day 18: Getting Read

Now that your script is in the best shape that you can make it, it's time to have a professional read it and give you notes. And the emphasis here is on *professional*. Just because your cousin Bubba watches a lot of TV doesn't mean that he is a qualified professional.

Who does fit in that category?

- A working writer or producer who works on sitcoms. If you do a little research and really put your mind to it, you will probably find that you are two degrees or less from a working sitcom writer or producer. Scan your family tree for someone who dated someone who is a former ex of someone who now is working on some show. Make that call and ask them if they would read your script in order to help you become a better writer. At this point, you are not submitting the script for a job; you're just looking to become a better writer.

- Have a teacher read your script. Many schools have screenwriting and sitcom writing classes taught by industry professionals.

- Pay someone to give you feedback. Many professional services will review scripts for money. These detailed synopses and critiques are called *coverage*. Some are very good and some aren't much better than cousin Bubba. Go to our Web site *(www.comedyworkshopS.com)* and click on "Sitcom Script Referral Service" for more information on how to get professional feedback on your script.

Sitcom Day 19: Final Rewrite

After getting professional feedback, you will probably need to do another rewrite. At the end of this rewrite, check your finished script one last time against the show's blueprint and make sure that it still fits in terms of character, structure, script formatting, story, and sets.

Then pat yourself on the back—you now have a finished script.

Other Comedy Fields

S tand-up and writing sitcoms aren't the only ways funny people can make money. Some other comedy fields:

- writing for other comics
- radio comedy
- improv
- TV warm-up
- humor essays
- motivational speaking

Part Three, "Funny Money," will explain how to go about getting these jobs, but before you can sell something—namely, yourself—you must be good at your craft. In approaching these other comedy fields, you should use the comedy techniques you've already learned, but with the following modifications.

Writing for Other Comics

While working toward their own success, many comics and writers make both money and connections by writing jokes for others. Screenwriter Irene Mecchi, coauthor of Disney's *The Lion King*, started by submitting

material to Lily Tomlin. Gabe Adelson, head writer on *Late Show with David Letterman,* started by writing material for headliners. Even David Letterman wrote jokes for Jimmie "J.J." Walker.

PRO TALK *with Gabe Adelson, head writer for* Late Night with David Letterman

"I was doing stand-up and had written material for various headliners over the years—just selling a line or two here and there. That led to submitting jokes to *Politically Incorrect,* where I ended up on staff."

When writing material for other comics . . .

- Capture the comic's style and voice the same way you would capture the voice of sitcom characters. The material must be customized for that particular comic. A joke that would get laughs for Rodney Dangerfield might bomb coming from Jay Leno.
- Riff off the subjects that are already in the comic's act rather than trying to come up with new topics. Instead, come up with fresh hits on their favorite topics, and give them different toppers.
- Write volumes of jokes, not just a couple of zingers.
- Make the jokes short—three lines or less.

Writing and Performing for Radio Shows

Companies such as Crystal Air and American Comedy Radio buy comedy material—fake commercials, celebrity impressions, song parodies, and current-event jokes. Here are tips from Chris Adams at Crystal Air Productions *(www.crystalair.com)* about the kind of material they are looking for.

- Celebrity parodies—but you must sound *exactly* like the person you are mimicking or don't bother.
- Jokes and other short, funny bits.
- One-liners on current news items.
- Human-interest-type stories, weird things going on in the news, and topics that DJs can talk about as well as have listeners call in about.
- Trivia questions with funny answers.

PRO TALK *with Chris Adams of Crystal Air Radio*

"Listen to a lot of radio and as silly as it sounds, don't change the station when the commercials come on. Listen to them because you might want to write some parodies of commercials. Also listen to what the DJs are doing and what the listeners are responding to on the morning shows. The biggest target demo for radio is adults twenty-five to forty-nine, so if you are within that range, you *are* the target demo. So, if you find something funny, chances are other people are going to find it funny as well."

PRO TALK *with Sue Kolinsky, comic/radio host*

"I got my radio job [*Mason and Kolinsky Anti Show* on WNEW FM102.7] because I was funny, I was from New York, where the show was, and I had a big sports background. We put people on our show who were funny or had a gimmick, such as Michael Sullivan Irwin, who created this character Coach, a politician with a lot of funny campaign promises. We used it as twenty-second spots. Send radio people a tape or a press release or just call and leave a message. I would call back if I thought it was interesting for the show. I didn't call back if I wasn't interested. DJs don't have secretaries. The best way to contact people is via e-mail."

mprov

"Stand-up comedy is a little too structured for me. I want to do improv, where you just get up there and be funny spontaneously."

Improv might look like people goofing around and saying funny things off the top of their heads, but in reality it is really one of the most highly structured forms of performing. I highly recommend that all comedy writers and stand-up comics take improv classes to hone their skills at character work, act-outs, and spontaneity. Improv actors are hired for sketch shows such as *Saturday Night Live*, TV commercials, voice-over work, game show hosting, TV warm-up, and more. Some of the benefits of improv are:

❑ It teaches you to be on your toes and in the moment. For a stand-up comic, this is an invaluable skill for handling hecklers, going with the flow, and calling the moment.

❑ It connects you to others. Stand-up is a party of one. It can be a lonely craft, while improv provides camaraderie and teaches you teamwork.

❑ It hones your craft of writing dialogue and making it sound more natural.

❑ It helps you create characters for your act-outs and sharpens your eye at capturing people's mannerisms. Very often we see something in life and know it's funny but don't know what to do with it. Improv classes give you a chance to flesh out a character by putting him or her into different situations in order to find the funny.

If you live near any major city or university, you will easily find an improv class, and if not, I would suggest starting one yourself. Check out our Web site for recommended improv books.

 ## TV Warm-up

Every TV show with a studio audience—sitcom, infomercial, game show—hires a comic to warm up the audience and keep them alive and laughing throughout the taping, which can go on for as long as six hours. Being a warm-up is more like cheerleading than like stand-up. It entails a lot of PG jokes and audience participation, in the form of games, gossip, games, prizes, questions like "Hey, where are you from?" or "Who came the farthest to get here?" and throwing candy at the audience when they get sleepy.

PRO TALK *with Wendy Kamenoff, comic, actress, warm-up*

"The job is like being a host at a cocktail party or a flight attendant—you've got to keep a lot of people happy. Comics that are angry and bitter need not apply. Producers tend to hire comics they know and trust. You can start out by volunteering to host or MC live shows and then send out a lot of letters with recommendations and video to TV producers."

Humor Essays, Opinion Pieces, and Articles

Magazines, newspapers, and Web sites will buy articles from beginning writers. Interesting stand-up premises can make interesting articles. Tips:

- Read a lot. Cynthia Heimel *(Sex Tips for Girls; If You Can't Live Without Me, Why Aren't You Dead Yet?)*, David Sedaris *(Barrel Fever; Naked; Me Talk Pretty One Day)*, and Ian Frazier *(Dating Your Mom)* are some of the great comedy essay writers.

PRO TALK *with Cindy Chupack, writer, TV producer*

"I wrote a lot for *Glamour*—a lot of the women magazines have space for essays. I have a male friend who wrote one for, like, a bridal magazine, about the role of the groom. There's a lot of room now in magazines and newspapers for that kind of thing and then it becomes a great little sample of your attitude and your voice. Whatever is going on in your life can be turned into a humor essay."

- Pick a magazine that *you* like and examine it the same way you did when researching your sitcom. Look at what kind of articles they buy, the length, the tone, the style.

PRO TALK *with Cindy Chupack*

"A lot of times when people write essays they sort of try to intellectualize things. When they're speaking they're so funny, human, and their observations are so natural and real. But when they write, they do something different. Let your real voice and humor come through your writing and be conversational. I have this one friend who I'm really funny with and I write her funny off-the-cuff letters. So whenever I got stuck writing I would think, 'Just pretend you're writing to Marie.' And then it's your natural voice, like you're talking to a friend rather than this big, nameless audience."

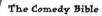

Turning Stand-up Topics into Articles and Essays

- Pick a topic, a story, or a situation on which you have a strong point of view. Or pick a topic that interests you and find your point of view by listing at least ten opinions about it.

> **PRO TALK** *with Sybil Adelman Sage, writer*
>
> "The philosophy and the point of the piece should be compatible with the publication. *Child* magazine is an upscale publication and you wouldn't write an article for them on the allures of being childless, or how to buy hand-me-downs, because you need to keep in mind the audience. I wrote a funny article for them about finding a nanny. The slant was that we mothers will do anything to keep a good nanny. We're sucking up to the nanny—the nanny drives whatever car she wants, the nanny gets the good steak, you get the leftovers."

- Choose a stand-up premise or an interesting opinion that fits the tone of the magazine and write your thoughts on it as if you were writing a letter to a close friend. For instance, if your premise was "It's weird that the same people who are against abortion are for the death penalty," that premise would work with a liberal magazine such as *Mother Jones* but not so well with *Parenting* magazine.
- When writing, outline your article in bullet points first. Each bullet point should substantiate an aspect of your point of view. As in writing a sitcom, the more detail you can put into the outline, the easier it will be to write the article.
- Do a burn draft of your article—using your outline as a map, write the entire article in one sitting as fast as you can.

The above will get you started and give you something to work with. But any professional can tell you that writing is about rewriting. The next part is the hard part—punch-up, polish, and tune. Look back to the details on writing a sitcom. First make sure that the structure works and that there is a logical flow of ideas. Next, make it funny. Then make it funnier. Take out anything that is superfluous, inauthentic, or not in tune with the tone of the magazine, and find someone you trust to give you feedback.

Motivational Humorist

Corporations pay big bucks to people who leave employees laughing *and* motivated. Motivational speaking is 70 percent entertainment and 30 percent message—sort of a funny sermon.

Crafting a successful speech is a trial-and-error process. My one-hour talk took four years to put together. I started out volunteering to speak for nonprofit organizations. At first I was so bad that some of these organizations should have paid me *not* to speak. Here are some basic tips to assist you in putting together your talk:

- Find a topic on which you are an expert, or at least think that you are an expert. This is not necessarily something that you went to school to learn, but rather a topic about which your life experiences have made you an authority. Just as you picked serious topics in your stand-up act to joke about, these topics should be serious as well. To find a topic, listen to what kind of advice you give your friends. How much of it actually works? Make a list of these topics.
- Do not sacrifice your message for a joke; it will diminish the power of your talk. When putting together your talk, go for the message first—then add the humor as an aside. Look at it this way—you're a funny person giving a serious speech.
- Always start your talk the same way you would start your stand-up act, by connecting with the audience. Connect with them by being personal and authentic right off the bat and zoning in on where they're at. I once made the mistake of trying to wake up a dead crowd by starting with a ton of energy. It had the opposite effect. Rather then riling them up, it overwhelmed them and pushed them away.
- Tell them up front exactly what your talk is all about and *then* go for the humor. To avoid the "Who the hell are you?" look, be very straightforward in your opening. Tell them who you are and what you are going to talk about, and then let the humor be a surprise.
- Never put down anything about anyone in the room. I made that mistake once, big time. I did a talk for an accounting firm, but before I spoke they showed this extremely long and boring home movie. So I opened with a joke about how long and boring the film was, not realizing that it was the CEO's home movie. Lesson one—never make a joke about the person who signs your check.

- Clean up your language. For some organizations, even *hell* and *damn* are unacceptable. If there is any part of my act that I am concerned about, I always run it by the client *before* I put my foot in my mouth.

- Corporate talks are a good home for stories, *if* they illustrate a salient point. Say what your point is, tell the story, and then say again what your point is. When telling stories, use act-outs to perform all the characters in your story.

- Speeches generally follow this structure:

  - —Identify their problem. Get specific information on the audience so you really know what issues they are struggling with. For example, "I understand that this company is going through a lot of change. They are hiring people and there is no more office space. This can get you stressed and make you want to slam the door to your office. But then again, you don't have an office. You don't have a door. You're working in a cubicle."

  - —Present yourself and your information as the solution to their problem. "I can show you how to make a humor choice and laugh your way out of stress."

  - —Qualify who you are and why they should listen to you. "I have had personal experience with this problem . . ."

  - —Tell them what they need to do what you propose. "This is what works in my life and should work in yours . . ."

PRO TALK *with speaker and author Lilly Walters*

"When creating a speech, ask yourself, what three things must the audience remember one year from now? Find a way to repeat those three things at *least* six times during your speech."

- End your talk with a "heart story." This is something that will move them emotionally and maybe get them to give you a standing ovation.

For more detailed information on how to put together your talk I recommend *Speak and Grow Rich*, by Dottie and Lilly Walters, or go to our Web site for links to speaker sites *(www.comedyworkshopS.com)*.

PART THREE

Funny Money

PRO TALK *with Woody Allen, quoted from* The Great Comedians, *by Larry Wilde (1972)*

"You like to write jokes and you like to tell them, and you do it. After that, it's pure luck."

So far this book has focused on the *show* side of show business. That will get you a few open mikes, a nibble at your scripts, and all the nachos you can eat. You must also focus on the *business* side if you want to have a moneymaking comedy career. Here's how to get your foot in the door, get your talent noticed, and get your parents to stop whining about spending $70,000 to send you to college.

Carter's 3-Step Comedy Business Strategy

Step 1: *Get good.*
Step 2: *Get noticed.*
Step 3: *Get paid.*

The way to become successful isn't a big mystery. The comedy business works just like every other business: *Get good*—develop a good product. *Get noticed*—advertise it. *Get paid*—duh. But many novices seem oblivious to this rather obvious 1-2-3 approach. They forget that timing, like everything else in comedy, is key. Putting yourself out in the marketplace before you're ready not only can hurt your career, it can even prevent you from ever having one. The good news is, everyone gets at least one shot. Someone important will read your script, see your act, or hear your pitch. The bad news is, someone important will read your script, see your act, or hear your pitch. If you aren't ready and if it isn't good, your first break might be your last.

"How long will I be struggling before I get famous?"

Being successful in comedy is very different from being famous. Becoming famous is actually easier than becoming successful at comedy. To get fifteen minutes of fame, you just have to do something outrageous. To get successful at comedy, you have to do an outrageous amount of work. Many people don't know who veteran stand-up Paula Poundstone is, but almost everyone recognizes the name of penis slicer Lorena Bobbitt. Cutting off someone's penis is quick and easy. Spending years perfecting an act, writing scripts, and waiting three hours to do three minutes at an open mike is long and hard. So, if fame and fortune are your only goals, start a pyramid scheme, live with O.J., rob a bank.

I fell into the trap of equating fame with success. For so many years I felt like a failure. It didn't matter if I got a standing ovation, had a great writing day, or even pulled in some big bucks doing comedy—I wasn't a household name. It took me a long time to realize that success is a state of mind. My critical voice that nagged, "But you don't have a sitcom," quieted down as I started focusing on small triumphs—like finding a great premise, writing new material, having a great set. Today I enjoy my career. Only about 1 percent of comics are famous, yet there are a lot of us out there making a fine living from the road, corporate gigs, TV appearances, writing for other comics, speaking, and, of course, writing books. Enjoy where you are—today.

"I'm not sure if I want to write comedy or perform stand-up. Can you tell me which one makes more money?"

If you are doing this for the money, I suggest starting an Internet company. That way you'll probably make a lot of money and nobody will scream, "You suck!" while you're working. I don't know any *successful* comics or writers who got in it for the money. We do it because that's what we do. That's what makes us happy. That's what we're passionate about. But to answer the question, here are some salary breakdowns as of 2001. For more up-to-date rates, get on the Internet and go to the Writers Guild, *www.wga.org,* or AFTRA, *www.aftra.com.*

Comedy Menu

Note. These prices are for people who are *not* household names. Once you're a known commodity you can get astronomical fees and a large bowl of red (and only red) M&M's in your dressing room.

Performing Comedy

❑ *Stand-up comic*

Opening act—$25 to $50 per night, or just dinner. Clubs usually
book a local comic who also MCs.
Middler—$350 to $750 per week, not including travel.
Headliner—$1,200 to $5,000 for the week, depending on your draw.
Cruise ship entertainer—$1,500 to $5,000 per week, plus the cruise.
Colleges—$750 to $3,500 for a one-hour show/one night.
Corporate—$750 to $10,000 for one hour/one night, squeaky clean.
TV appearance—union minimum is $617.

❑ *Improviser*

Sketch shows—usually split a cut of the door.

❑ *Commercial actor*

TV commercials—$682 day rate, plus residuals (residuals can
amount to many thousands or never happen).

❑ *Voice-over performer*

$639 per day plus residuals.

❑ *Warm-up for TV shows*

$750 per day, plus union perks such as health insurance.

❑ *Radio comedy*

$25 to $100 for jokes, song parodies, and bits.

Writing Comedy

❑ *Customized comedy material*

Writing for other comics—varies: Jay Leno pays $50 per joke;
Letterman pays $75 per joke.
Speechwriting—negotiable.
Ad copy—$300 to $700 per day.

❑ *Writing for TV*

Entry level staff on sitcom is $2,500 per week plus $7,500 per
episode that is produced. Usually there are twenty-two episodes

a season. Plus you get an additional $16,000 for every script you write, and about half that amount when it reruns. If the show goes into syndication you get a piece of that as well.

❑ *Punch-up*

> Punch-up guys come about once a week and make about $10,000 per day and are usually good friends with the show runner.

❑ *Screenwriting and directing*

> Original screenplay including treatment—$43,952 to $82,444. Story or treatment—$14,928 to $22,758.

❑ *Literary writing*

> Magazine articles—depending on the publication, $500—$2,000. Books—advance anywhere from $0 to $1,000,000+ against royalties. Standard paperback royalty payments are 7.5 percent of the cover price; hardcover royalties are from 10 to 15 percent.
> Internet writing—$20 to $50 per hour for specialty writing.

Managing and Booking

Managers get 15 percent of talent's gross.
Agents get 10 percent of talent's gross.
College and speaker agents take 15 to 30 percent of talent's gross.
Literary agents get 10 to 15 percent of the writer's gross.

Some of these salaries might seem like a lot of money, but when you deduct expenses, it's slightly less than what my grandfather made selling curtains. Let's say you get a writing assignment on a TV sitcom and make $16,000 for one script. That's your gross. Subtract from that your agent's commission, all the how-to-write books you had to buy, adult extension classes, copying, paper, phone bills, postage, messenger services, FedEx bills, faxes, computer diskettes, brass grommets to hold the pages together, flowers you bought the producer on her birthday, and the singing-telegram stripper you sent to the producer. Then divide that sum by all the hours you worked on the script plus all the hours you spent writing spec scripts. If you're lucky, you made about $5.40 an hour. So if you are in this funny business for the *money,* do yourself a favor and buy a lottery ticket—the odds of striking it rich are a whole lot better. If you do comedy because that's what you love, then you'll be happy whether you make money or not. And if you do make money—wheee!

A lot of times people end up getting jobs that they never could have anticipated. *Late Night* host Conan O'Brien wasn't known as a performer. He was a writer on *Saturday Night Live* when producer Lorne Michaels chose him to replace David Letterman on NBC's *Late Night with David Letterman.* Fritz Coleman was spotted at a comedy club and offered a job as KNBC's weatherman. In 1980 Seinfeld was plucked from the stand-up circuit to write for *Benson,* a popular sitcom, at a salary of $4,000 a week. He didn't last long but ended up the star of his own series, making millions of dollars. The moral of the story—don't be afraid to try out for anything.

Exercise: Finding Your Passion

Career choices are based on passion, not practicality. If you have followed the exercises in this book, by this time you might have performed a stand-up act, written a spec script, put together a one-person show, or perhaps just thought about writing a humorous essay. Maybe you started off reading this book wanting to write sitcoms, but later realized that writing jokes for other comics is more your thing. It doesn't matter what you chose to do, only that you love doing it. Whatever field of comedy you choose, ask yourself these questions:

1. Is this something that I would be happy doing ten hours a day, every day?
2. Could I do it for five years without making money and not give up?
3. Repeat question #2 and be honest.

   What two fields of comedy appeal the most to you?

1. _____

2. _____

Exercise: Writing Your Future

In order to get where you want to go, you need to know where you're going. The first time Jim Carrey performed at Yuk Yuk's Comedy Club he was booed off the stage. It took him two years to work up the nerve to go back. At nineteen, he caught the bus to Los Angeles. Failure wasn't an option. "I wrote myself a check for ten million dollars 'For Acting Services Rendered' and I kept it in my wallet until the day I earned it." Every journey begins with planning your destination.

1. Spend an hour writing a magazine article about your success—the story you want to appear in seven years. Be specific about which magazine would write about you. Are you on the cover of *Time* magazine, or are you being trashed in the *National Enquirer*? Be very specific about the details of your life.

    I did this exercise back in 1982. The title was *"Local Ocean Park Resident Skyrockets to Fame."* The article began like this—*Judy Carter, a struggling stand-up/actress, no longer has to struggle after being signed to one of the most lucrative studio deals around* . . . It went on not only to rave of my career success but to speak in great detail of the fancy restaurants where I had my meetings, my huge contributions to the arts, and my friend and trainer Arnold Schwarzenegger, *"who shaped my butt into the tight, hard, and high ass it is today."*

    Well, not everything came true—my career is in better shape than my ass—but it helped to have a vision.

2. Get very specific about your career goals.
    My ultimate career goals are

    _____

    _____

    _____

    _____

    _____

    In order to achieve my career goals, the actions I need to take are

    _____

    _____

    _____

    _____

    _____

    By (insert date) _____ I am committed to the possibility of

    _____

    _____

    _____

Now that you know where you are going, let's get on to Carter's 3-Step Comedy Business Strategy—get good, get noticed, get paid. These steps can and do overlap and it is not necessary to do them consecutively. You can get paid and get noticed while you're getting good. But nothing will last unless you make *getting good* your top priority.

Step 1:
Get Good

Whether you want to write comedy or perform it, getting good is a daily challenge, and you have to work at it all the time. It's not something you do when you *feel* creative. It's something you do no matter what, even when you're too busy, too tired, or too burnt out from your day job. You even do it when you're recovering from plastic surgery. Why? Because that's what it takes to get good.

Remember—every day that you don't work on your act or your script, some eager beaver is getting that much further ahead of you. The real competition comes in the everyday chore of working to get better at your craft. So when you are thinking about skipping a writing session, an open mike, or a workshop class, think of that comic out there who is showing up—prepared and sober.

Getting Good Tip #1: Create a Ton of Material

Imagine this. You finally get an agent to come see your act or read your script, and guess what? He liked it! You're in heaven, until you hear the scariest words in showbiz: "So, what else do you have?"

TV eats up material quickly. The good news is, there's a big and constant demand for funny stuff. The bad news—if you don't have a stockpile of it, then, "Next!" Maybe twenty years ago a comic could make a career out of seventeen minutes of material, or got by on the success of one script. Nowadays, however, an agent will only sign someone who has at least an hour of killer material, two killer spec scripts, and a lot of projects on the front burner.

Notice I don't say "material" or "scripts." You must have brilliantly funny *killer* material and *killer* scripts. Unfortunately, most comics and comedy writers don't create top-notch material in the first couple of years. I cringe when I look at what I did onstage during my first four years. It's not that it wasn't good or funny, it's just that it takes a lot of trial and error to come up with original material that truly reflects your vision and your voice and that reflects your persona.

Accumulating killer material can be an aggravating game of catch-up because even your best material will get old—fast. As soon as you say, "What's up with that Republican president?"—there's a Democrat in the White House. That funny TV commercial you like to parody is off the air, and suddenly the celebrity that you trashed for five minutes' worth of yucks is dead. Yesterday's hip is today's hack. Your *Golden Girls* spec script might be brilliant, but it isn't going to get you work today. You have to work on new material and new scripts *every day*.

Exercise: Keeping Current

- Make a regular time to work on your material. Rumor has it that Jerry Seinfeld set a timer and wrote until it rang.
- Be willing to throw out material—even if it kills. If you get a chunk that kills and you do it at every show, soon you will depend on that piece. You may even become frightened to perform without it. Take a courageous step and toss it out for a few months, to make room for another piece to add to your stockpile of killer material.
- Go through this book again and again, because each time that you read it you'll be at a different level of skill, and there's a good chance you'll get something new out of it each time.
- Write even if you don't *feel* like writing. Sometimes the darkest of moods will yield the freshest material. What you write might not end up in your act or a sitcom script, but you might be on your way to a great *New York* magazine piece, "50 Reasons to Go on Prozac."

Getting Good Tip #2 (for Performers): Get As Much Stage Time As Possible

There is no book, course, or formula that can teach you how to be a seasoned performer. As the Nike ad says, "Just do it." Comics with smart material but amateurish stage presence are called writers. If you want to be successful as a comic, get onstage, on *any* stage, as much as you can.

"But open mikes suck."

Stop whining about how bad open mikes are. Open mikes are comedy boot camps—the worse they are, the more seasoned you become. To get certified as a scuba diver, I went through a program that simulated every possible thing that could go wrong—losing my mask, losing my way, and even losing my air supply. Open mikes are the place where everything *does* go wrong. The mikes go dead, the audience is dead, and you die. That's OK. Better you learn how to deal with these bad situations at Comedy Night at Lou's Lobster House than during audition night at the Comedy Store. Because when you finally get that big agent to come see you perform, there's no guarantee that the audience won't be small, sleepy, or stupid. So do yourself a favor and start small. Hey, Rosie O'Donnell got her start doing stand-up in bowling alleys and Hamburger Hamlets.

Create Your Own Open Mikes

Not enough open mikes in your neighborhood? Hey, you're creative—start your own. One of my classes started their own comedy club at a hotel near the airport. They figured that the hotel bar had a built-in audience since people were stuck there. They worked out a deal with the hotel and charged a cover. Not only did they get paid, but other comics started calling them and suddenly they went from auditioning for spots to booking other comics. One tip—never do it on a sports night. Businessmen can turn ugly when someone turns off their game so the comics can perform.

> **PRO TALK** *with Kathy Griffen*
>
> "You have to promote yourself. I would rent a theater with a few other comics—Jeanane Garofalo, Dana Carvey—and we charged people one dollar. So people expected that this would be experimental—their expectations were low. If you can find your audience, that is more important than going for the biggest place. I would bomb at the Improv, so I thought, 'Where can I find my people?' I would perform for fifteen people at a coffee shop next door to the Improv, which felt better than bombing at the Improv."

Tips on Working Comedy Clubs

In the gravy days of doing comedy in the 1980s, there were hundreds of comedy clubs. As more stand-ups became available on TV, audiences dried up and clubs closed. Now it's almost easier to get a ride on *Air Force One* than it is to get a spot in the top clubs in Los Angeles and New York.

I asked owner Chris Mazzilli and former talent coordinator Delilah Romos of New York City's Gotham Comedy Club how to get a spot and how to make it pay off.

"What's the best way for a comic to make a good impression on a club owner?"

CHRIS: Don't go over the light when you audition. That drives me out of my mind.

DELILAH: Even if you're doing well—when the light comes on, get off the stage. It's a business and there are time constraints. When you are getting a lot of laughter and you see the light, say, "Thank you, good night my name is . . . ," and run.

"Anything else a comic should know to get on your good side?"

DELILAH: Stay out of the way of the waitresses and be nice to them. When you are self-absorbed you can come across as rude, and if they think you're rude, it will backfire when the manager or owner asks them who did well that night. Also . . .

Understand that there is a flow going on. Sometimes a comic has nervous energy and doesn't mean to, but gets in the way. When we do two shows a night, we have to reset the entire room and start a second show, so it helps when the comics keep out of the way. Introduce yourself to the manager and ask where he likes the comics to hang out so you don't get in the way.

Everybody likes harmony, so don't get cocky with the other comics. Try to be cordial and foster a sense of camaraderie.

When you call for feedback or booking info, leave your name and your phone number twice.

"What do you look for when you book a comic?"

CHRIS: I look for the smarter comic, the one with original autobiographical material. These people are unique—their history, who they are, where they come from.

DELILAH: Find your own voice and don't be clichéd. Do your homework—spend five hours a week watching comedy at clubs so that you learn who does what kind of material and which kind of material is overdone. Stereotypical jokes are just hacky. As a comic finds her own voice she gradually builds her own persona, and out of that grows genuine originality.

"What about language?"

DELILAH: Every club has its own character. Chris wants elegant upscale material. He doesn't want really blue jokes. Your language should be appropriate for your audience.

"What should a comic do to get booked into your club?"

CHRIS: Send in a tape—that's the step. It's rare that somebody who has only been doing comedy for one or two years gets booked. But there are those occasions when you see someone who is so good that you go, "They have it." I'd say it usually takes about five or six years to become a good comic. A professional comic can do well consistently in any kind of room, whereas a newer person who has a good ten to fifteen minutes can get thrown by something like a bad crowd. It doesn't make a difference what's going on in the room to the pros, they are that confident.

DELILAH: It's a long process. We don't book people with less than five years' experience, because we want polished acts. In New York there are a lot of venues where you can work out your material—in dough-nut shops, coffee shops, and supermarkets. Beginning comics should hang out at the club, meet as many people as they can, try to get a good recommendation, and persevere.

"Does having an agent help?"

DELILAH: The proof is in the pudding. If someone has an agent but isn't ready, that agent isn't going to be able to help them.

Getting Good Tip #3: Study Other Comics and Comedy Writers

You need to know what other comics and comedy writers are doing, and not just to prevent duplication. You must study the past and the present in order to find the wave of the future. Rent videos, read scripts, watch TV, hang out at clubs, go to festivals, and subscribe to *Variety*.

Getting Good Tip #4: Get Help

Once you work on something for more than five minutes you lose your perspective on it and need a fresh eye. Although writers, directors, impro-visers, and actors are always trying to improve their craft by taking classes, most stand-up comics seem to have an "I'm in this alone and don't need anybody's help" sort of attitude. However, most successful entertainers have a long list of classes, mentors, and comedy buddies who provided roadside assistance on their path to fame and fortune.

"But you can't teach anyone how to be funny, can you?"

No one can teach you *how to be* funny or talented, but if you *are* talented and funny, a professional you respect can help you develop your skills. And no matter how talented and funny you are, if you don't spend your waking hours asking, "How can I improve my craft?" chances are you *will* spend the rest of your life asking, "Would you like to hear our specials today?"

Get a Mentor

A mentor is someone who can give you feedback and point you in the right direction. Sucking up to people will get you everywhere in this business—especially if it's authentic. Contact and cultivate professionals who think like you but are higher up on the food chain. Seek them out. Buy them lunch. They'll admire your spunk, relive their own green-behind-the-ears days through you, and get a kick out of being a mentor.

How to Get a Mentor

Writers—get to know someone on a show by noting who wrote the episodes you liked and then e-mailing her or him a fan letter. Introduce yourself as a new writer and tell her specifically what you liked about her writing. Do *not* ask her to do something for you. Only if you get an e-mail back would it be appropriate to request a read of your script. At this stage, do not ask for help getting work. Ask for honest feedback. But if someone offers to introduce you to her agent—lucky you.

PRO TALK *with Rob Lotterstein, sitcom writer/producer*

"People contact me all the time over the Internet—'I'm twenty-two and I live in Ohio. I saw in your AOL profile that you're a writer. What show do you work on?' I've had people compliment me on shows I've written. One person asked if I would read his script. I asked him to mail it to me. I know what it's like being a beginning writer and I like helping people."

Performers—approach a successful comic and ask him if he could watch your act and give you honest opinions of your material. The top stars of comedy are usually too busy, but there are a lot of comics head-lining at comedy clubs who would be flattered by your attention if they are approached in a sincere manner. Remember, you're not looking to them to help you *get work,* but rather to help you *get good.*

I love it when someone sucks up to me in an enterprising way. I got an e-mail from a new Ohio comic, Bryan Emler. He found out that I was going to be playing three cities in Ohio and asked if he could do five minutes opening for me. In exchange, he offered to drive me to all my gigs. It was an offer that I couldn't refuse. I got a ride, pleasant company, and before you could say "Cincinnati," he had a solid twenty minutes from running things by me in the car.

Workshops and Classes

A good class offers a safe place to fall flat on your face, a chance to work on something risky rather than settle for the easy, hack joke. Classes give you a weekly structure, forcing you to show up and come up with new material. Even though I make my living at comedy—teaching, writing, and performing—I am constantly taking writing and improv classes to keep me tuned up.

Classes are also a great place to network. When one person breaks out of the pack and becomes successful, he often remembers the people who were with him at the beginning.

> **PRO TALK** *with Tom Shadyac, film director and former student*
>
> "When I was casting Eddie Murphy's movie *The Nutty Professor* I called in one of the students I met from Judy's workshop."

Tips on Picking a Class

- Audit the class first. Chemistry is important. At Comedy Workshops, we let everyone take a free class before signing up.
- Find out the teacher's credits. I wouldn't take a stand-up or writing class from someone who hasn't been somewhat successful doing it themselves.

- Does the class promote originality? If not, it might not be a good place for developing authentic material.

"What about hiring someone to write stand-up material for me?"

When I first started out I hired an expensive comedy writer to write me ten minutes of material. It was a joke all right, for the wrong reasons. That material might have worked for Bob Hope, but not for me It was that writer's vision of what I should say. Comics who can't create their own material are called actors. Once you become successful and have an identifiable persona, only then can people write for you. But the very nature of being a comic means that you have a burning desire to talk to an audience about something. No one can tell you what that something is and write it for you. Others can help you uncover it, add to it, and punch it up, but ultimately you are the one who has to have the ideas.

Where to find help:

- *Writers* can hire professional script readers to write *coverage* of their script. This is a detailed synopsis and opinion of your story. Go to our Web site for a list of companies that do this.
- *Performers:* The buddy method is the best way to create material. If you need a professional opinion of your act, go to our Web site for a list of contacts.

Internet Services

Every day there are more and more resources for comedy writers and performers on the Web. Go to the "links page" at *www.comedyworkshopS.com* for the latest comedy dot-com resources. Newsgroups are also a great resource of information. If you have any questions you can post them and someone will get back to you with answers. One of them in particular—*alt.comedy.standup*—has great tips and support amidst the bitching.

Getting Good Tip #5:
Set Challenging Goals

If your goal is starring in a sitcom, headlining a club, or making a million bucks, it's pretty much out of your control whether you reach that goal. That will depend on the depth of your talent, your willingness to persevere, and an awful lot of lucky breaks. But there are goals that you have full control over, such as how many hours you write, how much material you develop, and how many times you perform. Getting together an hour of stand-up material might *seem* out of reach, but if you created only seventy seconds of good material a week, in a year's time you would have an hour.

Exercise: Goal Setting

You might have become a comic to avoid time clocks and quotas, but if you're like many people, if left to your own devices you just cruise porn sites on the Internet. Make weekly commitments to write and perform.

Weekly Goal Sheet

This week I will

- write for _____ minutes each morning
- create _____ pages/minutes of new material
- perform _____ times
- try out _____ new jokes
- have a comedy jam session on _____
- call at least _____ new people to help my career

Go to *www.comedyworkshopS.com* for goal forms that you can print out.

Step 2:

Get Noticed

The way to get noticed is to promote yourself. Until you are so successful that you can hire a PR agent at $2,500 a month, *you* will need to be your own publicist. Even if you can afford to pay a publicist, don't cash out your trust fund yet. A publicist can only promote something that is *newsworthy*. And face it, a stand-up comic playing at an open mike isn't going to make the six o'clock news.

PRO TALK *with manager Bernie Brillstein*

"If you only have six or seven minutes, make sure that you're not going for cheap laughs—shock language and filthy humor. Look good. I don't mean pretty—I mean good. Look neat, have pride in your appearance—shine your shoes and put on a clean shirt. Have a beginning, a middle, and an end to each joke, which can't be longer than a minute. Put your personality into your material and make sure it's relatable."

If you get good, you *will* get noticed. The point of PR is making sure the *right* people notice you. There is certainly a glut of stand-up comics and comedy writers out there, but very few are truly excellent. In my generation of comics the great ones were, to name a few, Robin Williams, Jay

Leno, Jerry Seinfeld, Billy Crystal, Andy Kaufman, and Albert Brooks. They were the comic's comics. Watching their sets at the Improv was more important than cruising the bar for dates—that's how good they were. This was before the L.A. Improv was the breeding ground for TV development deals. Back then, comics followed their gut instincts rather than their agents' advice. I remember one night in 1975 when Albert Brooks took to the Improv stage at 11 P.M. and didn't get off until 3 A.M. A decade later, I still remember his premises—"Hey, you know how comics just do material that everyone can relate to? What if comics did material that no one could relate to? OK, you know how it's New Year's Eve and you are stuck in an elevator? Right?" He was a brilliant comic.

But until you are at the brilliant stage, there are ways to stand out from the pack while you are honing your craft.

Getting Noticed Tip #1: Highlight Your Persona

Letterman is a brand. So is Seinfeld. Everyone knows what kind of comedy they represent, and that brand of comedy is reflected in their material, clothes, and publicity. What is your brand of comedy? Whether you are a comedy writer or a stand-up, in order to stand out it is essential that you distinguish yourself by magnifying your brand of comedy—your identity, your image, your *persona*. It's not a cerebral decision you make about yourself. It's who you are—exaggerated times ten.

Richard Lewis created a readily identifiable persona of "angst" by wearing black, pacing the stage like a caged animal, and basing his jokes on his tortured life. Everything about him says, "I'm sick, I'm mentally disturbed, and I'm in a terrible state." He has a persona and that's his whole stance.

Is this a character he made up? No. In my interview with Richard, it became apparent that his persona is just an exaggerated version of who he is.

Kathy Griffen jokes about her abundant sex life: "Everything I do is all true and it's just my take on a situation." Kathy also highlights her persona by wearing tight, skimpy outfits that she practically pulls off while she does her act.

Finding your persona is a trial-and-error process. Phyllis Diller evolved her persona over years. When she first started out she looked like the woman next door. She told me, "That is what most of the female comics look like now. I realized that if I'm going to be onstage and they've got to pay to look at me, I better not look like the girl next door 'cause you can look at her for nothing."

Ms. Diller then took her dark hair and made it peroxide white. She started wearing shapeless dresses because "I wanted to tell them I was flat and I wasn't. I had a 38C. I have a million jokes about being flat—'For years I wore foam rubber and then one day I thought, maybe I erased them.' You can't do all those gags if they're looking at boobs."

She constructed her look wearing teeny little boots because she wanted them to cut her leg at the exact skinniest point on her ankle. In other words, "I wanted to have a lot of skinny-leg jokes. 'The last time I saw a leg like that there was a message attached.' 'Colonel Sanders loved my legs; in fact he brought out a special package of chicken in my honor. It had no breasts.' You've got to be the leader. You've got to decide who you are."

Many comics emphasize their persona by creating a slogan for themselves. When Roseanne Barr called herself the "domestic goddess" on her first Carson shot, her sitcom developed faster than you could say, "Poor trailer trash housewife mom." A monkey could have put together that sitcom because Roseanne did all the hard work—*she* defined *herself.* Her catchphrase not only suggested who she was and her point of view, but who her target audience was.

> **PRO TALK** *with Roseanne Barr (as told to me after a show at the Comedy Store)*
>
> "Stand-up is my therapy, Judy. I'm just really pissed off!"

A Writer's Voice

If you are a writer, you still need to hone your brand of comedy. Although writers are rarely thought to have a persona, they are said to have a voice. This term has always sounded weird to me because writers don't speak—they write, thus no voice. Yet the word *voice* is currently heard at every studio meeting. "I love this writer's voice." "His voice is very unique." "He has a very edgy voice." "Her voice is very clear." And yet in over forty-five interviews for this book, no one seemed able to define what it means to have a voice. So I won't try either. Instead, I will give you some examples. Trey Parker's voice (he is co-creator and writer for *South Park)* is different from Larry David's voice (he is creator and writer of *Seinfeld).* Both are extremely funny, talented, and edgy, but their hit on things is totally different. Parker puts his *South Park* little kids in big situations, while David's *Seinfeld* characters are big people in little situations. At the root of what we all do is something unique and constant—a sort of through line. It takes a lot of writing of what isn't us to find what is.

> **PRO TALK** *with Larry David*
>
> "I like to take something tiny that just expands and see where it goes."

Exercise: What Is Your Brand of Comedy?

In order to stand out from the pack, evaluate yourself.

1. What are your signature jokes? (Usually the jokes that get the biggest response.)
2. What type of audience do you feel most comfortable in front of (corporate types, college students, women, gays, Italians)?
3. What article of clothing suits you best? Rodney Dangerfield wears a rumpled coat and tie, giving him that "I don't get no respect" look.
4. Create an ad for your act that sums up what you do and targets your audience. What name would you give your show? Sandra Bernhard's stand-up show was called *Without You I'm Nothing.* This summed up the tone of her show. Six of my students got together and came up with *Six-Pack of Comedy* and had a clever flyer with their pictures on a six-pack of beer. What kind of picture would you have in the ad? Can you come up with a one-sentence phrase that sums you up?

Getting Noticed Tip #2: Have Professional Materials

You're doing a set at Comedy Night at Luigi's Italian Restaurant and someone says, "Hey, you were funny. I'm a TV exec. How do I get hold of you?" Do you *(a)* borrow a pen from him and scribble your phone number on the back of a napkin, *(b)* give him your business card, *(c)* get his business card?

I'd suggest both *b* and *c*. Do an Internet search on the guy to see if he is the TV exec in charge of something other than the mail room. And even if he *is* only working in the mail room, he probably knows someone. Anytime you are noticed *and* liked, you need to make something of it. The first step is to have promotional materials with you *at all times.*

Both writers and performers need the following:

■   *Stationary and business cards.* Make them look as professional as possible, which means resist the temptation to make them jokey. Performers, put a color picture of yourself on your business card so when that drunk audience member digs your card out of his pocket on Sunday morning, your picture and the word *comic* might stir brain cells.

- Just for performers: *8-by-10 black-and-white head shot* with your name and contact information. Newspapers prefer photos that have a white or light background. I wouldn't go wacky with the picture. If you look at all the successful comics, you'll notice very few of them are weird looking. As with everything else in life, handsome, cute, and attractive work best. Also have a few color pictures on your computer to e-mail to bookers, agents, or newspapers.
- *Résumé*—a listing of all your jobs, skills, and training.

"But what am I going to put on my résumé if I haven't had a job?"

Lie—no. Exaggerate—yes. List all the comedy clubs and colleges you've played. It doesn't have to say these were nonpaying gigs on amateur night. You've got to start somewhere. Writers, put on it any sort of writing jobs, newsletters, columns, spec scripts, and so on. On my first résumé I had parts I played in college, open mikes, my skills, my training, and my teachers. It was very, very short but got longer as I got work. If you really have nothing to put on a résumé, then just don't have one.

- *Biography*—a cute story of your life and career. Write it as it would appear in a magazine article about yourself. Keep it to one page or less, double-spaced, and make it entertaining, funny, and informative.
- Just writers: *writer's package.* This is a collection of writing samples that should be adapted according to the job opportunity. If you're up for *The Late Show with David Letterman* it would include top ten lists, current-event jokes, desk pieces, and remote ideas. If you are up for a sitcom staff position, it would be a spec script, and you can also add essay pieces if they reflect the tone of the show you're applying for.
- Just performers: *video.* This is your most important marketing tool. The video should be eight to twenty minutes depending on who you're sending it to, but don't count on anyone watching more than the first three minutes. Club owners and agents generally don't like edited tapes with cutaway shots to the audience. It looks like you're hiding something.

  - —Have a few versions of your act. I have a clean corporate tape, a women's issues tape, and a nightclub "let it rip" tape.
  - —The audio on your videotape must be clear. This gets tricky because if you use just the mike on the video camera, what you say will probably be hard to understand, while the conversation of the

drunks seated near the camera will be crystal clear. The best situation is to have two wireless mikes—one on you and one above the audience to get the laughs.

- •   —Keep your tape current. You need to look like your tape. One way to keep your tape up to date is to invest in a video editing system. I'm a gadgethead. I videotape practically every performance with a Sony three-chip digital video camera (DVCAM) with Azden wireless mikes. I keep my tape current by editing it on my computer using Adobe's Premiere and a Pinnacle Systems capture card.

PRO TALK *with New York City's Gotham Comedy Club's former talent coordinator, Delilah Romos*

"[On your demo video] we want to see that you can perform more than five to ten minutes. Like specializing your résumé for a specific job, check with the club to see what kind of tape they like and then send the appropriate one. A résumé and photo are helpful and they show that you are polished and professional. It's nice to see a professional package."

- ■   *Internet Web page.* Probably by the time this book is published, all your PR materials can be distributed via your Web site.

The following materials are more expensive and can wait until you have a clearer idea of your persona.

- ■   *PR packages.* Arrange all your promo materials in an attractive folder. Printing up personalized folders is very expensive, so be creative with labels instead. Even better, get a friend who is a graphic designer or an art student to give your materials a look that represents who you are. Your press package should include your biography, reviews, letters from happy clients and club owners, photos, flyers, and articles.

PRO TALK *with Michelle Marx, PR person who has represented Richard Lewis, Paula Poundstone, Rita Rudner, Robert Wuhl, Louie Anderson, and Judy Carter*

"A PR package needs to be built around a comic's persona with an interesting bio and the right picture. For example, with Richard Lewis, you think of an attitude. All black clothing and anxiety are very important parts of who he is. We heightened that in his PR package. You don't want a cheery picture of Lewis when his persona is anguish. You want dark and interesting. You want every piece of PR to capture what that comedian is portraying."

- *Design a flyer* that has a space to put the details of when and where you are performing so you don't have to redesign it every time you get a job. This flyer should visually express exactly who you are. When I first started out and was doing a mix of magic and comedy, I made a copy of an old-time magic flyer, "Carter the Great," that had a picture of me doing a death-defying escape from my grandmother's girdle. It got people's attention and made them laugh. Keep the background light so that your flyer will reprint well in newspapers.
- *Create postcards* with blank spaces so that you can add the "where" and "when" on a label. These are great handouts because they can fit in a pocket.

Getting Noticed Tip #3: Find Your Audience

Whether you're a writer or a performer you need to cultivate like-minded people who will *get* you. The audience for a New York–style comedy writer will be different from the audience for a Southern-style comedy writer. Not everyone will love what you do, but you need to find the people who will.

For performers, many of the gigs you get at the beginning of your career will be "bringer" gigs. That is, you can perform only if you *bring* five paying audience members to the gig. Beginning comics bitch and moan about these gigs, but they are your PR training ground. You must create your own fan base. If you can't or won't do it for yourself, why would an agent, manager, or producer want to do it for you? Bringer rooms are your training grounds for success. Unless you are Catholic, you are going to run out of relatives fast. You need to cultivate a following that isn't related to you. If you find that your material is hit-or-miss depending on the audience, don't change your act—change your audience. If you want to talk about being gay, then perhaps performing at a Southern Baptist church open mike isn't a good idea. Not everyone will like you, and that's OK.

PRO TALK *with T. J. Markwalter, vice president of Omnipop Talent Agency*

"I don't get suckered into how well the crowd is responding to somebody. If I think that they're very funny, very original, and very different, I will be very interested in working with them either way."

PRO TALK *with Kathy Griffen*

"I know that I'm not for everyone. I work well in big cities with gays and young people. I went on the road to work out material for my HBO special. It was a disaster. I was bombing with these Midwest audiences that didn't get me. So when I did my HBO special, I promoted it myself because I knew who I had to get to that taping. I got flyers to colleges, to the gay bars—people that I thought would like what I do."

Tips on Targeting Your Audience

- *Keep a database.* For writers, every contact, every tip needs to be saved in a database. For performers, every performance is an opportunity to expand your database. If people really like you, they will want to see you again, and you need their data to build your audience.

    It's difficult to get audience members to fill out data forms, and the old "Put your name on the mailing list at the back of the room" doesn't cut it. I suggest having drawings, contests, and free giveaways for those who do give you their info. It's not something you can do during your act, but certainly something that the MC can have fun with before and after it. Having a following will impress an agent and club owner more than the actual show. So once you get your fans' addresses, you must set up a system—such as the software database ACT—so that you can easily reach them. Go to our Web site for links and PR tips in setting up and running a comedy database.

■ *E-mail people about where and when you are performing.* Almost everyone has e-mail, and using it is free. It's a great way to let people know where you are performing without bugging them too much. Tips on e-mailing:

- • —Always have a "remove from list" option at the end of your e-mails.
- • —Never send anyone an attachment; it pisses people off. If you want them to see the fab flyer for your show, then post the flyer on the Web and e-mail people the link.
- • —Never show your e-mail list. Send all your e-mail "blind carbon copy."
- • —Put a short video of your act on your Web page. Just a tease. Never put your entire act on the Internet because it *will* get ripped off and there is no way to prevent that from happening. Go to our Web site for information on how to transfer your video to streaming Web video.

■ *Go to where like-minded people hang out*—colleges, bars, temples, gay bars— and hand out postcards and flyers. Don't assume because you hand someone a flyer that they will go to your gig. Talk to them.

■ *Donate time to charity.* Volunteering to do your act for a benefit is a great way to network and get a buzz out about what you do—plus it's great for your karma. Find a charity that you relate to and either produce your own fund-raiser or take part in theirs. I created a workshop for AIDS Project L.A. where I taught stand-up to people with AIDS. We called the project "HIV, <u>H</u>umor <u>I</u>s <u>V</u>ital." Twenty brave souls created material about living with AIDS and performed it at a comedy club. All the proceeds went to an AIDS charity. It created hope for the participants, raised consciousness and money, and it made the six o'clock news.

■ Can't find any place to do your act? Then *do it in the street.* Comic Michael Colyar spent nine years shouting his act to passersby on the boardwalk in Venice Beach, California. Producer Chuck Barris spotted him and put him on TV. Colyar went on to do an HBO special and Def Jam appearances, and became recognized internationally as the Star Search winner who gave away half of his $100,000 earnings to the homeless. Moral of the story—get out of the house.

> **PRO TALK** *with Frederick Levy, author of* How to Succeed in Hollywood Without Connections.
>
> "Network. Be willing to call or approach anyone and introduce your-self. You can't be shy. Contacts are the lifeline of Hollywood."

- *Network your brains out.* Do you see the same ten friends over and over again? If so, then join organizations that can assist you in expanding your circle of friends and potential audience members. I'm a member of the National Speakers Association, the Los Angeles Chamber of Commerce, the National Organization of Women, the Sierra Club, ACLU, SAG/AFTRA, and Women in Film, to name just a few. Always carry some discount or two-for-the-price-of-one coupons to your shows and hand them out at the events you attend. Networking at organizations can not only expand your audience base but also lead to other gigs and business opportunities.

Getting Noticed Tip #4: Work the Media

Whether you are having your first play produced or performing your stand-up act, it's important to get the media's attention. Ads are very expensive, but there are lots of ways to garner free publicity.

- *Send out press releases.* Tips on press releases:

  - —Make sure that the press release is in the right form, with proper contact information. At the top, put the contact information, then the header, then the usual who, what, where, when, and why. Write it so it can be reprinted as a newspaper article.

FOR IMMEDIATE RELEASE

[Event Date]
Contact:
[Put here all of your contact info, including e-mail.]

[Have a snappy, newsworthy headline here.]
"Stand-up comic gives pointers on how to not stress out during the holidays."
"Laugh-athon slated to raise money for needy children."

LOS ANGELES, CA—MARCH 21, 2001 [start with the location and date of the press release—then a one-page press release written like a magazine article. End with a phone number for people to call for more information.]

# # #

I don't know why, but press releases always end with # # #.

- —Find an interesting angle to what you are doing and turn that into a catchy heading. "New up-and-coming comic plays comedy club" will get your press release thrown into the nearest wastebasket. I wrote my most successful press release after I had done a few corporate gigs and decided I wanted to do more. The headline was "Fortune 500 companies turn to a stand-up comic to solve employee problems." The *Wall Street Journal* picked up on this press release and did a feature story on me. When it was published, the phone didn't stop ringing. A reprint resides at the front of my PR kit and it is still pulling in the jobs.
- —Don't have anything to publicize? Then create an event. One time right before I was to do my comedy/magic act at a club, I sent out a press release announcing that I would be hanging upside down outside a radio station, performing an escape from my grandmother's girdle. The press release was sent to the radio station and to women's organizations. The station did a tie-in and gave away free tickets and interviewed me for several days leading up to the event. A huge crowd gathered for the event. We handed out gobs of postcards promoting my gig at the club. I sold out the week and got featured with a picture and a story in the newspapers.

  At the time outrageousness was my thing; of course, it may not be yours. You can do wacky things, but you must remain true to yourself. Club owners will come up with crazy things that they want you to do, but don't do anything that goes against who you are.
- —Get your press releases to the right people and spell their names right. It takes extra time to call up the paper to find out exactly who the entertainment editor is, but the extra effort is worth it when your info gets into the right hands. Also make sure that you are sending stuff to the right publication. *Women's Journal* would be more likely to publish an article about sophisticated female comic Rita Rudner than about wild, disturbed comic Bobcat Goldthwait.

<u>PRO TALK</u> *with Michelle Marx, publicist*

"Press releases are important. A couple of times, they might be thrown into the garbage. But after a while it will create familiarity. You want your name to start hitting people. Just make sure they are well written and with purpose."

- *Get yourself free publicity on the radio.* If you are playing a comedy club, ask the owner to hook you up with radio stations. If you come up with a good angle, radio shows will put on newcomers who have a good angle and something funny to say.

  - —Create a contest with free ticket giveaways.
  - —Build a show around a holiday.
  - —Fax radio stations a joke a day.
  - —Create a funny character who has opinions on what is going on in town. This could even lead to paying gigs.

<u>PRO TALK</u> *with Michelle Marx, publicist*

"A lot of local radio shows have five o'clock funnies. Make a tape of what you do and send it in. Find interesting ways to send it to them. Anything that sets it apart from the rest of their stack of mail will help. Follow up with a phone call."

- *Send articles, jokes, and opinion pieces to newspapers, magazines, and Internet sites.* A lot of newspapers have a "Laugh Lines" column and it's a great way to get your name in the papers.

"But if my jokes get published, I won't be able to use them. Right?"

Not necessarily, but don't give away your best bits. Instead, use this as a way to get extra mileage out of current-event jokes that have a short shelf life. Send in a comment piece with your spin on the hot topics of the moment. For instance, if "road rage" is the flavor of the month, then write up funny ways to deal with road rage. You can write it as an article, a sidebar, a letter to the editor, or an opinion piece. It can end up in *Time* magazine, in your PR kit, or at the least as a writing sample that will help get you more jobs.

PRO TALK *with Michelle Marx, publicist*

"Go to the publications that reflect who you are. I wanted to make a marriage of the right publication to the right client. For example, Paula [Poundstone] is bright and writes well. I had her write opinion pieces for *Mother Jones*, the *L.A. Times*, *Entertainment Weekly*. It's about finding the people who would really relate to you and make them aware of yourself."

Getting Noticed Tip #5: Showcasing and Comedy Festivals

Comedy Contests

Contests are happening all the time. The prize money can be big and the attention they garner even bigger. And even if you lose, the exposure can still help your career. Sometimes the winner is not the most talented comic but the crowd pleaser who does hack song parodies on his guitar. "What if the *Brady Bunch* sang rap?!" Yeah, what if you had some jokes? Check our Web site for the dates and up-to-the-minute info on comedy festivals and writers' contests.

Writing Contests

There are hundreds of writing contests, workshops, and competitions in the United States, including all forms of comedy writing—plays, short stories, sitcoms, and screenplays. There are also many festivals that specialize. For instance, the Moondance International Film Festival is a competition for women screenwriters, filmmakers, playwrights, and short-story writers. The Detroit Black Writers Guild offers training and support to African American authors, sponsors an annual conference, and awards literary prizes. Go to our Web site at *www.comedyworkshopS.com* for listings of contests for comedy writers.

Comedy Festivals

Comedy festivals have become schmooze fests where comics and comedy writers network with other funny people, trade information, and rub elbows with industry types.

- *The U.S. Comedy Arts Festival,* in Aspen (around March), also known as the Aspen Comedy Festival, is put on by HBO. It's mostly a festival for high-level comics and the VIPs who Learjet in to see, ski, and schmooze. Besides presenting new talent to the industry, they honor the stars of comedy. They've done a Monty Python reunion, a tribute to Robin Williams, and a *Smothers Brothers Show* reunion, where they brought back all the original writers. If you can afford it and can find a hotel room, this high-end festival is a must-see.

> **PRO TALK** *with Judi Brown, talent booker for the U.S. Comedy Arts Festival*
>
> "I see over two thousand acts a year, both nationally and internationally—including stand-up, sketch, improv, theater pieces, and so on. I think that everybody sees somebody like me as just sitting in the back of the club with her arms folded—judging and jaded. Not true. I'm totally inspired with what I do for a living. There is nothing in the world that would please me more than if you were an absolute knock-out. When you're good, you make my job a lot easier. When I come back from Iowa, I have to pitch to my boss what I've found. If I come back and say, 'There was nothing there,' then I didn't do my job right. For us it's always about building relationships with talent and finding talent that we can nurture."

- *The Just for Laughs Montreal International Comedy Festival.* This is the biggest comedy festival in the world. It presents eight hundred artists, fifteen hundred shows, twenty countries, and takes place usually the last two weeks of July. This bilingual event presents everything from up-and-coming new faces to established stars of the business from North America as well as from the U.K., Ireland, Scotland, South Africa, Australia, New Zealand, Trinidad, and Holland.

<u>PRO TALK</u> *with Bruce Hills, Just for Laughs chief operating officer*

Judy: What comics get to be in the festival?

Bruce: If you've been doing open mikes for a couple of years, that's probably a little green for our festival.

Judy: Is there a lot of Industry at the festival?

Bruce: There are a handful of shows that are specifically programmed for the industry. The industry is looking for distinctive, funny comedians with something new to offer who can stand the pressure of having a TV show thrown on their shoulders, or at least to being a part of the cast. So, I'm not about to put people in the line of fire that aren't ready for that. Of course, there are the Dave Chappelles of the world. I saw his tape when he was seventeen and I said this guy is a superstar. He showed me four stand-up spots that were all different. Most comics send me the same stupid material on four sets trying to show me that they've been on four shows but also showing me they can't write more than eight minutes. Here's this kid that's brilliantly funny, original, who's not swearing.

Judy: You used a lot of words like *original, different,* and *distinctive.* Do you mean *what* they talk about, or *how* they talk about those subjects?

Bruce: It's both. There are some comics who have really wonderful, original deliveries, but when you *read* what they've just done on paper, it's not that brilliant. And then you have other people who have brilliant ideas but don't have a clue how to deliver it. They just stand there at a mike and bark out the material with no presentation and shitty clothes and three days of beard.

Judy: If a comic has been working out and they feel that they are ready, what do they do to get into the festival?

Bruce: We look at every single tape that comes in and we get anywhere from five hundred to eight hundred a year. We also go on the road and have a small staff in L.A. who screen comics for me to see on my trips to L.A. Plus, we go to New York a couple times a year, hold comedy competitions across Canada, and visit a handful of U.S. cities—Chicago, San Francisco, and Boston—every year.

Judy: Can you give some tips on what to do and what not to do on a videotape?

(continued)

Bruce: Have your tape reflect the type of material you do best. We have all kinds of different theme shows—gay, black, a nasty show, a Montreal show, a relationship show, a smart women's show . . . Know what your theme is and write it on the tape—"I have great *relationship* material, here's seven minutes of it." If you have a really crazy, dirty act and you're very good . . . *don't* send me the softened-down version, give me the best of what you do. If you're gay and you've got great gay material, don't send me the crossover set because you want to be booked on five shows instead of one. Show me the best gay material you have. There's a good chance that someone in the industry's going to be in every room that anyone performs at.

Judy: What about the quality of the tape?

Bruce: If you have a hard time understanding what the hell you're saying on a tape, how can you expect anyone else to get it? Don't send a tape like that to anyone. The sound should be clear, the picture should be pretty good, and you should be funny, *very* funny. If you use a camera that's stuck in the roof of a comedy club, don't run all over the stage so that you're out of half of the shots. Hire someone to shoot several of your performances over a period of a few days, then pick the best one and make plenty of copies of the tape. Sometimes I tell people, "You're really funny; send me a tape." And it comes in six weeks. It boggles my mind—in six weeks I can lose interest, forget, and book someone else. But if you don't think you're ready, don't send us a tape, because we'll probably write you off for a couple of years. We keep notes on every single person. I think we've got six or seven thousand notes in the computer. We can't see everyone, so if someone is shaking at the microphone and not original, we know they're not going to be a whole lot better in six months.

Judy: If you reject someone for one festival, do they have a chance for another one?

Bruce: Yes, as long as they're moving in the right direction. But they shouldn't send me the same tape that got them turned down—send me one that's a whole lot better. And if it takes three years to have a better one, then wait three years.

- *Big Stinkin Improv Festival,* Austin, Texas. BS is the largest annual improv and sketch comedy festival of its kind. Improv and sketch troupes from all over the world show their stuff to other performers, industry reps, and Texans. In addition, cutting-edge comics and Improv pros teach a variety of workshops. The festival is held in Austin, Texas, in October. Improv troupes can register online at *www.bigstinkin.com.*

■   *California Comedy Conference,* Palm Springs, California. Every year I hold a comedy workshop weekend where stand-up comics and comedy writers take classes, showcase, and network with industry professionals, such as agents, managers, studio executives, casting directors, producers, and top comedy coaches. Beginning comics and writers are welcome to attend. The comedy workshop weekend takes place in November. You can register at *www.comedyworkshopS.com.*

Showcasing for Comics

A showcase is a show produced by a comic or manager that is targeted to the industry. It's kind of like a debutante ball for comics—you're presenting yourself to the world, saying, "I'm good, I'm ready for the big time, and in ten minutes you're going to want me."

Showcases can be expensive and a lot of work. One way to keep the expenses down is to share your showcase with other comics of comparable ability. You have a better chance getting the industry out to see you and filling the audience with "normal" people when six or more comics are on the bill.

Six tips for producing a successful showcase:

1.   Hire a professional to design the flyers for your showcase. You don't want it to look like you're putting on an amateur night talent show. It doesn't matter how good you are if no one shows up.

2.   Mention in the flyer that there will be free food and drinks. It's a surefire way to get *lots* of industry people to your show. It's amazing what a bunch of rich people will do for free BBQ chicken wings and cosmopolitans.

3.   Make sure everyone who is anyone in the industry gets your flyer. In Los Angeles, the Breakdown Service *(www.breakdownservices.com)* will hand-deliver your promotional flyers or invitations to every active producer, agent, manager, and casting director in Los Angeles within seventy-two hours. This is the easiest way to get the word out. We do this at our workshop showcases at the Improv in L.A. and always get a good industry turnout.

4.   Fill the audience with civilians—nonindustry folks. Nothing is worse

than an audience of just industry people—they aren't known to be big laughers.

5. Even though this is a showcase, take risks with your material and be in the moment. Too often showcases come off dull because everyone is so overrehearsed that they lose their edge.

6. Professionally videotape the showcase. The next day call all the people who didn't show up and ask them if they would care to view the video.

Step 3:

Get Paid

"I've been doing a lot of stand-up and getting a good response. When is it time to quit my day job and do comedy full time?"

Generally, that depends on how easily you can adjust to being poor. The poorer and younger you are, the easier it is to do comedy full time because it doesn't entail a big change in your lifestyle. When you're in your forties and have a day job that pulls in the bucks, it's hard to give that up to live in an '86 Chevy Astro Van just so you can open for someone in Kansas.

PRO TALK *with Richard Jeni*

"I kept doing comedy even when I was bombing because I felt there was nothing else I could do. It was kind of like the film *An Officer and a Gentleman*—'I have no place else to go!' That kind of melodrama in your own mind is helpful. It's so hard at the beginning that if you feel you have other options you'll probably take them. But if you back yourself into a corner psychologically, like this is the last stop, there's no place else to go, then you'll stick with it."

Many comedy performers and writers work for free for many, many years before they see a paycheck. Screenwriter/director Nora Ephron wrote ten scripts that never got made before one of her unused screenplays drew the attention of ICM's Sam Cohn, who was looking for a writer to turn Karen Silkwood's life into a movie for Meryl Streep.

I was fortunate. When I was twenty-two, I got fired from my first job, as a high school teacher. This made me desperate—which was good. I had always had an act and had performed at frat parties and temple mixers throughout college. But I had given up performing the two years I spent teaching because I didn't have the time or energy. Being fired was the best thing that could have happened to me and my career. It was 1974, before the comedy club boom, and Playboy Clubs were the main venue for comics. When I called up the local Playboy Club to audition, they told me to talk to their talent booker, Irvin Arthur. I called him—a lot—but never got a return call. So I naively went to his office with my little magic act. I told his secretary, "Hello, I'm a magician/comedian and I would like to work at the Playboy Club." She told me that he never saw anyone without an appointment. So I sat in the reception area for five hours. Mr. Arthur must have felt sorry for me because he finally came out and invited me into his office. I did my act for him, right there in his office, and that night I had a gig at the L.A. Playboy Club—I got $50 and dinner! When Irvin quit his job, he became a manager—my manager—and he kept me working forty-five weeks a year for five years. Desperation can make you very determined.

Being ready means that not only is your work good but you are willing to put your butt on the line.

PRO TALK *with Michelle Marx, publicist*

"You have to keep going past the rejection. Don't take it to heart. When you put yourself out there it can make you feel naked. It helps to sometimes look at yourself as a business."

"How do I know if I am good enough to come to L.A. and get an agent?"

Even though you might be winning comedy contests, or your English teacher in Tuscaloosa, Alabama, thinks your scripts are really funny, don't immediately rush off to L.A. or New York. Mega manager Bernie Brillstein wisely suggests that new comics not show their act to any industry people until they are *better* than the competition. "If you are a kid from Ohio, then look at the competition in Cleveland. If you are better than anyone there, take a step out and go to New York to work at a few comedy clubs. If you still think you are good there, then believe me, someone will find you in a club or in L.A. You are not going to be discovered in Cleveland, but wait until you are ready."

For writers, the best way to get good is to keep writing, script after script, story after story, joke after joke. For comics, the road is the best place to work out your material. Comic Rocky LaPorte spent forty weeks a year on the road until he got a TV pilot and development deal with CBS. LaPorte won the Johnnie Walker comedy contest and signed with an agent, but it was four years before he felt he was ready to tackle L.A.

PRO TALK *with comic Rocky LaPorte*

"Everyone was telling me to go to L.A. and get on TV. I didn't do it because I knew l wasn't ready for L.A. I stayed on the road for four more years until I felt I was ready. You are ready when you have developed some depth and character, and can work *any* crowd. You have to bomb to succeed. Some comics spend all their time honing a ten-minute set that only works in New York. Then they go to Nashville, where their chunk on subways doesn't work because Nashville doesn't have subways. You have to know how to work *all* the states. The road is like college and you need it like an education."

Getting Paid Tip #1: Represent Yourself

Your First Agent Is You

In the beginning stages of a career you will meet agents who will want to represent or manage you. Very often these people have the same client list as Woody Allen's character in *Broadway Danny Rose*—plate spinners, dog acts, and a guy whose claim to fame is snorting nickels up his nose and out his mouth. (True story: my first agent.) These guys can sometimes bring you a couple of extra bucks, but in order to become successful before osteoporosis sets in, you need to get a really *good* agent.

Wouldn't it be great to have someone who looks after every detail of your career? Someone who can get you stage time and who knows what's going on in the business? Someone to negotiate your contracts and make sure that the checks don't bounce? Someone whose sole focus in life is making sure that you succeed? Guess what? Not only does this person exist, but you are about to sign on with him. Who is this agent extraordinaire? Take a look in the mirror.

If you are serious about a career in comedy, you must form your own agency—an agency that represents the interests of only one client: you. You will never get more personal attention than when you are the *only* client. And if you're working on commission and have only one client, you're going to do everything possible to try to get that client work so you can pay your bills.

"But I don't know anything about the business. Shouldn't my first step be getting a real agent?"

No. The first step is becoming really good at what you do *and* learning how to represent *yourself.* Eventually, you will have to *represent* yourself to an agent, so you must know how to sell yourself.

Most of us grow up with the dream that someone will discover us—recognize our talent and remove the burden of having so much unrealized potential. Women especially fall victim to this "Someday my prince will come" sort of thinking. If you think someone is going to come along and take over the business end of things so that you can just be creative, you're living in fantasyland. Repeat after me: "Nobody is coming." Nobody with half a brain is going to work that hard to get 10 percent of the kind of money you'll be lucky to earn right now. You want to be discovered? Discover yourself. Sign yourself. Represent yourself. Become the agent you've dreamed of getting.

"But Judy, practically all successful comics and writers have agents and managers."

Yes, they do. But all of them had something going on that interested an agent *before* that agent signed them. And that something they created for themselves. Even big stars can't afford to totally turn things over to someone else. The entertainment trade papers are filled with stories about big stars going bankrupt because they turned their businesses and careers over to agents and managers who then mismanaged their affairs. Garry Shandling sued his manager and friend, Brad Grey, for $100 million, alleging that Grey improperly leveraged his relationship with Shandling to benefit his other business interests and clients. Grey countersued Shandling for $10 million, accusing Shandling of "aberrant and irresponsible behavior." Every agent and manager's number one client is themselves, so if you want to be top dog, you have to look out for your own interests and not trust someone else to do it.

Even if you get a good agent who has a lot of connections, unless you personally nurture and maintain those contacts, you'll lose them when you lose the agent—and you will lose an agent (or ten) over the course of your career. Agents use the "Let's throw everything against the wall and see what sticks" policy. They court you, sign you, and then, if *you* don't get something going, dump you.

PRO TALK *with Phyllis Diller*

"If an agent had a brain in his ass he'd be doing it himself. An agent doesn't want you until you're making at least $5,000 a week. An agency doesn't want you until you are making a million a week. They are interested in one thing, money. They are not in the business of developing talent. You are. You are the only one who is ever going to know what is right for you."

"Changing agents is like rearranging the deck chairs on the *Titanic*."

—ANONYMOUS

"Don't people need to have relatives in the business?"

It helps to a certain point. People will give a relative or a friend a break, but if you don't have the talent, drive, and business savvy to back up a nepotistic opportunity, you'll never be more than so-and-so's cousin. Look what being related to a star did for the acting careers of Sly Stallone's and Tom Hanks's brothers. Didn't know that they had brothers in the business? You get my point.

Starting Your Own Comedy Management Business

In the eighties, I dumped my never-return-a-call agent and decided that I would manage my own career. I created the management firm of Keller-Stevens. I made it legal by getting a DBA (doing business as) and hired a professional to design my logo, contracts, and stationery. My manager's name became "Pam Keller." Pam was tough as nails, with a heavy New York accent and a no-nonsense approach to booking her favorite and only client—me. Putting people on hold was an important component of looking like a successful management firm. Radio Shack supplied me with a hold button and Muzak for my phone. I developed the character of Pam's secretary, "Doris," in my improv class. Doris was a bit ditsy but had all the charm that Pam lacked. "Keller-Stevens Management, may I help you?" Of course, all of these characters were really me, sitting in my bathrobe in my converted garage and talking in different voices.

Keller-Stevens Management (nobody, including me, ever knew who "Stevens" was) got me a lot of work. I remember one club owner saying, "Pam, saw Judy when I was in L.A. and I don't think she has any talent." Any other agent would have offered the club owner another client: "If you don't like Judy, what about Rita Rudner?" But Pam didn't take no for an answer. "How could you judge her when she was trying out new material?" Pam scolded him. "Look at her videotape at least. Do you think I'd waste my time managing her if she wasn't brilliant!" Cut to—Pam got me the job.

Pam reached the peak of her career when I was playing in Indianapolis. David Letterman called the club asking about the mysterious Pam Keller, whom he had never met. But this deception became too confusing when other comics called and asked Pam to manage them too. It was also difficult when Pam and Judy had to be in the same place. Pam was the only manager in history who never "did lunch" with anyone. This method of representing yourself is recommended only to those with a strong sense of adventure and several personalities. The rest of you will probably do better using the buddy method.

You and your comedy buddy go into the management business together and make calls on each other's behalf. This works especially well if the two of you are not competing for the same jobs. For instance, one of you is a performer and the other is a writer, or you are different genders. It's a lot easier selling someone other than yourself.

<u>Pro Talk</u> *with Richard Jeni*

"I have a corporation. It is not a company in the sense that you can drive by the Richard Jeni building in downtown L.A., but I am incorporated. Which is ironic because one of the reasons people become comedians is to avoid traditional business activities. But the minute you become even a little successful, suddenly you find yourself running a company and having employees. A person chooses to have a company because they want to operate at a certain level. I spend a tremendous amount of time dealing with people, publicity, money, and managers and agents and all that crap. Your first goal is becoming successful, and your second goal is trying not to fall off your perch and go back down."

Setting Up Your Company

Whether you are starting your business alone or with a buddy, you will need to make it official by registering your company, creating a mission statement, and having proper contracts, stationery, and basic office equipment. This is not an unusual practice. Most successful performers form their own companies to create, develop, and produce projects for themselves. If you're sitting there whining, "But, I'm just not the business type," heed the wise words of Joan Rivers—"Grow up!"

Getting a Name

Your company name should reflect what you do. Mine is Comedy Workshop Productions. Pretty clear about what it is that we do. My friend Carmen McKay is a corporate humorist and her company name says it all, Corporate Comedy. You don't have to be as literal as I was, but your company name should reflect your tone or style. David Letterman's company is Worldwide Pants. The name reflects his irreverent style. Garry Shandling is obsessed with his hair. Name of his company—How's My Hair?

Exercise: Creating Your Company Name

You don't want your company name to limit you. For instance, if you want to do dramatic acting as well as stand-up comedy, you probably don't want your company name to be Butt Funny Inc. This exercise will help you explore *all* possibilities before deciding on a company name.

Do a mind map (see page 183 on how to mind map) of your career. Put what you currently like doing the most in the center balloon. Then write down all the offshoots. Keep creating circles, and include all of your career hopes and dreams. When you think you're finished, push yourself to go further. Spend at least two days on this. Then play with the words on the page and whatever other words come to mind to find the right name for your company.

Write the name of your company here:

_____

Create a Mission Statement

A mission statement describes the services, intentions, and possibilities of your company. It should include what you do and what you plan on doing.

My friend Carmen McKay, who created the company Corporate Comedy, guided me and my "staff" (my comedy buddy and my assistant) in coming up with the mission statement for my company. The three of us wrote down words that described what the company did as well as ideas about what we could do in the future. On a bulletin board, we tacked up forty-five little pieces of paper—each with a descriptive word—and then narrowed them down to the most important ones: *comedy, books, workshop, projects, inspire, educate, transform, film, theater, TV, clubs, Internet, laughter, entertainment worldwide, authenticity.* After a little rearranging we ended up with our mission statement:

> Comedy Workshop Productions creates comedy projects that inspire, educate, and transform others in the mediums of film, theater, TV, clubs, books, the Internet, and workshops where people learn how to spread laughter and entertainment throughout the world coming from their own authenticity.

Making It Legal

Once you've decided on your company name and mission statement, it's time to make it official by filing a fictitious business name statement with the city clerk's office. This is also called a DBA (doing business as). Rules are different depending what city you live in, but in Los Angeles, it costs approximately $10 and you have to file a fictitious business name statement with a newspaper and run it for a week. Call around because some papers are cheaper than others. Some newspapers specialize in doing the filing for you.

"Why do I need to get so legal-schmegal with all of this?"

You may not be *Dreamworks,* but you are going to be issuing contracts using your company name, and if there is any trouble in collecting money, you need to make sure that you've crossed your *T*s and dotted your *I*s.

Office Hours

All businesses need regular hours. If you have been working on getting good, you probably have regular writing hours. Now you need to also schedule, and commit to keeping, regular office hours—even if your day job is an office job.

Office Equipment

Get yourself the basics:

- phone with an answering service
- pager/cell phone
- Internet service and e-mail
- fax/copier
- computer/printer

Signing Your First Contract

Sign up your management company's first artist—yourself. Then make sure that artist pays you. Managers get 15 percent of their clients' gross income. Use that money to pay for phone calls, Internet services, office equipment, and other items and services that will enable your company to grow.

Write down the specific career goals you will achieve for your client (you), such as "book open mikes to develop his craft," "create showcases," "make showbiz big shots aware of him," "focus on booking the corporate market." Make it official by writing out a contract of intent, and then sign it. Congrats, you have just signed your first client.

Getting Paid Tip #2: Diversify

The first question anyone in power will ask is, "What has she done?" "Nothing" is not a good answer. It's hard to find someone in Hollywood who will give a job to an unknown. Showbiz big shots are more likely to pay attention to you if someone else in showbiz has already noticed you.

"But Judy, this sounds like a catch-22. Nobody will give me a break unless someone else gives me a break. What should I do?"

It costs *a lot* of money to produce a TV show and no one is going to risk those millions on an unknown. However, there are other respected fields that welcome newcomers and will give you that all-important first break—theater, radio, public access TV, the Internet. Nowadays it's not enough to just be a stand-up comic or a sitcom writer. You have to diversify, expand into other fields. That way, when you finally do meet with a powerful agent, manager, or producer, you'll be able to say, "I'm a stand-up comic and I'm *also* a published writer, I have a regular spot on a radio show, and I'm making a buck on the college market. I would like to show you my comedy reel. It's a compilation of shorts that I wrote, produced, starred in, and directed, which is airing today on channel 52." This gives an agent something to work with.

PRO TALK *with Michelle Marx, publicist*

"Stay aware of what's going on around you that might provide clever opportunities. Be timely. I pitched a show about Richard Lewis giving 'wrong advice' on Valentine's Day to MTV and they went for it. We had people write in weeks ahead for wrong advice. It got a few weeks of MTV airtime for him and reinforced his persona to our target market."

Become a Produced Playwright

Can't get anyone to read your sitcom scripts? Produce them yourself as plays. In 1984 I wrote, produced, and starred in a musical with a cast of eight, *Goddess of Mystery*. When my play got rave reviews in the *L.A.*

Times, L.A. Weekly, and *Variety,* the phone started to ring. I was called in to audition for TV parts. *The Merv Griffin Show* (a talk/variety show of the seventies and eighties) booked me to perform a part of the play, and Warner Bros. TV offered me a development deal to convert the play into a sitcom. Not bad results for just renting a ninety-nine-seat theater.

PRO TALK *with Ellen Sandler, executive producer of* Everybody Loves Raymond, Coach, *and many others*

"I got into sitcoms by writing and coproducing a one-act play with two actors. One of them was living with Danny DeVito at the time and he brought everyone down from *Taxi* (the hit TV sitcom) to see it, and I got hired to write for *Taxi* with my partner."

Whether you are doing a one-person show or have a cast of many, workshop your project before you take it public. Director/manager Irene Penn took Sherry Glaser's one-person show *Family Secrets* on the road for three and a half years before she felt it was ready to go to New York. And how do you know when something is ready? Ms. Penn says, "It's instinct. After workshopping your project, take it to venues that have similar audiences. Since we wanted to end up with a New York show, we took the play to Miami, Fort Lauderdale, Coconut Grove, because most of the people there are retired ex–New Yorkers."

PRO TALK *with Irene Penn, producer/director*

Judy: What's better, doing a play in Los Angeles or New York?

Irene: Los Angeles has a certain mold for actresses. If you look like Candy Bergen, you are ready for L.A. If you don't fit into that mold, then take the play to New York because they look beyond appearances to deeper emotional issues. If you are doing an edgy piece, you'll get noticed there.

Become a Published Writer by Having Your Work Appear in Newspapers, Magazines, and Trade Newsletters

Being published is very prestigious and none too difficult. A weekly column is a great way to publicize yourself. Every profession has trade magazines. Determine which ones your target audience reads and write a humor piece for them. For instance, I wrote an article for the *Jewish Journal.* In the byline I included my contact info, phone number, and e-mail, and I ended up getting all the temple mixers I could stand. Hey, it's a living. Dave Barry started by writing a humor column for the local paper. It attracted attention and was rerun elsewhere. One thing led to many others. In 1983 he joined the staff of the *Miami Herald.* He's also written over twenty humor books and won a Pulitzer Prize for commentary journalism.

PRO TALK *with Cindy Chupack, producer/writer*

"I submitted a personal essay to a New York magazine and it got published. My TV writing career was launched when a sitcom producer saw that piece. I eventually got a staff job on the sitcom *Coach.* Years later my essays, which I had continued writing, were key in getting me the job on HBO's *Sex in the City.* I had written *Coach* and *Everybody Loves Raymond,* but the only sample that could show them that I could do this show were these essays about dating and sexual ethics. It was those essays that got me the job of co–executive producer." *(Note.* Ms. Chupack was nominated for an Emmy for her work on *Sex in the City.)*

Self-Publish Your Own Book

You don't have to wait for Simon & Schuster or some other big publishing house to publish your book because you can self-publish it or get your work published on-line. Authors generally receive royalties of 7 to 10 percent of paperback sales from major publishers. Self-publishers, on the other hand, can see as much as a 50 percent return on investment; however, that means that the author has to pay in advance for the bookbinding, artwork, publicity, and editing. There are also Internet sites such as *www.fatbrain.com* that will sell what you write over their Web site and take a percentage. For more information on the self-publishing market, a good resource book is Dan Poynter's *The Self-Publishing Manual* (Para Publishing, $19.95).

Produce Your Own CD

Workshop student Amy Borkowsky thought that her overly protective mother's messages on her answering machine were so funny that she played them in her stand-up act. When audience members requested copies of them, she produced a CD of them and created a Web site *(www.sendamy.com)*. Amy eventually took time off from her day job to promote the CD and got a lot of radio stations to play portions of it. Cut to—Amy featured in *Life, Jane, Mademoiselle, Newsday,* and on the *Today Show, Lifetime,* and MSNBC. In one year she has sold over a hundred thousand copies of her CD and received offers to develop a sitcom based on her relationship with her mom. As Amy told me, "I didn't do it for the money. The money just showed up. I did it because I really believed in the project and it became a passion for me."

Producing your act or short stories on CD is cheap and something you can do on your computer with the right software. (See our Web page for details on producing your own CD.) CDs cost about fifty cents each and are a great addition to your PR package as well as a great source of revenue.

Become a Regular Guest on the Radio

Comic Robin Roberts was hired as a writer and voice performer for DJ Rick Dees at Los Angeles radio station KIIS FM through sheer luck. "Rick's producer came across my picture and résumé, called me, and asked me to record a bit with him over the phone. He liked it, and invited me to join the Cast of Idiots, Rick's staff of radio comics. I got $50 for each piece I wrote and an additional $50 for performing it. Best of all, I could do the job over the phone in my underwear."

Be the Star of Your Own Public Access TV Show

Have an idea for a TV show but no one will buy it? Do it yourself. Public access really provides the best opportunity for someone who doesn't have the Hollywood package—the agent, financing, and so forth—but is dedicated. With enough time, chutzpah, and sometimes money, anybody can produce a show. People do watch—sometimes even the right people.

In 1992, Colin Malone, a struggling stand-up comic, and his friend Dino Everett were working at a video store in L.A. when they decided to create a half-hour public access show. *Colin's Sleazy Friends* has hit cult rage status and is now one of the most talked about in southern California, with mainstream celebrities such as Drew Carey and Janeane Garofalo joining porno stars and weird acts. It is one of the few access programs that air in a regular weekly time slot—Wednesdays at midnight, taking away viewers from Letterman and Leno. And now with the help of the True Blue Network and satellite television, millions view it worldwide.

Check with your local public access station for their production procedures.

Produce, Direct, Star in, and Distribute Your Own Comedy Videos

You want to write, act, and direct? So do it. The price of high-quality digital video equipment is rapidly dropping, which means anyone can start their own comedy production company and distribute their videos via the Internet. Trey Parker and Matt Stone of *South Park* fame created a short Christmas cartoon that they sent as a Christmas video to Hollywood Studios. Cut to—a deal with the Comedy Channel. Writer Eric Kaplan created an Internet animated series for Icebox.com, *Zombie College.* The series was then bought by Fox Broadcasting Company, marking the first time a show created for the Net has been purchased by a major television network. After Gene Laufenberg's dark-comedy ten-minute film *Sunday's Game* premiered on ifilm.com, Laufenberg signed a two-picture deal with Fox 2000.

Become a Star in the College Market

The college market books acts based on talent, not connections. Anyone can submit a tape to the NACA (National Association of Campus Activities, *www.naca.org*) or the smaller APCA (Association for the Promotion of College Activities, *www.apca.com*). Both organizations arrange showcases directly with the college buyers; they have regional conferences; plus they both meet once a year at a national conference. Campus buyers attend the showcases looking for entertainers, agencies, presenters, and services for their school programs. Performers can submit a video after completing an application and sending in a fee. The organizers at the NACA are obligated to watch at least the first three minutes of every tape submitted;

the APCA will watch twenty minutes of each tape and return all fees if you are not selected. There are also special college agents who represent comics. They generally take a cut of 15 to 30 percent of the fee. They look for clean one-hour acts that are aimed at the seventeen-to-twenty-two age range. For more information see the Appendix at the back of this book.

PRO TALK *with Bruce Smith, president of Omnipop Talent Agency*

"Most college comics audition for the college market through an agent but a lot of comics represent themselves. The selection committee is basically locked in a room for a week and goes through all the tapes. It leans more to the conservative than you'd think."

Become a Successful Corporate Humorist

Every day there are business meetings in your area that hire entertainers. If you have material that would be appropriate for a certain company, contact that company directly. One of my students was the greeter at Banana Republic. She based her stand-up act on her job. I suggested that she ask her boss to let her do five minutes at their next corporate meeting. She killed and went on to do national Banana Republic meetings for the big bucks. Another student, Ann Lippert, had a routine about shopping at Home Depot. She submitted her tape and got a gig at their Christmas party.

When calling a company make sure you are giving your spiel to the right person. Ask for the *event planner.* Usually someone in Human Resources will know who that person is.

Submit Jokes to Greeting Card Companies

Many greeting card companies pay for jokes and create the artwork themselves. There are many card companies on-line, such as *bluemountain.com* and *kinkycards.com.* Contact each company to find out their submission procedure.

Getting Paid Tip #3: Get Professional Contacts

It's nice if your aunt Edith thinks your spec script is really funny, but it's fantastic if the executive producer of a hit NBC sitcom feels that way. Unfortunately, big shots will return a call only if

- you're a name who's already making gobs of money
- they saw your schtick or read your script and liked you
- you're introduced to them by someone they know and respect
- you're a relative
- you're a friend of a relative
- you're a friend of a friend
- you give sexual favors freely

"There are never any industry VIPs in the audience on open-mike night at Shakey's Pizza Parlor, and my relatives are all in the heavy farm equipment business. How will I ever get an introduction to a big shot?"

There are only six degrees of separation between you and the head of comedy development at ABC. The trick is to find the right six people.

"But shouldn't I get a **real** *agent first before I approach these people?"*

The people who are your six degrees of separation can be agents, but most successful people make things happen *before* they get an agent. You're much more attractive to an agent if some VIPs are already nuts about you.

PRO TALK *with Rob Lotterstein*

(When sitcom writer Rob Lotterstein was just starting out, he wanted to find a professional working writer to read his spec script.) "I called Jeff Stepakoff, who was a working TV writer. I met him because my friend Larry had a friend named Mark. Mark was friends with this guy David, and David's girlfriend's best friend, Michelle, grew up with Jeff. I got his number from Michelle and said I was Michelle's friend. He was very happy to hear from me, read my script, gave me tips, and introduced me to other people in the industry. Everyone is connected to someone in the industry."

Warning! Don't do the "Six Degrees of Separation" exercise (page 328) until you are ready and are really good, otherwise you will burn contacts—fast.

PRO TALK *with Richard Lewis*

"My first break was meeting David Brenner at the Improv in New York and we became fast friends. He taught me a lot about the business and kept me from foolishly burning bridges. He advised me to wait six months before coming to the Improv and to go perform in some of these hellholes. I would drive hours to do five or ten minutes—and do it night after night. After six months I did an open-mike night at the Improv and I was head and shoulders above the rest of the group. Don't burn your bridges needlessly. Give yourself some time to perfect your craft."

When you go after the big shots, make sure you have your persona nailed and your material down. When David Letterman was working the Comedy Store in Hollywood, he was managed by Buddy Morra. Buddy would watch Letterman's act every night and wouldn't let anyone see him for years. He made sure he had developed his own style and felt confident before he brought any VIPs to see him.

PRO TALK *with David Letterman, talking in* Esquire *about Jay Leno's impact on his work*

"Well, you go to the Comedy Store night after night and you see these people, like yourself, floundering to develop an identity. One night I saw a guy named Jay Leno onstage [and] I thought I just might as well go home. Because his attitude and his style were so crystallized and so right on the money and he had such good observations. I mean his entire life and existence seemed to be a set-up and then he would provide the perfect punchline. I thought, 'Jeez, that's the way it ought to be done.' So I really started patterning my material after him."

Warning! Do not contact big shots until you are ready. Look at all contacts as a one-shot deal—blow it and you don't get a second chance. So make sure you are ready to give it your best shot.

PRO TALK *with Cindy Chupack, producer/writer*

"Sometimes when I've really critiqued a script the writer will say, 'Can I give it to you again after I do the rewrite?' Then it becomes this ongoing job for me. When you give someone a script, that's your one shot, and just take whatever advice or critique they can give you. If they like it, try to find out if there's anybody else that they think you should send it to. But unless they offer to read a rewrite, don't ask them to read it a second time."

Exercise: Six Degrees of Separation Game

Ask or e-mail all of your friends, relatives, acquaintances, and one-night stands for any information about *anybody* that they might know in the entertainment industry. Spend some time working on your approach so you seem professional. They might not know anyone but might know someone who knows someone who knows someone. Any tip or introduction will help.

Gather your contacts and call them. Look at it this way. If you really are that good, you're doing them a favor, since discovering you makes them look real good.

Getting Paid Tip #4: How to Get Big Shots on the Phone

Have you ever been frightened to call up someone? Phone phobia is normal. Sure, it's easy when you're making a request on someone else's behalf, but self-promotion is hard. Yet you must make an attempt to build personal relationships with the movers and shakers in show business. That means you have to get off your ass and get on the phone—but don't be an ass on the phone.

Getting Past the Secretary

This is one of the weirdest ways I bypassed the secretary.

ME: This is Judy Carter. I would like to talk to Mr. Big Shot, please.
SECRETARY: Can I tell him what this is regarding?
ME: I need to talk to him personally. It's regarding his lab test results.

Faster than I could say "herpes," I was on the phone with Mr. Big Shot. But misrepresenting yourself can open a whole other can of worms. Honesty is the best policy.

Here are some tips on calling the big shots, from my publicist and friend Michelle Marx:

- Don't go barging into people's offices. "Hello, Security?"
- Don't be overly annoying.
- Remember that everyone's very busy. If someone doesn't pay attention to you, don't take it personally. Realize they are busy or don't care—*yet.* Don't get bent out of shape and mail them a dead rat just because they didn't return your twenty phone calls. You might not have a life, but they do.
- Be pleasantly persistent. Keep up a stream of e-mails, press releases, flyers, and faxes, but make sure they are professional, to the point, and friendly. Then give the people freedom to respond in their own time, even if it does take a couple of years. At least you are getting your name out there.

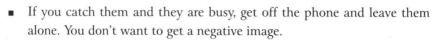

- If you catch them and they are busy, get off the phone and leave them alone. You don't want to get a negative image.
- Have your six-degrees-of-separation person call the big shot first and rave about you. If your contact won't do that but said that you can use her name, then use it all that you can. That contact—who is the second cousin of your ex-boyfriend, who lives around the block from your high school algebra teacher—is not just an acquaintance but your best friend. "Hello, my name is Joe Nobody and I was referred by my good friend Susie Somebody. I believe that Mr. Big Shot is expecting my call."
- And finally, to get to Ms. or Mr. Big Shot, become best friends with the secretary. Treat all secretaries as if they are the most important people in the world, because at this point in your career, they are. All showbiz secretaries are moguls in training. It's to their benefit if they find the next big comedy star and bring her to their boss's attention.

Finding the Right Agent

Trying to find the right business agent, manager, or producer for your career is as difficult as marrying the right person. There has to be chemistry. Not everyone will like you. When I first attempted to get an agent for my first book—*Stand-up Comedy: The Book* (Dell Books, 1989)—I was rejected by everyone. And I do mean everyone. They all told me the same thing: "This book has too narrow a focus." But I found an out-of-work book agent in my Weight Watchers meeting who liked the project. She submitted it to every publisher and it was rejected by everyone—except one. The book is currently in its seventeenth printing and has had a shelf life of over twelve years. It only takes one person. You have to find that one person.

Before you approach an agency, research the company. Know everything about them—their clients, their successes, their failures. Not everyone is right for you and you have to know which agents will represent your "brand."

PRO TALK *with Bruce Smith, president of Omnipop Agency*

"My preference is for them [comics] to approach us knowing as much about the company as possible. I am flattered and immediately become stupid. 'Gee, I had no idea you knew so much about us . . . ' I'm just ga-ga that somebody actually did their homework. Half the time, people send out form letters, head shots, and tapes to a million places, and there's nothing personal about it. It's like a hooker offering to sleep with you."

Exercise: Selling Yourself to an Agency

Before you pitch yourself to a manager or an agent, you need to see yourself as they do—a commodity. In this exercise, you are going to recreate an agency's staff meeting where they decide on new clients.

Gather four or five friends and have them pretend to be agents at a staff meeting. You're going to pretend to be an agent as well, someone who just saw your act or read your material, and you're going to pitch why fellow agents should sign you up. It could sound like this: "I just saw this comic who is doing some very edgy material that really appeals to a young audience. A lot of his material is about being a high school teacher and I can see sending him out on the college circuit to develop his material and then cashing in on him in a sitcom—sort of a cross between *Friends* and *Welcome Back, Kotter.*"

Have your fellow agents ask questions about this prospective client, such as

- How are you going to make money with him/her?
- What is his/her vision of where he/she wants to go?
- What's his/her overall attitude?

If you find it hard to pitch yourself, you might find it easier to start this exercise by pitching someone who is established. If you just saw a new comic named Robin Williams, how would you go about pitching him?

What to Do When You Get a Big Shot on the Phone

When speaking to Mr. Important Person Who Can Change the Course of Your Career, do you ever feel stupid? When you get off the phone do you want to slam your head into a trash compactor? Then before you dial that number, you better plan what you're going to say after "hello."

Carter's 7 Steps to Successful Negotiations

1. When you call a VIP, have a short and witty introduction of who you are and what you want, mentioning the person who recommended you. Practice with a friend before you make the call. Do *not* make any big requests at this point, such as, "I want you to sign me to your agency." You can say, "I want people such as yourself to be aware of what I'm doing because I'm looking for representation." Or, "I'm looking to get into the college market."

2. Ask them, "What are your concerns?" This will create an opening for them to give you the negatives, which is important information for you to have.

3. Repeat their concerns to them. *Never* defend, and never address their concerns. Instead, mirror them. For instance, let's say Big Shot says, "There isn't a lot of work for women in your age range." It's very difficult not to take this sort of comment personally, but rather than defending yourself, mirror their concern back to them. "So, you don't think there are jobs in my age range? Is that what you mean?" Resist the temptation to defend ("But there are a lot of women getting work in my age group"). Everyone wants to be heard and taken seriously. Very often, once someone really believes that you've heard what they said, their concern vanishes. If you can truly mirror someone's concerns back to them it makes you powerful—as long as you do it without whining, crying, or defending. By the way, this also works well with *any* relationship. Go for complete understanding first.

4. Empty them of their concerns. "Do you have any *other* concerns?" "I'm very busy now and have a stack of papers on my desk and don't even have time to look at new people." And mirror those concerns back, "I get that you are an extremely busy person."

5. Only *after* you have emptied Mr. Big Shot of his concerns do you rephrase what you want, *taking into consideration their concerns.* "I get that you are very busy. I could send you my short, eight-minute video, which would knock your socks off. Then, if you want to see more, I could send you the longer one. I find that there is a large market for what I do, especially because I'm getting a buzz from my weekly radio show and my column in the *Pasadena Weekly.*"

6. Go in for a request. Make this a small request. "Would you be willing to

watch my video?" "Can I put you on the comp list for my show?" It would *not* be appropriate to ask in an initial conversation, "Will you represent me?" or, "Would you invest in my project?" Go for something that can get an easy yes.

7. Make your request time and date specific: "I will messenger my tape over this afternoon." Push for a specific time and date: "How about if I call you on Friday at two P.M.?" How many times have you got off the phone with someone who sounded really enthusiastic and then nothing happened? You probably got a "Hollywood no." Unless you get a time and date commitment for the next step, they might as well have said no.

Here is a real-world example where I used this technique and I went from "concerns" to signed contract in fifteen minutes.

It was a job for a one-hour concert at a women's business group in Sacramento. They liked my tape, but were dragging their feet about booking me.

These were Ms. Big Shot's concerns: "Judy, we like what you do but quite frankly, last time we had a comic, we really didn't have a very big turnout."

I mirrored her. "So, you're concerned that you're not going to get a big turnout and you're not going to sell tickets. Is that right?"

"Yes, it is."

"Any other concerns?"

"Well, we lost, quite frankly, we lost money last time."

I said, "Oh, how much money did you lose?"

And she said, "Well, we came out about seven hundred and fifty dollars short."

"OK, got it. Any other concerns?"

"No, that's it."

I then repitched, taking into consideration her concerns: "Well, in getting people to come, I can supply you with all the postcards and flyers plus a list of the places where they should be put. And how many people did you have come to the show last year?"

"Five hundred people."

"So, you had five hundred people come, and how much did the comic charge you?"

"The comic charged us last year fifteen hundred dollars."

I said, "And you lost seven-fifty."

She said, "Yes."

I said, "I'll tell you what . . . how about if I charge you seven hundred and fifty dollars less, so that if you have the exact same number of people come this year, you won't lose any money? So, I will only ask you for a guarantee of seven hundred and fifty dollars. Anything above and beyond that, I will take eighty percent of the door. Do you agree to this?"

"Yes, I agree."

I faxed her a contract and within fifteen minutes, I had a signed contract.

This way, I addressed her concerns, creating a win-win situation where she knew that she would not take a loss no matter what. End result—the concert was totally sold out and I came away with 80 percent of the door, amounting to $2,700 for my show. Both of us ended up extremely happy.

The Hollywood No

In Hollywood no one wants to blow someone off, because down the line, they might end up being a big star. You need to understand the dynamics of the Hollywood no. If someone says, "I'd love to watch your tape," but you can never get them on the phone again, most likely you've been given a Hollywood no. Stop calling them, but still pursue these people by keeping them in your information loop via e-mail and faxes. You never know when a Hollywood no will turn into a Hollywood maybe somewhere down the line.

> **PRO TALK** *with Judi Brown, talent coordinator for U.S. Comedy Arts Festival (Aspen)*
>
> "If somebody shows an interest in you, keep in contact with them. Send them a thank-you card. Send them an update. 'I'm doing this, I'm doing that . . . ' Nurture that relationship and always keep them in the loop. You never know when they might have something for you."

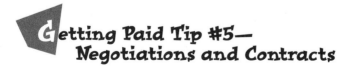

Getting Paid Tip #5— Negotiations and Contracts

Negotiating for yourself doesn't have to be a traumatic experience if you use the seven-step negotiation formula above.

"When someone wants me for a gig, how do I figure out what to charge them?"

There is no one right price for a gig. At the beginning of your career don't expect more than a burger. But if you are making people laugh and are fairly clean, someone will soon ask you how much you would charge to do your act at their event or to write something for them. Don't talk money until you're clear on what exactly it is they need and what their budget is.

1. Ask them what they want you to do before talking money and get them to be specific. If they say, "I want you to perform at a roast for my dad," questions should include

   - —How much time do you want me to do?
   - —Do you want me to also MC?
   - —Do you want me to write custom material?

2. Ask them, "What is your budget?" "We can give you $500." "My usual fee is $750. How firm are you? How about meeting me halfway? Do you have a budget to pay for my writing and MCing fees?"

3. If they won't budge on the money, go for some perks—not stock options, but small perks. If they won't give you more money, maybe they will give you an extra dinner for a friend, a hotel room, gas money, a hooker.

4. Fax or e-mail them a contract or a deal memo within fifteen minutes. Don't give people a chance to think and change their minds. You can download different contracts from my Web site at *www.comedyworkshopS.com.*

Getting Paid Tip #6: Turn One Job into Many

It takes a lot of work to get one gig. And just as you want to have many hits off one setup, you want to roll that one job into many.

1. Promote every job that you have. Club owners love comics who bring in customers. Inform the booker in writing of all the work that you are doing to promote the gig.

2. Book a return engagement *before* you leave. Even if it's a year away, don't leave without getting back into their calendar.

3. Request a "happy letter" from them to include in your PR kit. Make sure you send a SASE for their convenience. Sometimes after working at a corporate event, I get e-mailed compliments from people in the audience. I then ask them to fax me their blank stationery and permission to reprint their praises on their stationery to include in my PR kit.

4. Ask for referrals. If you did a good job for someone, ask them if they have any associations, friends, clients, and so on who would enjoy your act.

5. When performing out of town, send local agents, speaker bureaus, and college bookers free tickets to your show and schmooze with them afterward.

6. Write at least one thank-you note a week to the people in your life—your family, your friends, and that person on the street who gave you a quarter for the parking meter when you didn't have any change. Then move that appreciation to the people in your career. That agent who got you a job, the waitress who took the time to give you feedback on your act, the secretary who took the time to give you an address where to send your tape. The more you appreciate what you have, the more you will have. I am mentoring a fifteen-year-old high school student who has a lot of reasons to be resentful about her lot in life. She has no father and lived in one room in a motel in Compton with her four siblings and her mother, who was on welfare. By writing one thank-you note a week, she went from a whiner to a winner. Sometimes she's had to scour a dismal week to find that one person. But no matter how bad things were, when she looked hard enough, there was always someone to thank. She told me how people responded to her notes of appreciation: "They cry with happiness." She has learned a very important lesson in life—to get it, you have to give it.

Pro Talk *with Judi Brown, manager*

"A good friend of mine, George Lopez, just walked out of a comedy club with thirty-five thousand dollars. It was all about him building the [Hispanic] market, building the price in the market, and continuing to come back to a comedy club every six months. Find your market and do everything to promote yourself because club owners will continue to reward you if you can prove that you are a draw. Even if you're featuring [middle act], if you sell tickets and bring people into the club, the club owner will reward you and in years to come you could find yourself cutting eighty percent door deals."

And Finally . . .
How to Get All the Attention and Love You Could Ever Want

You want to get noticed? Notice others. If I did it all over again, one thing I would do differently would be to connect more and be more giving to others. When I started out, I was self-absorbed, needy, and insecure. Good qualities for comedy, bad for friendships. I viewed other comics as my competition rather than as my comrades. I didn't help them with their acts; I hoarded my audition tips as well as my accolades. I wasn't a bitch, I was just scared. Or maybe I was both.

Energy needs to flow from the comic *to* the audience. They've paid for *you* to give it to *them.* So many comics are so desperate for attention and jobs that they become energy vampires on and off the stage. They are looking outside themselves for fulfillment and compliments. Some even need the audience to *give* energy to them. But if a comic comes onto a stage or into an office *needing,* they will not get *anything.* And even if they do get something, it will never be enough. Have you ever had a great set but your focus was on the one sour face in the second row?

I learned on one cold, snowy New York night that taking the time to notice others is the key to *real* success.

I was the opening act at New York's Bottom Line for the Roches, a band that was on *Saturday Night Live* a lot. The audience was full of show-biz VIPs who schmoozed and talked loudly while I was onstage. I made some jokes about it to the civilians in the first row, but the big shots continued to talk during my act. And if that wasn't bad enough, when I got offstage I found out that the club owners had let these VIPs in and kept my seventy-five-year-old aunt Edith and her family standing in the snow outside. I went backstage in a fury. A woman asked me, "What's the matter, honey?" I burst out crying. She pulled me into a small backstage bathroom. This complete stranger sat on the toilet in this tiny New York cockroach-infested bathroom, holding me on her lap while I sobbed on her shoulder. "That's OK, honey. I know how hard it can be." When I looked up I realized, "Oh my God, you're Gilda Radner." At that time, Gilda was a big star on *Saturday Night Live.* She was there to introduce the band, but took the time to care for a complete stranger. Gilda Radner died of ovarian cancer in 1989.

How do you want to be remembered? Some of the people reading this book will become stars, be written about, and be the butt of other comics' jokes. But sometimes it's the little moments, when we take the time to recognize others, that we truly are a superstar.

Appendix

Comedy Services

Judy Carter's Comedy Workshops Productions—
www.comedyworkshopS.com.

Services Available

- Stand-up and comedy writing workshops (eight-week and weekend workshops)
- Comedy consultations via phone, e-mail, video, or audiotape
- California's Comedy Conference—a weekend spent with some of Hollywood's best and brightest. Attend workshops taught by industry professionals and get a chance to showcase your act in front of agents, managers, producers, sitcom/film writers, network and studio executives and casting directors—all while networking with other comics and writers. Beginning comics and writers are welcome to attend. Usually held in November in Palm Springs, California.

Comedy Supplies

- Instructional CDs, tapes, and videos—including *Five Steps to Writing Jokes, Stand-up Comedy Techniques, The Business of Comedy, Achieving Comedy Career Success,* and more
- Joke writing software—designed to assist you in writing jokes, preparing set lists, and cataloguing jokes

For a free brochure, contact us at 800-4-COMICS (800-426-6427) or *info@comedyworkshopS.com.*

Visit *www.comedyworkshopS.com* for up-to-date information and an array of resources and services for comedy performers and writers.

U.S. COMEDY CLUBS

Comedy clubs change all the time. For a complete up-to-date listing, go to *www.comedyworkshopS.com.*

Alabama
The Comedy Club at the
  Stardome
1818 Data Drive
Hoover, AL 35244
205-444-0008
www.stardome.com
stardome@stardome.com

Arizona
Improvisation
930 E. University Drive
Tempe, AZ 85281
480-921-9877
www.improvclubs.com

Laff's Comedy Cafe
2900 E. Broadway
Tucson, AZ 85716
520-881-8928

California
Improvisation
8162 Melrose Ave.
L.A., CA 90401
323-651-3625
www.improvclubs.com

The Brea Improv
945 East Birch Street, Brea
  Market Place

Brea, CA 92821-5832
714-529-7878

Comedy Store
8433 Sunset Blvd.
West Hollywood, CA 90069
323-656-6225
www.thecomedystore.com

The Ice House
24 N. Mentor Ave.
Pasadena, CA 91106-1745
626-577-1894
www.icehouseonline.com
icehousecc@hotmail.com

The Comedy & Magic Club
1018 Hermosa Avenue
(near 10th Street)
Hermosa Beach, CA 90254
310-376-6914

Laugh Factory
8001 W. Sunset Blvd.
West Hollywood, CA 90046-2401
323-656-1336

Sweet River Bar & Grill
248 Coddingtown Ctr.
Santa Rosa, CA 95401-3506
707-526-0400

Comedy Spotlight at
  Hornblowers
1559 Spinnaker Drive
Ventura, CA 93001
805-658-2202

LA Connection Comedy Theatre
13442 Ventura Blvd.
Sherman Oaks, CA 91432-3828
818-784-1868
www.laconnectioncomedy.com

Mixed Nuts Comedy Club
5040 Pico Blvd.
Los Angeles, CA 90019
323-933-2106

Tommy T's
1655 Willow Pass Rd.
Concord, CA 94520-2611
925-686-5233
www.tommyts.com
tommyts1@aol.com

Maestro's
2323 San Ramon Valley Blvd.
San Ramon, CA 94583
925-743-1500
www.maestro.com

Palookaville
1133 Pacific Ave.
Santa Cruz, CA 95060
831-454-0600

Punch Line
444 Battery Street
San Francisco, CA 94111
415-397-4337
www.punchlinecomedyclub.com

Cobbs Comedy Club
2801 Leavenworth St.
San Francisco, CA 94133-1129
415-928-4445
cobbs@ccnet.com

Rooster T. Feathers
157 West El Camino Real
Sunnyvale, CA 94087
408-736-0921
roostertfeathers.com
bookings@roostertfeathers.com

Colorado
Comedy Works
Wende Curtis
1226 15th Street
Denver, CO 80202
303-595-3637
www.comedyworks.com
Slcatcw@aol.com

Wit's End Comedy Club
8861 Harlen
Westminster, CO 80031
303-430-4242
witsend@aol.com

Loonee's Comedy Corner
1305 N. Academy
Colorado Springs, CO 80909
719-591-0707
www.loonees.com

Delaware
Comedy Cabaret
Wilmington, DE
302-652-6873

District of Columbia
The Improvisation
1140 Connecticut Ave.
Washington, DC 20036
202-296-7008
www.dcimprov.com

Florida
Miami Improv
3390 Mary Street #356
Coconut Grove, FL 33133
305-441-8200
www.miamiimprov.com
contact@miamiimprov.com

Uncle Funny's
9160 State Road 84
Davie, FL 33324
954-474-5653
*www.sofloridacomedyscene.com/uncle
    funnys.html*

McCurdy's Comedy Club
3900 Clark Road
Sarasota, FL 34233
941-925-3869
www.mccurdyscomedy.com
mccurdyscomedyclub@juno.com

Sidesplitters Comedy Club
12938 N. Dale Hwy
Tampa, FL 33618-2806
813-960-1197
www.sidesplitterscomedy.com

Laugh-In Comedy Café
College Parkway and Winkler
    Road
Fort Myers, FL 33919
479-LAFF (5233)

info@laughincomedycafe.com
www.laughincomedycafe.com

Groucho's
785 S. Babcock St.
Melbourne, FL 32901-1890
321-724-1220

Comedy Zone
Miami, FL
305-672-4788

Comedy Zone
2900 N. Monroe St.
Tallahassee, FL 32303
850-386-JOKE(5653)

The Comedy Zone
Mandarin
I-295 and San Jose Blvd.
Jacksonville, FL 32257
904-268-8080
www.comedyzone.com

Coconut's Comedy Club
3311 U.S. Highway 98
    North
Lakeland, FL 33805
863-687-2678

Coconut's Comedy Club
6100 Gulf Blvd.
St. Petersburg, FL 33706
727-360-5653

Wacky Weaver's
1801 Tarah Trace
Brandon, FL 33510
813-661-5527
800-386-JOKE (5653)

GIGGLES at Sidelines
250 Apollo Beach Blvd.
Apollo Beach, FL 33572
813-641-1217
www.gigglesclubs.com

GIGGLES at Poseidon Restaurant
and Lounge
2035 S.E. U.S. 19
Crystal River, FL 34429
352-563-1184

GIGGLES at Holiday Inn
3209 S. Atlantic Avenue
Daytona Beach Shores, FL 32118
904-761-2050

GIGGLES at Sheraton Four Points
151 E. Washington
Orlando, FL 32801
407-841-3220

GIGGLES at Holiday Inn
Wheelhouse Restaurant and
Lounge
55 Tamiami Trail
Punta Gorda, FL 33950
941-639-4041

GIGGLES at Duffers Sports Bar
and Night Club
6940 U.S. 27 North
Sebring, FL 33870
863-382-6339

GIGGLES at the Rare Olive
Restaurant and Night Club
300 Central Avenue
St. Petersburg, FL 33731
727-822-7273

GIGGLES at Holiday Inn—
Kennedy Space Center
4951 S. Washington Avenue
Titusville, FL 32780
321-269-2121

GIGGLES at the Best Western
Admiral's Inn
5665 Cypress Gardens Blvd.
Winter Haven, FL 33884
863-324-5950

Comedy Corner
West Palm Beach, FL
561-833-1812

Georgia
Uptown Comedy Corner
2140 Peachtree Road N.W.
Atlanta, GA 30309-1314
404-350-6990

The Punchline
280 Hilderbrand Drive
Atlanta, GA 30328
404-252-5233
www.punchline.com
comedy@punchline.com

The Comedy House Theater
2740 Washington Rd.
Augusta, GA 30909
706-736-9190

Hawaii
Big Island Comedy Club
Box 945
Kailua-Kona, HI 96745
808-329-4368
members.comedy.com/hawaii
hawaii@comedy.com

Idaho
Funny Bone
404 S 8th Street
Boise, ID 83702
208-331-2663

Illinois
Jukebox Comedy Club
3527 W. Farmington Road
Peoria, IL 61604-4705
309-673-5853
www.jukeboxcomedy.com

Barrel of Laughs
10345 S. Central Ave.
Oak Lawn, IL 60453
708-499-2969

Comedy Comedy
Naperville, IL
630-226-9700

Comedy, Etc.
I-64 and Highway 159
Fairview Heights, IL 62208-0000
618-628-4242

Riddles Comedy Club
15750 S. Harlem Ave.
Orland Park, IL 60462-5279
708-444-0234

Improv Olympic
3541 N. Clark St.
Chicago, IL 60657
773-880-0199
improv@enteract.com

Second City & Second City Etc.
1616 N. Wells

Chicago, IL 60614
312-337-3992

Zanies
1548 N. Wells St.
Chicago, IL 60610
312-337-4027

Indiana
Cracker's Comedy Club—
    Downtown
247 South Meridan Street
Indianapolis, IN 46225
317-631-3536
www.crackerscomedy.com

Snickerz Comedy Bar
5535 Saint Joe Rd.
Fort Wayne, IN 46835
219-486-6323

Funny Bone Comedy Club—
    South Bend
1290 Scottsdale Mall
South Bend, IN 46614-3471
219-299-9999
www.sbfunnybone.com
www.funnyboneusa.com (complete
    listing of clubs)

One Liners Comedy Club
50 Airport Pkwy.
Greenwood, IN 46143-1438
317-889-5233
www.onelinerscomedy.com

Wisecrackers
Merrillville, IN 46410
219-769-6311

Iowa
Spaghetti Works
310 Court Ave.
Des Moines, IA 50309
515-243-2195

Funny Bone—Des Moines
8529 Hickman Rd.
Des Moines, IA 50322-4321
515-270-2100
www.funnybone.com

Penguins Comedy Club
Downtown Cedar Rapids at 209
    1st Ave. S.E.
Cedar Rapids, IA 52405
319-362-8133
www.penguinscomedyclub.com

Kentucky
Comedy Caravan
1250 Bardstown Road
Louisville, KY 40204-1333
502-459-0022
www.comedycaravan.com
tss@bellsouth.net

Louisiana
Funny Bone
Rich Miller
4715 Bennington Ave.
Baton Rouge, LA 70808-3114
612-331-4360
www.funnybone.com

Maine
Comedy Connection
16 Custom House Wharf
Portland, ME 04101
207-774-5554

www.mainehumor.com/comedy00.html
theoffice@mainehumor.com

Maryland
Comedy Factory
36 Light Street
Baltimore, MD 21202-1001
410-752-4189

Winchester's
102 Water Street
Baltimore, MD 21202-6315
410-576-8558
comedyclub102@aol.com

Tracy's Comedy Club
Baltimore, MD 21222
410-665-8600
www.tracyscomedyclub.com

Massachusetts
The Comedy Connection
245 Quincy Market Building
Boston, MA 02109
617-248-9700
www.comedyconnectionboston.com
comedyconnect@hotmail.com

Nick's Comedy Stop
100 Warrenton St.
Boston, MA 02116-5622
617-423-2900

The Comedy Studio
114 Columbia St.
Cambridge, MA 02139-2730
617-661-6507
www.thecomedystudio.com
rick@thecomedystudio.com

Dick Doherty's Comedy Vault
@ Remington's Restaurant
124 Boylston St.
Boston, MA 02116
800-401-2221
www.dickdohertycomedy.com

Dick Doherty's Comedy Escape
@ China Blossom Restaurant
Rte. 125/133
North Andover, MA 01845
800-401-2221
www.dickdohertycomedy.com

Dick Doherty's Comedy
    Escape
@ Randolph Holiday Inn
Rt. 28
Randolph, MA 02368
800-401-2221
www.dickdohertycomedy.com

Michigan
1891 Room at the Holly Hotel
Doubletree Hotel
Holly, MI 48442
248-634-5208
www.hollyhotel.com
george@hollyhotel.com

Mainstreet Comedy Showcase
314 E. Liberty Street
Ann Arbor, MI 48104
734-996-9080
www.aacomedy.com
admin@aacomedy.com

Russo's Comedy Club
11225 S. Saginaw St.
Grand Blanc, MI 48439

810-695-1671
russos@comedy.com

Mark Ridley's Comedy Castle
269 East 4th
Royal Oak, MI 48067
248-542-9900
www.comedycastle.com
MRidley750@aol.com

Joey's Comedy Club
36071 Plymouth Rd.
Livonia, MI 48150-1441
734-261-0555
www.joeyscomedyclub.com

Gary Field's Comedy Club
2580 Capital Ave. S.W.
Battle Creek, MI 49015-4196
616-965-4646

Saginaw Comedy Club
218 N. Hamilton
Saginaw, MI 48602-4216
517-799-9555

Shooters
8845 Gratiot Rd.
Saginaw, MI 48609-4810
517-781-6333

The Other Place
738 S. Garfield
Traverse City, MI 49686-3428
213-941-0988

Bea's Comedy Kitchen
541 East Larned
Detroit, MI 48226
313-961-2581

Chaplin's East Comedy Club
34244 Groesbeck Highway
Clinton Twp., MI 48035

Comedy Den
2845 Thornhills, S.E.
Grand Rapids, MI 49546
616-949-9322
rcdow@comedy.com

Second City Comedy Theatre
2301 Woodward
Detroit, MI 48201
313-965-2222
Fax: 313-471-3466
www.secondcity.com
SCDet@aol.com

Back Door
313 Ashmun
Sault Ste. Marie, MI 49783
906-635-1547

Connxtions Comedy Club
2900 N. East St.
Lansing, MI 48906
517-482-1468
edp@connxtionscomedyclub.com
www.connxtionscomedyclub.com

Dr Grins@The Bob
20 Monroe, N.W.
Grand Rapids, MI 49503
616-356-2000
klemmen@thebob.com

Big Red's Comedy Club
Oxford, MI 48370
248-628-6500

Minnesota
Acme Comedy Company
708 N. 1st St.
Minneapolis, MN 55401-1133
612-338-6393
AcmeComCo@aol.com
www.acmecomedycompany.com

Knuckleheads
402 East Broadway
Bloomington, MN 55425
612-854-5233
www.knuckleheadscomedy.com

First Street Station
102 6th Ave. S.
St. Cloud, MN 56301-3621
320-252-4538

Mississippi
Boomtown Casino Biloxi
676 Bayview Ave.
Biloxi, MS 39530
228-435-7000
www.boomtownbiloxi.com
btbxm2@datasync.com

Missouri
Stanford and Sons
504 Westport Rd.
Kansas City, MO 64111-3012
816-561-7454
www.stanfordandsons.com
stanford@aol.com

Funny Bone—Saint Louis
940 Westport Plz.
Saint Louis, MO 63146-3108
314-469-6692
www.funnyboneusa.com

Deja Vu
405 Cherry St.
Columbia, MO 65201
573-443-3216
www.topofthevu.com

Nebraska
Funny Bone—Omaha
705 N. 114th St.
Omaha, NE 68154-1515
402-493-8036
www.funnyboneomaha.com

Jokers
1314 Jones St.
Omaha, NE 68102
402-345-4584
402-345-4703
comedylift@comedy.com

Nevada
Riviera Comedy Club
2901 Las Vegas Blvd. S.
Las Vegas, NV 89109-1931
702-794-9247

Catch a Rising Star—Silver
  Legacy Casino
407 N. Virginia St.
Reno, NV 89501-1138
775-325-7469
www.silverlegacy.com

The Comedy Stop at the Trop
Las Vegas, NV 89109
702-739-2714
www.thecomedystop.com

The Improv—at Harrah's Casino
3475 Las Vegas Blvd. S.

Las Vegas, NV 89109-8922
702-369-5000

Reno Improv—Hilton
Reno, NV 89595
775-789-2078

New Hampshire
Dick Doherty's Comedy Escape
Gilford, NH 03249
800-401-2221

New Jersey
Rascals Comedy Club
1500 Highway 35 South
Ocean Township, NJ 07712
732-517-0002

Catch a Rising Star—N.J.
Hyatt Regency Hotel
102 Carnegie Ctr.
Princeton, NJ 08540-6200
609-987-8018

The Comedy Stop at the Trop—
  Atlantic City
Tropicana Casino
Atlantic City, NJ 08401
609-822-7353

Comedy Cabaret
Holiday Inn—Runnemede
Runnemede, NJ 08078
856-312-1113

Bananas Comedy Club
Holiday Inn
283 Route 17 South
Hasbrouck Heights, NJ 07604
201-727-1090

Stress Factory
375 George St.
New Brunswick, NJ 08901-2003
732-545-4242
www.stressfactory.com

New Mexico
Laff's Comedy Cafe
Albuquerque, NM 87111
505-296-5653
www.laffcomedy.com

New York
Stand-Up New York
236 West 78th Street
New York, NY 10024
212-595-0850
corncobq@aol.com

Gotham Comedy Club
34 W. 22nd St.
New York, NY 10010-5805
212-367-9000
www.gothamcomedyclub.com

Gladys's Comedy Room
145 West 45th Street
New York, NY 10036
212-832-1762

Dangerfield's
1118 1st Ave.
New York, NY 10021-8339
212-593-1650
www.dangerfieldscomedyclub.com

The Comic Strip
1568 2nd Avenue
New York, NY 10028
212-861-9386

www.comicstriplive.com
comicstriplive@aol.com

Caroline's
1626 Broadway
New York, NY 10019
212-956-0101
www.carolines.com
ckalinoski@carolines.com

Comedy Cellar
117 MacDougal St.
New York, NY 10012
212-254-3480

Duplex
61 Christopher Street
New York, NY 10014
212-255-5438
duplexnyc@aol.com

Broadway Comedy Club
334 W. 46th St.
New York, NY 10036
212-977-1000

New York Comedy Club
241 E. 24th St.
New York, NY 10010
212-696-5233
www.newyorkcomedyclub.com

McGuire's Comedy Club
1627 Smithtown Ave.
Bohemia, NY 11716
516-467-5413

Comedy Works
37 Route 9W
Glenmount, NY 12077
518-465-8811

Pip's
2005 Emmons Ave.
Brooklyn, NY 11235-2707
718-646-9433

Funny Bone—Buffalo
Boulevard Mall
Buffalo, NY 14226
716-838-2800

Lake Ontario Playhouse
103 W. Main
Sacketts Harbor, NY 13685-0000
315-646-2305

The Comix Cafe—Tonawanda
3163 Eggert Rd.
Tonawanda, NY 14150-7156
716-835-4242

Comix Cafe
3163 Eggert Rd.
Buffalo, NY 14150-7156
716-835-4242

Comix Cafe
Rochester, NY 14623
716-424-5243

Comedy Cellar
Estee Adorim
117 MacDougal St.
New York, NY 10012-1267
212-254-3480
www.comedycellar.com

Bananas Comedy Club—
   Poughkeepsie
679 South Rd.
Poughkeepsie, NY 12601-5652

914-462-3333
www.bananascomedyclub.com
bananascomedyclub@aol.com

Boston Comedy Club
Tom Nikki
82 W. 3rd St.
New York, NY 10012-1008
212-447-1000

Governor's Comedy Club
90 Division Avenue
Levittown, NY 11756
516-731-3358

North Carolina
The Comedy Zone—Charlotte
5317 E. Independence Blvd.
Charlotte, NC 28212-0543
704-227-2909
www.comedyzonecharlotte.com
newcomedyzonedeb@aol.com

The Comedy Zone—Greensboro
1126 S. Holden Rd.
Greensboro, NC 27407-2307
336-632-9880
www.thecomedyzone.com

Charlie Goodnights
861 W. Morgan St.
Raleigh, NC 27603-1613
919-828-5233
www.charliegoodnights.com
jp@rightangledesigns.net

Comedy Club
3410 Buccaneer Dr.
Nags Head, NC 27959-9699
252-441-7232

North Dakota
Comedy Gallery
Grand Forks, ND
701-772-2222
cklingo@comedy.com

Ohio
Funny Farm Comedy Club
1620 Motor Inn Dr.
Girad, OH 44420-2422
330-759-4242
www.funnyfarmcomedyclub.com
funnykidd@aol.com

Wiley's Comedy Club
101 Pine St.
Dayton, OH 45402-2925
937-224-5653
www.wileyscomedyclub.com
moonpierob@hotmail.com

Go Bananas
8410 Market Place Lane
Cincinnati, OH 45242
513-984-9288

The Improvisation
2000 Sycamore
Cleveland, OH 44113
216-696-4677

Jokers Comedy Cafe
8900 Kingsridge Dr.
Dayton, OH 45458-1619
937-433-5233
www.jokerscafe.com
lmgrigs@aol.com

Hilarities
1546 State Rd.

Cuyahoga Falls, OH 44223-1302
330-923-4700

Funny Bone
145 Easton Town Center
Columbus, OH 43219
614-471-5653
www.funnybone-columbus.com

Oklahoma
Tulsa Comedy Club
6906 South Lewis
Tulsa, OK 74136
918-481-0558
www.hotcomedy.com/tulsa.html

Oregon
Harvey's Comedy Club
436 N.W. 6th Ave.
Portland, OR 97209-3613
503-241-0338
www.harveyscomedyclub.com

Pennsylvania
Laugh House
Philadelphia, PA 19107
215-440-4240
www.laughhouse.net
laughhouse@aol.com

The Comedy Works
6200 Nathan Hale Court
Bensalem, PA 19020
215-741-1661

David Stein's Comedy Outlet
1741 Papermill Rd.
Reading, PA 19610-1207
610-373-4242
www.steinproductions.com
seve@epix.net

Comedy Cabaret
625 N. Main Street
(on top of Poco's Restaurant)
Doylestown, PA 18901
215-345-5653
www.comedycabaret.com

Villa East Comedy Club
2331 Lincoln Hwy. E.
Lancaster, PA 17602-1113
717-397-4973

Comedy Cabaret
Bala Cynwyd, PA 19004
610-664-4451

Comedy Cabaret
Bensalem, PA 19116
215-676-5653

Funny Bone
Pittsburgh, PA 15219
412-281-3130
www.funnybonelive.com

David Stein's Reading Comedy
    Outlet
at the Sheraton Reading Hotel
Papermill Rd.
Wyomissing, PA 19610
610-376-3811

Rhode Island
Comedy Connection
39 Warren Ave.
East Providence, RI 02914
401-483-8383

South Carolina
The Comedy House Theater

14 Berryhill Rd.
Columbia, SC 29210-6431
803-798-9898

South Dakota
Filly's Comedy Shoppe
445 Mount Rushmore Rd.
Rapid City, SD 57701
605-348-8300

Tennessee
The Comedy Catch at the Cafe
3224 Brainerd Rd.
Chattanooga, TN 37411-3501
423-622-2233
www.chattanooga.net/comedy
comedyctch@aol.com

The Looney Bin Comedy Club
2125 Madison Ave.
Memphis, TN 38104-6501
901-725-5653
www.loonybincomedy.com
laughing@bellsouth.net

Zanie's Comedy Showplace
2025 8th Ave. S.
Nashville, TN 37204-2201
615-269-0221

Texas
River Center
849 East Commerce Rm. 893
San Antonio, TX 78205
210-229-1420

Spellbinder's Comedy Club
10001 Westheimer
Houston, TX 77042
713-266-2525

The Comic Strip
6633 N. Mesa St.
El Paso, TX 79912-4427
915-581-8877

The Comedy Showcase
12547 Gulf Freeway
Houston, TX 77034
281-481-1188
www.thecomedyshowcase.com
us@thecomedyshowcase.com

Corral Club
621 Hemphill St.
Ft. Worth, TX 76104
817-335-0196

Houston's Laff Stop
1952 West Gray
Houston, TX 77019
713-524-2333
www.laffstop.com
shavedhead@earthlink.net

Hyena's Comedy Club—Arlington
Arlington, TX 76011
817-226-5233

Hyena's Comedy Club—Fort
  Worth
Fort Worth, TX 76106
817-877-5233

Improvisation
Addison, TX 75001
972-404-0323
www.improvclub.com
addison@improvclubs.com

Capital City Comedy Club
8120 Research Blvd. #100

Austin, TX 78205
512-467-2333
www.hotcomedy.com

Comedy Sports Playhouse
P.O. Box 49486
Austin, TX 78765
512-266-3397

Froggy Bottoms
5131 Aberdeen Ave.
Lubbock, TX 79414
(806) 785-4477

Utah
Laugh's Comedy Cafe
Ogden, UT 84401
801-622-5588

Johnny B's Comedy Club
177 West 300 South
Provo, UT 84601
801-377-6910

Vermont
The Comedy Zone
60 Battery Street
Burlington, VT 05401
802-658-6500

Virginia
Comedy Club
109 S. 12th St.
Richmond, VA 23219-4011
804-643-5653
www.comedyclub.net
qnofcomd@mindspring.com

Thoroughgood Inn Comedy Club
Bayside Shopping Ctr.

Virginia Beach, VA 23451-0000
757-460-8399
www.tgicomedyclub.com

Washington
Comedy Underground
222 So. Main St.
Seattle, WA 98104
206-628-0303

Comedy Underground
100 South 9th Street
Tacoma, WA 98402
253-272-2489
www.comedyunderground.com

Giggles Comedy Club
5220 Roosevelt Way N.E.
Seattle, WA 98105
206-526-5653

Laff's Comedy Cafe
1221 North Howard
Spokane, WA 99201
509-484-2356

Laff's Comedy Cafe
Bellevue, WA 98009
425-568-1647

Best Western Inn Tower Comedy
   Club
Richland, WA 99353
509-946-4121

West Virginia
The Comedy Zone
Ramada Inn
South Charleston, WV 25303
304-774-4641

Wisconsin
Funny Bone
2801 S. Oneida St.
Ashwaubenon, WI 54304-5748
920-498-2663

Skyline Comedy Cafe
Appleton, WI 54915
920-734-5653
www.skylinecomedy.com

Funny Business Comedy Club
117 State St.
Madison, WI 53703
608-256-0099

Laugh Lines Comedy Club
6722 Odana Rd.
Madison, WI 53719
608-833-1055

Comedy Cafe
615 E. Brady St.
Milwaukee, WI 53202
414-271-5653

College Showcases

National Association for Campus Activities
13 Harbison Way
Columbia, SC 29212-3401
Phone: (803)732-6222; fax: (803)749-1047
www.naca.org
lour@naca.org

   NACA serves nearly 1,200 member colleges and universities, as well as close to 600 associate member talent agencies, performers, and product specialties firms working in the college market. Talent agencies, management firms, performers, and promotion or product specialties businesses interested in getting involved in the college market will benefit from a National Association membership. To join, go to their Web site or call for more information.

Association for the Promotion of Campus Activities
1131 South Fork Drive
Sevierville, TN 37862
1-800-681-5031
www.apca.com

   The Association for the Promotion of Campus Activities is a national campus buyers organization that holds showcases and supplies entertainment information to campus talent buyers throughout the United States. Last year, over 135 schools and 750 campus buyers attended the APCA national conference showcases looking for entertainers, agencies, presenters, and services for their school programs.

College Bookers

The following are agents, speakers' bureaus, and production houses that book comics and humorous speakers primarily for the college market.

6 Mile Records (843) 766-4575
comedy, pop/modern rock music, record company

Adair Performance (888) 452-3247
children/family programs, comedy, folk music/acoustic/coffeehouse, jazz music/new age, lecture, mime, novelty/variety/interactive

Admire Entertainment, Inc. (877) ADMIRE U (236-4738)
comedy, lecture, novelty/variety/interactive, training/development

Agency for the Performing Arts (310) 888-4291

comedy, country music, jazz music/new age, pop/modern rock music, R&B/soul music

Agent 0007, Inc. (781) 259-0007

comedy, country music, dance artists, novelty/variety/interactive, pop/modern rock music, world/international music

AKA PROTEUS.COM (402) 420-6984

lecture

Alive! with the Arts (410) 882-1191

concert production services, comedy, folk music/acoustic/coffeehouse, hip-hop/rap music, jazz music/new age, multicultural programs, pop/modern rock music, R&B/soul music, specialty advertising products, world/international music

Ambassador Agency (615) 370-4700

comedy, folk music/acoustic/coffeehouse, gospel/contemporary Christian music, lecture, novelty/variety/interactive

American Academy of Mime (949) 858-5500

children/family programs, comedy, lecture, mime, novelty/variety/interactive, theater/Broadway

AMG Entertainment, Inc. (717) 394-7218

novelty/variety/interactive

Ampa Events (800) 358-5451

comedy, dance artists, hip-hop/rap music, novelty/variety/interactive, pop/modern rock music, R&B/soul music

An Affair with Jean-Paul, LLC (973) 218-2413

children/family programs, comedy, dance artists, lecture, novelty/variety, R&B/soul music

Andrew Becker Enterprises, Inc. (888) 99-HYPNO (4-9766)

novelty/variety/interactive

Andrew Potter Productions (781) 863-6389

comedy, lecture, motion pictures, multicultural programs, novelty/variety/interactive

Artists United (770) 321-0042

comedy

Atlantic Entertainment (617) 327-3048

blues music, comedy, novelty/variety/interactive, pop/modern rock music

Auburn Moon Agency (800) 566-6653
comedy, folk music/acoustic/coffeehouse, gospel/contemporary Christian music, lecture, motion pictures, multicultural programs, pop/modern rock, R&B/soul music, novelty/variety/interactive

B.O. Productions, Ltd. 011-44-1189-403516
comedy

Bass/Schuler Entertainment (773) 539-8100
blues music, children/family programs, classical music, comedy, country music, hip-hop/rap music, jazz music/new age, lecture, mime, multicultural programs, novelty/variety/interactive, pop/modern rock music, R&B/soul music, world/international music

Bennett Communications (615) 826-6993
art exhibits, blues music, children/family programs, classical music, comedy, gospel/contemporary Christian music, jazz music/new age, lecture, multicultural programs, training/development

The Black Comedy Tour (215) 855-8557
comedy, hip-hop/rap music, lecture, R&B/soul music

Blade Agency (800) 367-1700
comedy, country music, folk music/acoustic/coffeehouse, jazz music/new age, novelty/variety/interactive, pop/modern rock music, R&B/soul music

Blue Onion Collective (412) 731-3372
comedy, folk music, pop/modern rock music

Brave New Workshop (612) 377-8445
comedy, novelty/variety/interactive

Brian Howard (310) 962-9362
comedy, novelty/variety

Britton Greenstein Loyd Management (610) 828-7537
blues music, comedy, children/family programs, dance artists, folk music/acoustic/coffeehouse, mime, multicultural programs, pop/modern rock music, theater/Broadway, world/international music

Bruce Smick Amusements, Inc. (800) 332-2377
children/family programs, comedy, mime, novelty/variety

Burly Bear Network (212) 293-0770
art exhibits, comedy, motion

pictures, Web/broadcast/satellite programming

C. J. Johnson/Brian Brushwood Entertainment (800) 462-4424
children/family programs, comedy, novelty/variety/interactive

C.R. Entertainment, Inc. (516) 897-6116
blues music, comedy, concert production services, country music, folk music/acoustic/coffeehouse, gospel/contemporary Christian music, hip-hop/rap music, jazz music/new age, novelty/variety/interactive, pop/modern rock music, R&B/soul music, training/development, Web/broadcast/satellite programming, world/international music

Campus Outreach Services (610) 989-0651
lecture

CAMPUSPEAK, Inc. (303) 745-5545
lecture

Capital Speakers Incorporated (800) 220-3052
children/family programs, comedy, lecture, multicultural programs, novelty/variety/interactive, training/development

Chameleon Productions (407) 859-9300
comedy, country music, dance artists, gospel/contemporary Christian music, novelty/variety/interactive, pop/modern rock music, R&B/soul music

Coffee Enterprises, Inc. (808) 488-1776
lecture

Comedy West (888) 897-2256
comedy, pop/modern rock music

Concert Ideas, Inc./Harris Goldberg Management (800) 836-2000
blues music, comedy, concert production services, country music, folk music/acoustic/coffeehouse, hip-hop/rap music, jazz music/new age, pop/modern rock music, R&B/soul music

CTM Entertainment (780) 489-0954
comedy, lecture, novelty/variety/interactive

Cutting Edge Entertainment (888) 221-6538
comedy, concert production services, folk music/acoustic/coffeehouse, novelty/variety/interactive, pop/modern rock music

Dave Schwensen
  Entertainment (440) 967-
  0293
children/family programs, comedy,
country music, folk music/
acoustic/coffeehouse, lecture,
novelty/variety/interactive,
pop/modern rock music, travel

DCA Productions (800) 659-
  2063
children/family programs, classical
music, comedy, country music,
folk music/acoustic/coffeehouse,
gospel/contemporary music, hip-
hop/rap music, jazz music/new
age, lecture, mime, multicultural
programs, novelty/variety/
interactive, pop/modern rock
music, R&B/soul music, theater/
Broadway, world/international

Dead Tree Press (973) 300-
  0090
blues music, comedy, country
music, folk music/acoustic/
coffeehouse, multicultural
programs, novelty/variety/
interactive, pop/modern rock
music, publications, world/
international music

DeirdreFlint.Com (215) 574-
  5730
comedy, folk
music/acoustic/coffeehouse

Disability in Media Everywhere
  (973) 244-0394
lecture

Don Buchwald & Associates
  (323) 602-2340
comedy, lecture,
novelty/variety/interactive,
theater/Broadway

Don Law Agency (617) 547-
  1940
comedy, folk
music/acoustic/coffeehouse, hip-
hop/rap music, jazz music/new
age, pop/modern rock music,
R&B/soul music

Dramatic Marketing
  Associates—African
  American Drama
  Company (415) 333-
  2232
comedy, folk music/acoustic/
coffeehouse, jazz music/new age,
lecture, theater/Broadway

Duff Entertainment (773)
  342-3833
comedy, concert production
services, novelty/variety/
interactive, pop/modern rock
music, R&B/soul music

Eirene Productions (651)
  748-8119
lecture, theater/Broadway

Entertainment Connection,
  Inc. (800) 793-0085
blues music, comedy, mime,
pop/modern rock music,
novelty/variety/interactive,
training/development

**Entertainment Solutions, Inc.
(888) 738-9950**

comedy, lecture, motion pictures,
novelty/variety/interactive,
pop/modern rock music

**Eric Buss—Master of Foolology
(818) 543-0038**

comedy, novelty/variety/
interactive

**Everything But the Mime (407)
856-2412**

children/family programs, comedy,
folk music, jazz music/new age,
lecture, novelty/variety/interactive

**Fantasma Productions, Inc.
(561) 832-6397**

comedy, jazz music/new age,
pop/modern rock music

**Fogg Entertainment (614) 451-
1100**

comedy, jazz music/new age,
lecture, pop/modern rock music,
novelty/variety/interactive

**Full Tilt Management (402)
558-8790**

blues music, comedy, country
music, folk music/acoustic/
coffeehouse, multicultural
programs, pop/modern rock music

**G. G. Greg Agency (216) 692-
1193**

blues music, children/family
programs, classical music, comedy,
country music, dance artists, folk

music/acoustic/coffeehouse,
gospel/contemporary Christian
music, hip-hop/rap music, jazz
music/new age, lecture,
multicultural programs, novelty/
variety/interactive, R&B/soul
music

**G. L. Berg and Associates (507)
645-0585**

children/family programs, comedy,
folk music/acoustic/coffeehouse,
gospel/contemporary Christian
music, jazz music/new age,
lecture, mime, multicultural
programs, novelty/variety/
interactive, pop/modern rock
music

**GFI Entertainment (650) 343-
9334**

comedy, folk
music/acoustic/coffeehouse, hip-
hop/rap music, lecture,
multicultural programs,
pop/modern rock music

**Good Guy Productions (877)
353-5351**

comedy, concert production
services, country music, folk
music/acoustic/coffeehouse, hip-
hop/rap music, lecture, novelty/
variety/interactive, pop/modern
rock music, R&B/soul music,
theater/Broadway, training/
development

**Horton Smith Management
(877) 682-1395**

blues music, children/family programs, classical music, comedy, dance artists, gospel/contemporary Christian music, jazz music/new age, lecture, multicultural programs, theater/Broadway

ICM Artists, Ltd. (212) 556-5602
comedy, lecture

Illusions of Garry Carson & Kelsey (888) 732-4027
comedy, novelty/variety/interactive

The Improv Asylum (617) 263-1221
comedy, novelty/variety/interactive, theater/Broadway, training/development

Jason Mystic Entertainment, Inc. (651) 578-1288
children/family programs, comedy, novelty/variety/interactive, pop/modern rock music, theater/Broadway

Joey Edmonds Agency (773) 871-1444
children/family programs, comedy, gospel/contemporary Christian music, lecture, multicultural programs, novelty/variety/interactive, pop/modern rock music

Jus' Wiggin Entertainment (800) 417-4943
comedy, multicultural programs

Kaleidoscope Entertainment, Inc. (800) 71-SCOPE (7-2673)
children/family programs, comedy, concert production services, folk music/acoustic/coffeehouse, gospel/contemporary Christian music, lecture, novelty/variety/interactive, pop/modern rock music, theater/Broadway, training/development

The Karkut Entertainment Group (570) 421-2834
children/family programs, comedy, country music, folk music/acoustic/coffeehouse, lecture, multicultural programs, novelty/variety/interactive, pop/modern rock music, specialty advertising products, training/development

Ken-Ran Entertainment (972) 690-6099
comedy, country music, lecture, novelty/variety/interactive, pop/modern rock music, R&B/soul music

Kismet Productions (937) 873-9927
comedy, country music, folk music/acoustic/coffeehouse, jazz music/new age, lecture, pop/modern rock music, R&B/soul music

The Klages Agency, Inc. (800) 876-6315

blues music, comedy, folk music/acoustic/coffeehouse, lecture

Laugh Riot Productions (917) 364-2244
comedy, theater/Broadway

Laughing Matters (404) 681-1378
comedy, novelty/variety/interactive, theater/Broadway, training/development

Laughs on Us—Stand-Up Comedians (508) 947-9528
comedy

Lefton Promotions, Inc. (800) 737-1995
children/family programs, comedy, lecture, mime, novelty/variety/interactive

Lordly & Dame, Inc. (617) 482-3593
lecture, multicultural programs

Marcos Productions, Inc. (888) 779-8951
children/family programs, comedy, gospel/contemporary Christian music, mime, novelty/variety/interactive, pop/modern rock music

Margaret Parry Presents (307) 875-6836
comedy, lecture, novelty/variety/interactive, training/development

Metropolitan Entertainment Group (973) 744-0770
blues music, comedy, concert production services, country music, folk music/acoustic/coffeehouse, hip-hop/rap music, jazz music/new age, pop/modern rock music

Neon Entertainment (800) 993-NEON
children/family programs, comedy, concert production services, folk music/acoustic/coffeehouse, lecture, novelty/variety/interactive, pop/modern rock music

New York Entertainment (212) 586-1000 x306
comedy

Olson Entertainment Group, Inc. (888) 747-5634
comedy, folk music/acoustic/coffeehouse, novelty/variety/interactive, pop/modern rock music, R&B/soul music

Omnipop, Inc. Talent Agency (516) 937-6011
comedy, lecture, novelty/variety/interactive, pop/modern rock music

On the Road Booking Company (212) 302-5559
comedy, dance artists, pop/modern rock music, theater/Broadway

OUTmedia (718) 789-1776
children/family programs, comedy,
dance artists, gospel/
contemporary Christian music,
lecture, multicultural programs,
novelty/variety/interactive,
pop/modern rock music,
theater/Broadway

**Outright Speakers and Talent
Bureau** (800) 294-3309
comedy, lecture, theater/
Broadway

Paradigm Entertainment Group
(800) 992-8676
comedy, country music,
gospel/contemporary Christian
music, hip-hop/rap music, lecture,
novelty/variety/interactive

Paradise Artists (805) 646-
8433
children/family programs, comedy,
folk music/acoustic/coffeehouse,
jazz music/new age, novelty/
variety/interactive, pop/modern
rock music

The Party People, Inc. (800)
958-9915
children/family programs, comedy,
lecture, motion pictures,
novelty/variety/interactive,
theater/Broadway

PB & J Management (323)
876-1340
comedy, jazz music/new age,
novelty/variety/interactive

**Pelican Marketing and
Management, Inc.** (716)
381-5224
children/family programs, comedy,
folk music/acoustic/coffeehouse,
novelty/variety/interactive,
pop/modern rock music

Pet Shop Productions (617)
655-9022
comedy

Planet Ant, LLC (313) 506-
9115
comedy, lecture, motion pictures,
pop/modern rock music

Portland Night & Day (503)
630-2568
comedy, folk
music/acoustic/coffeehouse,
lecture, novelty/variety/inter-
active, world/international music

Prince/SF Productions (415)
731-9977
comedy, dance artists, folk
music/acoustic/coffeehouse, hip-
hop/rap music, lecture, multicultural programs, pop/modern
rock music, R&B/soul music

Pro Management, Inc. (978)
579-5900
blues music, comedy, concert
production services, country
music, dance artists, pop/modern
rock music, R&B/soul music,
theater/Broadway,
world/international music

Professional Magic Presentations (612) 378-2200
comedy, novelty/variety/interactive

R. P. Program Group (717) 762-6000
comedy, lecture, novelty/variety/interactive, training/development

Red, Black and Green Promotions (201) 871-8995
comedy, lecture, hip-hop/rap music, novelty/variety/interactive, pop/modern rock music, R&B/soul music

Rising Star Promotions (877) 704-STAR
blues music, comedy, country music, gospel/contemporary Christian music, novelty/variety/interactive, pop/modern rock music

Russ Peak Presentations (800) 381-5858
comedy, lecture, novelty/variety/interactive

S.C. Entertainment (212) 929-0630
blues music, children/family programs, classical music, comedy, country music, gospel/contemporary Christian music, folk music/acoustic/coffeehouse, jazz music/new age, lecture, multicultural programs, pop/modern rock music, R&B/soul music, theater/Broadway, world/international music

S.T.A.R.S. Productions (973) 300-9123
comedy, hip-hop/rap music, jazz music/new age, multicultural programs, pop/modern rock music, world/international music

Santa Barbara Speakers Bureau (805) 682-7474
lecture

Silver World Wide Entertainment (212) 284-3660
art exhibits, concert production services, hip-hop/rap music, multicultural programs, novelty/variety/interactive, pop/modern rock music, Web/broadcast/satellite programming, world/international music

The Smith Agency, Inc. (616) 791-8298
comedy, concert production services, folk music/acoustic/coffeehouse, novelty/variety/interactive

Sophie K. Entertainment (877) 664-8559
blues music, comedy, folk music/acoustic/coffeehouse, multicultural programs, pop/modern rock music

SpeakOut Speakers, Artists, Exhibits and Films (510) 601-0182
art exhibits, children/family programs, comedy, concert production services, dance artists, folk music/acoustic/coffeehouse, hip-hop/rap music, jazz music/new age, lecture, motion pictures, multicultural programs, theater/Broadway, training/development, world/international music

Speaker Resource Center, Inc. (312) 641-6362
comedy, lecture, training/development

Stage 9 Productions (248) 414-7690
blues music, comedy, country music, gospel/contemporary Christian music, folk music/acoustic/coffeehouse, jazz music/new age, novelty/variety/interactive, pop/modern rock music, R&B/soul music, world/international music

Starleigh Entertainment (877) STARLEIGH
blues music, children/family programs, comedy, concert production services, folk music/acoustic/coffeehouse, jazz music/new age, novelty/variety/interactive, pop/modern rock music, R&B/soul music

Stefinity Entertainment (310) 393-3995
children/family programs, comedy, lecture, motion pictures, novelty/variety/interactive, theater/Broadway

Stephanie Romm Productions, Inc. (845) 255-0553
children/family programs, comedy, folk music/acoustic/coffeehouse, novelty/variety/interactive

Summit Entertainment (888) 925-7073
comedy

Supreme Talent International (800) 677-2731
comedy, jazz music/new age, lecture, pop/modern rock music, theater/Broadway

T.V.F.M. (818) 398-2481
blues music, comedy, folk music/acoustic/coffeehouse, motion pictures, pop/modern rock music, record company, theater/Broadway

Talent Network, Inc. (412) 264-4727
comedy, pop/modern rock music, novelty/variety/interactive

Thomas Ball Entertainment (800) 556-9567
comedy, folk music/acoustic/coffeehouse, lecture, novelty/

variety/interactive, pop/modern rock music

Three Rivers Agency (724) 873-1816
comedy, concert production services, hip-hop/rap music, novelty/variety/interactive, pop/modern rock music, R&B/soul music

TimeOut Productions (304) 623-6322
novelty/variety/interactive

Tri-Media Marketing (800) 736-6616
specialty advertising products

Twenty-First Century Speakers (888) 421-2368
lecture, multicultural programs, training/development

Victoria Sanders and Associates, LLC (212) 242-9485
art exhibits, comedy, lecture, multicultural programs

Voices (253) 813-3581
lecture, multicultural programs, novelty/variety/interactive, training/development

Well Done Productions (703) 620-0567
children/family programs, comedy, novelty/variety/interactive

William Morris Agency (310) 859-4000
comedy, country music, folk music/acoustic/coffeehouse, gospel/contemporary Christian music, hip-hop/rap music, lecture, pop/modern rock music, R&B/soul music

Youthstream Media Networks (480) 350-9362
comedy, lecture, motion pictures, multicultural programs, pop/modern rock music, training/development

The Writers Guild Registration Service

(Reprinted with permission from the Writers Guild of America West.)

The Writers Guild's Registration Service (or Intellectual Property Registry) registers over 30,000 pieces of literary material each year, and is available to members and nonmembers alike.

Writers are invited to submit material to be archived by the Writers Guild to protect their work. For more information on this service, contact the Registration Department at (323) 782-4500.

Registrable Material

- Registrable material includes scripts, treatments, synopses, outlines, written ideas specifically intended for radio, television, and theatrical motion pictures, video cassettes/discs, and interactive media.
- The WGA Registration Office also accepts stage plays, novels, and other books, short stories, poems, commercials, lyrics, and drawings.

Procedure for Deposit

- Materials may be submitted for registration in person or by mail.
- The Registration Office must receive

    1. One (1) unbound, loose-leaf copy of material on standard, 8½-by-11-inch paper.
    2. Cover sheet with title of material and all writers' full legal names.
    3. Social security number (or foreign equivalent), return address, and phone numbers of authors.
    4. Registration fee: WGAw and WGAE members, $10. Nonmembers, $20.

- When the material is received, it is sealed in an envelope and the date and time are recorded. **A numbered receipt is returned serving as the official documentation of registration and should be kept in a safe place.**
- Notice of registration shall consist of the following wording: REGISTERED WGAw No._____ and be applied upon the title page.
- Member Stamp. At the time of registration, WGAw members may request that a maximum of two (2) copies of the material being registered be stamped with the legend "MEMBER WGAw." The stamp indicates only that one or more of the writers listed as an author on the title page was a WGAw member at the time the material was registered with the title page bearing the stamp. There is no additional fee for use of the stamp.